TALK
UNDER
THE
BEAN
ARBOR

豆
棚
閒
話

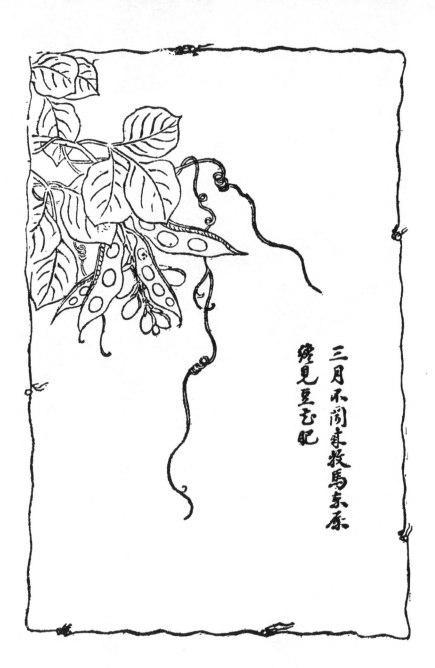

三月不閒年牧馬東原
總見豆玉肥

Idle Talk under the Bean Arbor

A SEVENTEENTH-CENTURY
CHINESE STORY COLLECTION

Compiled by Aina the Layman

WITH COMMENTARY BY
Ziran the Eccentric Wanderer

EDITED BY
Robert E. Hegel

UNIVERSITY OF
WASHINGTON PRESS
Seattle and London

Idle Talk under the Bean Arbor was made possible in part by grants from the Chiang Ching-kuo Foundation for International Scholarly Exchange and from the James P. Geiss Foundation, a private, nonprofit operating foundation that sponsors research on China's Ming dynasty (1368–1644).

Illuminating the Ming

Additional support was provided by the William H. Matheson Trust for the Liselotte Dieckmann Professorship in Comparative Literature at Washington University in St. Louis.

UNIVERSITY OF WASHINGTON PRESS
www.washington.edu/uwpress

LIBRARY OF CONGRESS CATALOGING-IN-PUBLICATION DATA
Names: Ainajushi, author. | Hegel, Robert E., 1943– editor.
Title: Idle talk under the bean arbor : a seventeenth-century Chinese story collection /
    compiled by Aina the Layman; with commentary by Ziran the Eccentric Wanderer ;
    edited by Robert E. Hegel.
Other titles: Dou peng xian hua. English | Seventeenth-century Chinese story collection
Description: 1st edition. | Seattle : University of Washington Press, [2017] |
    Includes bibliographical references and index.
Identifiers: LCCN 2016025839 | ISBN 9780295999975 (hardcover : alk. paper)
Classification: LCC PL2698.A4 D68 2017 | DDC 895.13/4—dc23
LC record available at https://lccn.loc.gov/2016025839

COVER AND FRONTISPIECE: The Climbing Beans, from *Doupeng xianhua*, Hanhailou ed., fig. 1a. Reprinted from Zhang Mangong, *Gudian wenxue banhua*, 79. Inscription:

For three months no sound of the cavalry's approach,
All I see are fattening beans across the Eastern Plain.

In gratitude

For the inspiration offered by three great translators:

Patrick Hanan

David T. Roy

Burton Watson

CONTENTS

Acknowledgments

It was through the writings of Patrick Hanan that I became aware of the significance of *Idle Talk under the Bean Arbor*, and so his name properly appears first in our dedication. But David Roy, indefatigable translator of the Ming novel *Plum in the Golden Vase* (Jin ping mei cihua) and provider of innumerable notes on cultural and stylistic matters, inspired our efforts to include explanations for what would have been obvious to the original readers of these stories. And Burton Watson, with whom I spent memorable hours talking while a graduate student, long ago set the standard for making old texts come alive while retaining something of their original grace in the less flexible grammar of English. Our failures to reach that standard have been remedied repeatedly by our copy editor Laura Iwasaki, who has our sincere gratitude for her persistence in getting just the reading we sought. Thanks, too, to Nancy W. Cortelyou, senior project editor for *Idle Talk*, and to the anonymous reviewers for their many helpful queries and suggestions, all of which significantly improved our renditions.

Once again I am grateful to Lorri Hagman, executive editor at the University of Washington Press, for her wonderful curiosity about texts and her unwavering support for this and other projects. From its beginning, this collection of translations was a joint undertaking of past and present graduate students at Washington University in St. Louis, and one from the University of Oregon, without whose good cheer and hard work it might have taken many years to complete. They translated ten of the dozen stories here very rapidly over the summer of 2015, leaving only two for me to render, with excellent help from Xu Yunjing. Aina's troublesome turns of phrase, his local colloquialisms and slang, even his obscure literary references challenged us all. Several thoughtful friends and colleagues have helped immensely in turning these obstacles into comprehensible English. They have been named singly in footnotes and elsewhere, but let me thank them here again:

with Washington University in St. Louis connections, Li Qiancheng, Liang Xia, Wang Wei, Xu Yunjing (and her father, Xu Jinlian, in Suzhou); and at the University of Oregon, Ren Chaoyi and Chen Yue.

Robert E. Hegel
St. Louis, April 2016

Introduction

GOSSIP AND EXAGGERATION IN AINA'S SHORT STORIES

Robert E. Hegel

By around 1660, when the collection *Idle Talk under the Bean Arbor* (Doupeng xianhua) appeared, China already had a long and creative tradition of fiction in the classical literary language, and the vernacular story, too, had enjoyed a century of popularity.[1] But *Idle Talk* is unique. First, its overall structure makes the collection more closely resemble Chaucer's English *Canterbury Tales*, Boccaccio's Italian *Decameron*, or the medieval Arabic *Thousand and One Nights* than any other story collection in Chinese of its time. *Idle Talk* links its numerous narratives together with a frame story and a continuing motif that is also unprecedented: the growth and maturation of runner beans. No other Chinese story collection produced before the turn of the twentieth century had this sort of framing device or even passing references to a single image from one story to the next.

Second, not only are the narrators here identified with certain traits and interests, but so, too, is the audience characterized, and the telling of tales is dramatized to a degree that is unprecedented in premodern Chinese literature. Storytellers here address their audiences directly, and their listeners' responses range from delight and approval to disgust and disbelief.

Even more strikingly, the stories told under the bean arbor are exceptional for their thematic contrariness. Although other writers of the seventeenth century experimented with narrative forms and regularly provided ironic visions of society's ills, the stories in *Idle Talk* repeatedly dash the reader's expectations with dramatic plot twists and ironic inversions of characters famous in history, legend, and more conventional narratives in this form. The first session is a grotesque account of female jealousy, followed by the total rewriting of a romantic legend about an ancient couple. The third session twists images of merchants as necessarily clever, and the fourth traces the unexpected career of the wastrel son of a wealthy household. In the fifth, a self-styled man of principles is clearly not the moral equal of a carefree beggar—who accepts his destiny to be so. In the sixth session, Buddhist monks commit vicious crimes in order to earn more contributions from the unsuspecting faithful, while officials at all levels seem utterly benighted in their policies and actions. The seventh rewrites an ancient legend about loyalty to the state and suggests terrible outcomes for those who refuse to recognize changes of government. In the eighth, a more obvious allegory, the physically blind fare better in life than do their self-deluding but sighted contemporaries. Justice may be done in this world, but session 9 argues that it is accomplished more often by coincidence than through administrative competence. Cheating—a recurring theme throughout the collection—gets its comeuppance in session 10. In the eleventh, the dead must produce goods for sale in order to stave off starvation for the living, while the final story in the collection is a devastating exposé of the irrelevance of self-congratulatory philosophizing in a time of postwar political tensions. Heroic historical figures are regularly debunked here, their "real stories" from earlier texts reinterpreted as mere subterfuge meant to conceal their cowardice and selfishness. Truly moral behavior may be found in unexpected places, but even then, only rarely. Each session is followed by general comments, but these, too, contain mutually contradictory statements, especially about the author and his intentions. It would seem that both he and his commentator collaborated to leave only ambiguous hints that might clarify their motives, forcing their readers to figure these out on their own.[2]

INNOVATIONS AND CONVENTIONS

Aina's frame tale presents a plausible, even homely situation. In the first heat of late spring, an older villager builds a makeshift arbor for his climbing beans. As they grow, their leaves form a light canopy over the ground below. With any breeze at all, the shady space becomes a cool refuge from the burning summer sun. Villagers gather there to chat, and before long they begin to tell one another anecdotes and stories to pass the time. Like gossip at other times and places, exaggeration abounds as each speaker attempts to create a tale at least as entertaining as the ones that came before. Nine different narrators speak during the dozen sessions that make up this collection, and each one carries on at least some conversation with his frequently argumentative audience. Differences in theme and diction are somewhat consistent with the varied characterizations of the speakers.

In literary terms, *Idle Talk* is rightly seen as a creative turn from the vernacular short fiction produced in such profusion by Feng Menglong (1574–1646) and Ling Mengchu (1580–1644) during the 1620s and 1630s. Altogether their five earlier compilations comprise 198 stories. Feng's were mostly adapted from earlier tales in the classical language or historical incidents. Ling's stories are similar elaborations on other texts from China's vast narrative and theatrical traditions. Feng experimented with grouping his stories into contrastive pairs in his first collection and, by the third compilation, into contrastive pairs and mutually reflective groupings of up to eight stories.[3] *Idle Talk* took this experimentation in new directions with its frame story by integrating explicit references to growing beans throughout the collection. Its author also generally paired these stories so that they would reflect on each other; the two halves of the set (sessions 1–6 and 7–12) are also symmetrical to a degree.[4]

Feng, Ling, and Aina all wrote in a vernacular narrative form known as the *huaben*. During the twentieth century, in an effort to uncover the creative spirit of China's masses in contrast to the formal writings of the elite, literary historians began to explore the country's rich oral traditions, storytelling in particular. Topics narrated by professional raconteurs were mentioned in guidebooks to cities of the Jiangnan or lower Yangzi River region dating from the twelfth to thirteenth centuries, and many could be matched to written vernacular stories of later periods. Literary scholar and fiction writer Lu Xun (1881–1936) proposed using the term *huaben* on the assumption that these later stories were "prompt books" that the professionals had used when telling their tales.[5] Ming period examples that revealed significant literary polish were designated *ni huaben*, or "imitation prompt books," based on the theory that they were adaptations by educated authors of tales told by less cultured professional raconteurs. These narratives, and most novel-length vernacular writings as well, were ostensibly scorned by members of the educated elite, who passed them off as suitable reading only for youths and women. Subsequent research has revealed that professional storytellers—past and present—rarely used scripts during their narratives, and that the authors of the mature vernacular stories were generally highly educated men who had failed to find careers through the civil service examinations. Moreover, since most late Ming period short stories were adapted from classical-language tales, their relationship to oral composition is unknowable at this remove in time, although it is probably significantly less direct than previously supposed. Rather than being totally new creation (if that is ever possible), China's vernacular literary tradition is the result of textual adaptation. Nowhere can we see more sophisticated, self-conscious use of this technique than in these stories by Aina.

Idle Talk stories are similar in length to those of his predecessors. As did they, Aina drew upon rich linguistic sources to enliven his tales. He freely incorporated expressions and grammatical structures from the classical literary tradition, technical language of all sorts, and colloquialisms of the lower Yangzi area. Yet Aina's style is often more demanding than that of his predecessors. His several narrators may tell us what characters think as well as what they say and do. These raconteurs regularly draw wry moral lessons from their successes and failures, a device drawn from practices perfected in earlier seventeenth-century Chinese fiction. References to classic historical, philosophical, and religious texts are frequent throughout the collection, although most are parodied to one degree or another. Aina's rewritings of earlier stories and legends tend to skew the originals to such extents that what had conventionally seemed heroic appears to be petty and venal—and the opposite, as notorious butchers of the past might be presented as merely following Heaven's plan to cull the excess population from human society.

Perhaps even more curious is the range of narrative structures in these twelve sessions. Some loosely follow the pattern worked out for the vernacular story by Feng Menglong several decades earlier, "the kind that concerns itself with a single character in a single action and which serves to provide entertainment."[6] But in marked contrast to Feng's stories, several sessions are themselves collections of short anecdotes rather than one sustained story. Sessions 1 and 2 are parallel in their assemblage of brief tales on single themes. Session 10 begins with descriptions of a place, Tiger Hill, or Huqiu, in Suzhou, continues with a number of satirical poems, and then proceeds to the first of its two linked stories, which begins only after the session is well under way. And session 12 incorporates only one brief anecdote into an otherwise rambling lecture, interrupted by numerous challenges and questions from the audience—following the form of an oral performance, but without the story. Why include these oddly formed pieces in a collection of vernacular tales? The commentary at the end of the last session—presumably written by a friend of the author's—suggests that Aina dashed off these tales in very short order. Although this may be factual, the other unconventional features of this collection suggest that these structural exceptions, too, were deliberately provided to provoke a sense of strangeness among readers.[7] We need to reread, and to read back and forth, in these tales if we are to catch their range of meanings. Like earlier stories in this form, these, too, convey didactic messages. But these have a special urgency. In an age of suspicion and political tensions—the early Qing, when the new rulers were anxious to nip any resistance in the bud (as our "old gent" narrator observes at the end of the final session)—subtlety had to be the watchword. All stories here are presented as *xianhua*, "idle talk" or "chitchat," a term that recurs frequently throughout the collection, as if to disavow any serious political concern. Aina would have us read very carefully to apprehend his message or to realize—like the monk of session 6 or the retired official in session 10—that we, too, have been tricked, and there is no way out of Aina's narrative mazes save to recognize the cleverness with which we have been baited.[8]

Aina had a clear sense of history: his stories regularly hint at parallels between times past and contemporary situations. His themes include retribution in a Buddhist sense, the more Confucian virtues of loyalty and filial concern, and the sense of community and compassion that transcended sectarian distinctions in traditional Chinese values. Often these themes are interwoven, with the benefits of filial action visible in later generations. Aina's combination of themes can create confusion as well. The collection begins with tales of horrendous jealousy on the part of women. Yet the young men in the audience challenge the narrator on his misogyny: surely not all women are like that. And the narrator concedes. But women are seldom depicted positively in this collection. Many are victims of male brutality. Even the pitiful account of the renowned ancient beauty Xishi in session 2, murdered for her apparently guileless skill in enticing men, is more about male callousness and greed concentrated in the minister Fan Li. The story overturns romantic legends about the couple and exposes a world in which such pretty tales no longer have a place, exploitation occurs without censure, and violence lurks behind every relationship.[9]

Aina's tales return to one point consistently: authority corrupts, whether at the personal level or in government. Few conscientious administrators appear here—they all seem ready to connive their way to more power and privilege. Confucian rationales do not excuse civilian administrators—military commanders are just as vulnerable to nefarious schemes—and rulers are seldom perspicacious enough to forestall even the most disastrous outcomes of their plans. Despite good intentions and generous behavior among the many, the basic meanness of a self-centered few tends to undermine virtually all social institutions mentioned in his stories. *Pian*, meaning "trickery" or "swindling," is a term that recurs in virtually every story and describes all too many relationships. It is easy to conclude that Aina held a deeply cynical view of his contemporaries.

THE EARLY QING LITERARY WORLD

To a degree, *Idle Talk under the Bean Arbor* embodies trends visible in other writings of the period. The horrors of the recent dynastic transition loom behind many writings of the late seventeenth century. Natural disasters and official malfeasance occasioned rampant banditry throughout the Ming state from the late 1620s through the 1640s. The raids brought widespread dislocations and suffering, with further mass slaughter and devastation caused by the numerous uprisings of starving peasants and attendant upon the systematic Manchu conquest of the 1640s through the early 1660s.[10] Reflections on that chaotic time appeared on the stage and in fiction, some commenting directly on recent events, and others accomplishing the same effect by noting parallels with other times of dynastic crisis.[11] Indeed, the seventeenth century witnessed a growing movement toward structural change and thematic experimentation in various literary forms that expressed no more reverence toward earlier models than these stories do toward the political and cultural values of the past. *Idle Talk* was hardly the only such response to warfare and devastation that came to rely heavily on satire and irony and increasing engagement with literary games.[12] Another example is the dramatist and impresario Li Yu (1610/11–1680): as a publisher and a bon vivant, he was well known among the cultural figures of the lower Yangzi region during the early Qing. He may also have been a friend of the pseudonymous Aina. A man of great taste but of no political stature, Li Yu wrote short stories and then adapted some for the stage, although several had begun as his plays in the first place. He experimented with divisions into chapters and often with wickedly witty reversals of conventional themes that confounded readers' expectations.[13] Nor were reevaluations of historical events confined to literature during the early Qing period, when a new creativity arose among historians as they began to see China's past in a new light. In a long narrative poem, "Sorrows of Ten Thousand Ages"

(Wan'gu chou), Gui Zhuang (1613–1673) assumes an "ironic and irreverent tone in his review of all of Chinese history . . . until he gets to the Ming, when the need to lament overrides the urge to debunk exalted narratives."[14] The poem also justifies Gui's choice to avoid political involvement, as did many elite survivors of the dynastic transition, whether or not they retained Ming dynasty sympathies.

IMAGINING AN AUTHOR

Idle Talk was compiled by a man identified only as Aina Jushi, Aina the Buddhist Layman. "Aina" is not really a name; it means "a cassock woven with artemisia" of the sort that might be worn by one of the Buddhist faithful.[15] As a robe worn over one's regular clothing, this *aina* might signify a disguise, an assumed identity rather than an expression of faith on the part of the author. Nor is "Jushi" precise in its meaning as a form of address. Any educated man in retirement might take it on, regardless of how engaged he might be with Buddhist practice. According to the final comment in the collection, Aina was unsuccessful in landing a position in the Qing administration, presumably because he did not pass the highest level of civil service examinations. However, there is no knowing if this happened because he failed or whether he chose not to participate for political reasons. He turned to writing poetry, plays, and fiction to relieve his frustrations, the commentator avers. But in his foreword, Aina admits to not being fond of writing verse, and indeed, most of the original poetry in the collection is unapologetic doggerel. Thus we have two contrasting versions of Aina's talents and his oeuvre bookending the collection. Because medical texts are mentioned several times in the stories, one scholar speculates that Aina practiced medicine to earn a living.[16] The commentator portrays him as widely traveled and, more to the point, suggests that Aina was a keen observer of people and places. Given his penchant for incisive description and terse but effective characterization, this suggestion seems borne out by his fiction.

The commentator does not specify *when* Aina traveled, which would seem to be of some relevance to understanding the darkness in these tales. That, at least, seems to be no mystery: these twelve linked stories reflect a time when the mid-century dynastic transition and its accompanying horrors were a vivid memory only to members of the older generation. They identify Aina as one of them. The narrator of session 9 spent several years in Beijing, where he became familiar with police corruption. This might have been based on firsthand knowledge if Aina had lived in the capital while studying for the triennial civil service examinations, as many young men did. Significantly, the institutions he describes all date from the late Ming. The narrator of session 11 also tells about events of at least two decades before, presumably the 1640s, that he ostensibly witnessed personally. Given this testimony, we can conclude that Aina was probably born between 1610 and 1620 and lived at least fifty years, through the 1660s or beyond. Any traveling he might have done would have brought him in contact with proof that the world of his youth, the Ming empire, was falling apart—with grim evidence of the consequences of political disorder virtually everywhere.

However, that time is past in the settings of these stories. Several pointedly refer to current social tranquility, suggesting that this era of peace was most likely new and not well established—only the young men at the bean arbor gathering, presumably in their early twenties, seem uninformed about the political transition. The final session reveals their fear that the strict new Manchu government might suspect that even their harmless gatherings could have seditious intent, which prompts them to discontinue their storytelling sessions. Most likely, the 1660s would have been the only period during the author's lifetime when the lower Yangzi region was relatively free from bloodshed and suffering. Memory is called upon in several of these tales—their author's memories may well have engendered the violence and misery narrated here. Aina is seldom unclear about the general causes for callous disregard for human life—narrow self-interest brings out the very worst in everyone in these tales—but his fiction is much more ambiguous about how to restore or maintain social harmony. Some readers identify Aina as a Ming loyalist, although these stories portray no better time in the past. Moreover, at several points, the various speakers refer to the idea that Heaven allows or even encourages destruction in order to wipe away the excesses of humanity. This would seem to be a grim proposal that this mid-century period of death and destruction should be accepted without regret, a marked contrast to the attitude of the poet Gui Zhuang mentioned above. Aina's narrators repeatedly exhort their listeners to accept the status quo, which would suggest that Aina himself was not opposed to Qing rule—or at least not to the relative stability that it imposed.[17]

And yet *Idle Talk* is not all bleak or even consistently negative. Aina was not simply a misanthrope—irony and sarcasm abound throughout the collection. With session 8 as a prime example, the reader finds slapstick comedy here, and sly wit, along with tremendous erudition. Even the grim first-person accounts in session 11 are capped by stories marked by ghoulish humor. His references to classical texts and Buddhist scriptures are precise and always apt—clearly he was well read, as his commentator observes. Their common human foibles render his characters remarkably familiar to readers today. But Aina's stories also present cultural details now appreciated only by scholars specializing in the period. He seems to have known a great deal about the cultural centers and tourist spots of his day, the Jiangnan cities. He knew the slang of the brothel and the gambling house and the terminology of judicial courts and Buddhist monasteries, as well as the technical language of all major philosophical schools of his time. He also knew something about medicine, and about beans—their varieties, their cultivation, and how best to prepare them for eating—as he reminds his readers throughout the collection. He seems to have had a special relationship with Suzhou: in addition to the fairly negative picture he paints of the spongers of Tiger Hill in session 10, in the session 2 he refers to the ancient king of the state of Wu, Fu Chai, as a "Suzhou phony." It may be that he had bad experiences there, but since the earlier master of the short story, Feng Menglong, was so extensively identified with that city, these references may be another backhanded indication that Aina was deliberately deviating from the literary model established by his famous predecessor. But for all their superficiality, at least Suzhou people do not suffer from the bad breath his storyteller attributes to the people of the old region of Yue, modern Zhejiang!

Aina's stories persuasively capture the tenor of a troubled age and embody the work of a major storyteller in whose hands a mature literary form was parodied and adapted even further. And although he offers pithy comments about lapses of judgment and unethical conduct, it is the profound and troubling ambiguity of his narrators' moral stances that catches the reader's imagination most frequently. This conclusion is brought home in the collection's final story, in which a pompous tutor in the Confucian classics, a self-styled philosopher who holds forth in the longest session of the twelve, proceeds to establish what he considers the orthodox version of cosmology and ethics, to the dismay of his listeners. They ask him straightforward questions about the logic and fairness of his assertions, which he regularly fails to answer convincingly. The effect is to call into question the entire orthodox Neo-Confucian (Lixue) intellectual project. This implies challenges to the civil service examinations and the administrative structures that were theoretically based on that system of thought.[18] Aina seems utterly disaffected with the dominant political ideology and with Confucian personal ethics as well, evidence for which can be found throughout this collection.

The Commentator and Other Voices

Each session in *Idle Talk* is followed by comments attributed to a second writer known only by a pseudonym, presumably a close acquaintance of the author's.[19] The commentator purports to understand Aina's intentions in writing. In this, he follows the pattern established by fiction commentators earlier in the seventeenth century, but unlike Ye Zhou (Ye Yangkai) (fl. 1595–1624) and Jin Shengtan (1610–1661), Ziran "the Eccentric Wanderer" does not instruct his readers on how to read as stridently as the pioneers in this practice did. Nor does he criticize weak points in the narrative. Instead, Ziran agrees with Aina on the sorry state of society, amplifies his mentions of earlier literature, and offers suggestions on elaborations on the theme of each session or on its ethical applications.[20] In addition, he provides hints about the author's life from an insider's perspective. This is a practice that would not be fully exploited until the middle of the eighteenth century in the Zhiyanzhai commentaries on manuscripts of the monumental novel *Honglou meng* (Dream of red mansions or Dream of the red chamber), better known now in English as *Story of the Stone* (Shitou ji), written by the author's relatives.[21] It is in part through Ziran's comments that we can be sure that Aina did live through the Qing conquest and can glimpse the individual experience that lies behind these tales. Clearly the commentator shared similarly horrifying memories—and the author's explicit desire to strengthen a sense of survivorhood among China's aging population.

Commentator and author are only two of the several voices exploited here. The same elderly man, a teacher in a local elementary-level school, provides three of the stories (sessions 1, 2, and 11). His education comes not only from books but also from the experience of having lived through the chaotic dynastic change. Members of the audience, especially a number of the young men, ask him about his experiences and how, from this perspective, he reads such important questions as relations between husbands and wives. A neighbor tells the stories in sessions 3 and 4. The raconteur of the stories in sessions 5, 9, and 12 may well be the owner of the bean arbor, the host for these gatherings. The perspective in session 10 seems to be the voice behind the entire collection, serving a function similar to that of the general narrator in more conventional collections of Chinese vernacular stories.

One of the storytellers (sessions 6, 7) is a young man, confident and knowledgeable, the possessor of strong opinions. Another storyteller (session 8) is not particularly learned but ostensibly has a good memory: he retells a story nearly verbatim that he had heard from a Buddhist monk. (This is another example of the self-conscious use of ambiguities in this collection. Do we readers hear any of the young man's voice, or is it all that of the monk he channels?) First-person accounts figure importantly in these tales, but the experience is often presented at second- or third-hand, creating quotations within quotations within quotations.[22] Only the speaker of the final session claims altruistic intentions behind his presentation, but that self-styled Confucian scholar's impassioned lecture on philosophical abstractions apparently mystifies and irritates his listeners. Worse yet, his presence suggests that the authorities, too, might hear of these informal meetings and become suspicious of their intent. This makes the most sense if we understand that the background for these gatherings is an age when local uprisings were seen as having brought down the Ming and the new Qing government was wary of all unannounced assemblies, no matter how small. Without making his worries explicit, here Aina reveals his ongoing concern that tranquility in life, as in his fiction, is indeed transient. Like the readers of Gui Zhuang's poems, we are left to reread and ponder the relevance of his messages to us in our day as well.

A Note on the History of the Text

The oldest extant version of *Idle Talk under the Bean Arbor* was printed in a relatively expensive, nicely illustrated, large-format wood-block edition around 1660, to judge from internal evidence. Fragments of one copy are housed in the National Library of China in Beijing. A subsequent edition, published by the printer Hanhailou in the lower Yangzi River valley, appeared somewhat later, probably still early in the Kangxi era of the Qing period (1662–1722).[23] This imprint carried a number of illustrations, several of which are reproduced here. After slight editing to make a few portions of the text easier to read, the collection was also published in Suzhou by the commercial printer Shuyetang in 1781. Recent reprints, of which there are a number, are based on one or the other of these versions. It appears that *Idle Talk* has moved beyond the classroom and scholarly study to gather a growing audience among the general literature-reading public in China today. Several versions of the collection can even be found online.[24] Unfortunately, online editions usually are not annotated and may contain errors or misreadings of dialectical turns of phrase and idioms that are no longer current. Yet even if inadequate for academic purposes, they are making this remarkable collection widely available for the first time ever.

The primary text for these translations is the Taiwan Sanmin edition, which seems to reproduce the Hanhailou edition quite faithfully. It also includes notes explaining obscure terms, colloquialisms, and institutional details now known only by historians of the period. All were compared with a Shuyetang edition or the variorum edition reprinted in *Xihu jiahua deng sanzhong*.

Curiously, session 12 was one of the first Chinese stories to be translated into a European language—apparently because of a misunderstanding. It appeared in Jean-Baptiste Du Halde's (1674–1743) *Description géographique, historique, chronologique, politique, et physique de l'empire de la Chine et de la Tartarie chinoise* (known in English as *The General History of China*) under the title "Dialogue où un Philosophe Chinois moderne nommé Tchin, expose son sentiment sur l'origine et l'état du Monde." The historian seems to have mistaken this parody for a sincere exposition on contemporary philosophy. That text, in several English-language editions as well as in French, circulated quite widely and—ironically—may have contributed to the broadly favorable view of China as a land of rational and humanistic governance among the learned circles of western Europe in the early eighteenth century.[25] Although a complete French translation of the collection appeared recently, only one of the *Idle Talk* stories was translated into English during the twentieth century.[26]

One more bit of book history: Feng Menglong published his three collections in the 1620s, and two more collections of forty stories each by Ling Mengchu followed within a decade.[27] But with the fall of the Ming dynasty, all these major collections disappeared in China. In their place, an anthology of forty stories selected from the works of Feng and Ling, *Miraculous Visions, New and Old* (Jin gu qiguan), was printed and reprinted regularly from perhaps as early as 1640 into the twentieth century.[28] By contrast, Aina's *Idle Talk* was reprinted less frequently but seems to have been fairly widely known among later writers. A collection of classical-language stories inspired by Aina's tales, *The Little Bean Arbor* (Xiao doupeng), appeared around 1800. In its preface, dated 1795, the writer mentions owning a copy of *Idle Talk* as well.[29] An 1805 printing of a sequel to the very popular *Story of the Stone* has a preface that apparently copies a number of phrases from the preface reprinted in this volume.[30] Other references to the collection indicate the ongoing presence of Aina's unique compilation on the literary scene throughout the Qing period.

FORMAT OF THIS VOLUME

The early edition presented here begins with two prefatory pieces, one by a pseudonymous editor and a second ostensibly by Aina himself, perhaps with his commentator (although some scholars read them as one and the same individual). The twelve storytelling sessions follow, each composed of several related tales, with or without the intrusion of a general narrator using the voice of the author. To signal changes in narrators within sessions, we have occasionally inserted titles for stories within stories. Each session is followed by a "General Comments" section with entries from the original commentator that vary considerably in length and focus. Some critique the stories, others comment on the author, and some do both. The set of translations is followed by a brief "Afterthoughts on the Stories" section in which the translators offer reflections and suggestions on ways of approaching each session. The "Historical and Cultural References" section provides more detailed information concerning institutions, terms, and people mentioned in individual sessions (organized alphabetically). This is followed by a glossary of Chinese characters for names, titles, and terms.

Terms of Measurement and Titles

Terms of Measurement

chi = a little less than one English foot
jin = approximately 1.3 English pounds
li = approximately one-third English mile, or half a kilometer
liang = around one ounce (silver)
qian = one-tenth of an ounce, a mace
shi = around 160 English pounds, or 72 kilos
sui = one year of age (counting one *sui* at birth)

Titles

Translations of military and administrative titles and offices are from Charles O. Hucker, *A Dictionary of Official Titles in Imperial China* (Stanford: Stanford University Press, 1985).

Chronology of China's Historical Periods (Dynasties and States)

Legendary Rulers
    Yao   2357–2255 BCE?
    Shun   2255–2205 BCE?
    Yu   2205–2197 BCE?

Xia   2070–1600 BCE?

Shang   ca. 1600–1046 BCE

Zhou   1046–256 BCE
   Western Zhou   1046–771 BCE
   Eastern Zhou   770–256 BCE
   Spring and Autumn Period   772–476 BCE
   Warring States Period   475–221 BCE

Qin   221–206 BCE

Han   202 BCE–220 CE

Three Kingdoms   220–80

Jin 265–420

Northern and Southern Dynasties   420–589

Sui	581–618
Tang	618–907
Five Dynasties, Ten Kingdoms	902–79
Song	960–1279
Northern Song	960–1127
Southern Song	1127–1279
Yuan	1271–1368
Ming	1368–1644
Qing	1636–1911

IDLE
TALK
UNDER
THE
BEAN
ARBOR

豆
棚
閒
話

Doupeng xianhua, Hanhailou ed., fig. 2a, from
Zhang Mangong, *Gudian wenxue banhua*, 77.

Doupeng xianhua, Hanhailou ed., fig. 1b, from
Zhang Mangong, *Gudian wenxue banhua*, 76.

Preface

The revered master Aina is a gentleman of refinement of the present. In the distant past, he would have been called an "eccentric scholar."[1] He is blessed with the talents of ten thousand individuals, like those who composed poems while walking seven steps or while folding their arms eight times.[2] His marvelous wisdom is comparable to that of someone with three ears—two long and one short.[3] For some time now, his conversations have so astonished those near him that they could not help but stand up in awe. He has been as able to distinguish himself from the multitude as an awl sticking out through a bag. Recently, the proud dove has become even more prideful,[4] and the lazy dragon has become playful. Being unable to sell his bellyful of "The *Classic of Poetry* states . . ." or "So said Confucius . . ." did not preclude his manifesting his divine abilities in other ways. Despite having a multitude of brothers and comrades in associations and groups, why should he join them in their farcical activities?[5] What is worse, in an assembly of apes and monkeys, it is difficult to find a snake that can be charmed differently from the rest. While eking out a living in difficult and demeaning ways, how can one wait for the hare that will run headlong into a stump?[6] He may instead include chinaroot and cockscomb in his medicinal concoctions and turn all his giggling and scolding into texts.[7]

He brashly upended the twenty-one histories, looking for accounts of insignificant matters. He closely studied the eighteen arhats' discourse on cause and effect, seeking always the sweet aftertaste of the olive.[8] He hastened through old legends, replacing one name with another, quietly righting the wrongs of history. He overturned settled cases—although the hat of a Mr. Dong might be put on the head of a Mr. Xue, a more attractive image then appears.

Because Scholar Su had a bellyful of resentment,[9] he invoked Master Dongfang to indulge in mockery with his clever tongue.[10] So adept at taking the bell from the neck of the tiger,[11] Aina can even do somersaults on its back. His skill in carefully linking the plots is like that of threading pearls, with their treacherous labyrinthine pores, by an ant's antennae.[12] His stories make one burst out laughing or as suddenly shed tears—all of them are thought-provoking—surpassing the medical prescriptions written by all the immortals across the seas.[13] Whether about what is wrong or what is right, they instantly inspire reverence among readers, like the Buddha's sermons and lessons in the Bamboo Grove.[14] His stories would turn the snoring Zai Wo away from playful amusements and from stretching out after a meal.[15] Even the unsmiling Yanluo would not fail to applaud him in public when he realizes their twists of plot.[16] Reading these tales will prompt one to gulp down three measures of good wine in the depths of a long night, or sip a cup of tea brewed with rainwater when gentle breezes blow. If you doubt what I say is true, I invite you to read on.

—Dashed off by Whistling Crane of the Empty Heavens

Translated by Li Qiancheng

Foreword

Written by Layman Aina from Shengshui
Commentary by Ziran the Eccentric Wanderer from Yuanhu

Thus said Aina: Xu Jutan, a poet of an earlier generation in my home area, had a volume titled *Doupeng yin*, or *Rhymes from the Bean Arbor*.[1] His poems in ancient style, regulated verse, and quatrain forms all dealt with delightful events and unusual happenings from throughout the world, both ancient and modern. They were cherished and appreciated for many years. What a pity that now, with the man gone and those times long past, they are no longer extant. Nevertheless, when autumn winds blow and the beans ripen, gentlemen of noble character and elegance are still able to recite one or two couplets, which allows us to return to his times in spirit.

I am not fond of writing poetry, so I chose some delightful and hilarious episodes from events of the past and arranged them here randomly to supplement his "bean arbor" idea. Hence, I preface this endeavor with one of Jutan's poems. The poem says:

> In my thatched cottage in the west, with nothing to do,
> Nowhere can I find a cool place to escape from the heat.
> In the sixth month, the ponds are always shallow;
> In the woods, third-year saplings have not yet grown tall.
> Growing beans, the arbor can well provide a cool nook
> Surpassing pavilions near water, and fragrant besides.
> The evening breeze gathers old folks south of the rivulet:
> They playfully chat through the twilight as cicadas call.

Translated by Li Qiancheng

Jie Zhitui Sets Fire to His Jealous Wife

The lower Yangzi River valley is low-lying. Although the weather there is generally mild, the fourth month is known as the yellow mold season because of the rain, and the fifth and sixth months are known as triple sweltering days, when the relentless sun beats down from high in the sky. People traveling along the road have sweat running down their backs, and their foreheads are baked dry by the sun. Even at home, people groan from the heat until they have no breath left in their lungs, but there's nowhere to escape it.

The rich families have the best way of fending off the heat with their cooling pavilions or open-wall halls on the water, where they fan themselves and relax for refreshment. The second-best method belongs to the mountain monks and wild men who let their hair hang long, wear loose-fitting garments, and pass the time of day under the tall pines. The common folks of the middling sort have little choice but to find some goat's-eye bean seedlings in the middle of the second month and plant them in empty spaces around the house.[1] They put up some wooden stakes or bamboo poles, form them into an arbor, and tie them together with twisted-grass rope all around like silk festoons. Within a fortnight, the seedlings sprout and the vines wind their way around the bamboo poles. Before long, they fill in the arbor, making it airier and cooler than a man-made pavilion.

Young and old, men and women, they all bring out their benches, set up their chairs, or spread out their summer sleeping mats and settle down under the bean arbor. They fan themselves and enjoy the breeze. The older men chat about the government gazette, comment on local news, or spin stories. Some men comment on the women in other families—whose mother was virtuous, whose wife is a shrew—and generally talk about jealous women more than about virtuous ones. The women like to chat about one another's husbands, which gentleman is good and which is not—generally most women are jealous, while few truly love their husbands. As you can see, the word "jealousy" is constantly in the mouths—and turning around in the hearts—of men and women alike, day in and day out. Rather than tell you a tale about something else, let me start with "jealousy," and you can listen to your heart's content. The story will not fail to fulfill the intention behind building this bean arbor. So please, relax and listen to my tale.

One day, several young lads and a few older gents were lounging around under a bean arbor. One of them was holding a fan in his right hand and some kind of book for leisure reading in his left. When he reached a particularly exciting passage, there was a five-word quatrain. Suddenly he slapped his fan on the bench and exclaimed, "This is too much, it's just too much!"

An elderly gent stood up and asked, "What was that about?"

The lad handed him the book and pointed to the lines. "How can it say, 'The bite of a green bamboo viper, / The stinger on the rump of a yellow bee, / Neither is as poisonous / as the heart of a woman can be'? The poet must have been bullied by a woman for no reason to be as savage as that. Could a woman's heart really be more venomous than those two poisonous creatures?"

The elderly gent responded, "You young lads haven't experienced anything like it. You've never left home or traveled around, and you haven't even met a lot of people or heard many stories about it. So how could you believe it? I've already started my fifth decade and would rather stay a widower than marry again. I've traveled the roads and I've seen plenty, and I've heard many stories about such women too—every place seems to have its own type, with its own brand of savagery, and every woman has her own type of venom. I won't bore you with all the details, but there was a man who knew about such things. He wrote *A Mirror of Jealousy*, which contains stories about shrews and their behavior since ancient times as well as true events that he had seen and heard more recently. The author had the book printed, and it spread everywhere. He intended to let his male readers know about shrewish behavior so they would be on their guard and to warn women to examine their hearts and discipline themselves—so men and women could live together in peace. For this book he earned considerably more merit than Tripitaka did when he fetched the holy sutras from the West.[2] But who would have guessed that once women started to read the book, and understood that 'jealousy' had been around since ancient times, that they would think they were supposed to be jealous? They thought the deeds described in *A*

Mirror of Jealousy were commonplace. They started to develop their own ideas, to do things new and really novel. Before long, they wanted the author to add not just another supplement to the book, but two or three—their desires would not be satisfied until they were called heroes of 'the women's way.'"

Another elderly man piped up, "What this book describes are jealous acts that are in the past. What's so strange about that? There's also jealousy that lingers for thousands of years until the woman becomes a ghost or a deity—that's what's really rare."

The lad saw that the two old gentlemen were speaking knowledgeably, so he saluted them and begged them, "That's what we want to hear about!"

One of the old men said, "This is a long story. Boil some pots of first-class Songluojie tea and some top-grade tender Longjing tea, and bring me a few plates of tasty pastries, and then I'll tell you the tale."

The lads said in unison, "Nothing hard about that. We have it all. Now please tell us the true story, and don't tell us some old lies just to swindle us out of some tea and snacks. We're still young and not widely read, but we want evidence from others before we'll believe you!"

Slowly, the old man unfolded his fan, balanced it on the corner of the bench, stood up, and began his story.

THE OLD MAN'S TALE

In a certain month of a certain year, my partners and I bought some medicine to resell in Shandong. We rode with our donkeys and carts until we came to a big river several *li* south of the market town of Linji in Zhangqiu County, Ji'nan Prefecture. There were long lines of ferries and livestock on both sides of the river, traveling to and fro, and nothing struck me as unusual. There were lots of women, some going and some coming. The homely ones traveled across as if nothing was happening, but the ones with some looks dared not cross. Once the good-looking women reached the river, they pulled locks of hair down from their temples, stuck rank grass in their hair buns, and put on old, worn-out clothes. They dared not take the ferry until they looked a mess. Before they got on, they scooped up dirt and mud and smeared it on their faces, all to ensure they could cross safely. If a woman with some pretentions to looks wasn't willing to destroy her appearance when she reached the middle of the river, a great muddy wave would roll up and crash against the boat, dirtying her clothes and wetting her cargo.

Sometimes the waves would pull the woman into the river, and not even her shadow would ever be seen again.

What kind of monster would commit such an evil act? I made some discreet inquiries at a nearby inn. Since the people there all needed to cross the river, they were afraid of it and didn't dare talk about it directly. Only one elderly fellow teaching at a private school was willing to tell me.

How Jealous Woman Ford Came to Be

This spirit originated long ago. In the Tang dynasty someone wrote *Notes on the Strange*, which said, "This river crossing is called 'Jealous Woman Ford.'"[3] During the Taishi reign of the Jin dynasty, a man named Liu Boyu had a wife surnamed Duan, who was called Mingguang.[4] She had a very jealous nature. One day, Boyu drank a few cups of wine on an empty stomach and started to recite, without realizing it, several lines from Cao Zijian's "Rhapsody on the Luo River Goddess" in front of her.[5] The lines went like this:

> In appearance, she lightly flutters like a startled swan,
> Curvets like a roaming dragon.
> Her luster is more brilliant than autumn chrysanthemum,
> Her resplendence is more luxuriant than spring pine.
>
> She is dimly descried like the moon obscured by light clouds,
> She drifts airily like whirling snow in streaming wind.
> Gaze at her from afar,
> And she glistens like the sun rising over morning mists,
> Examine her close up,
> And she is dazzling as lotus emerging from limpid ripples.
>
> Between plump and thin, she strikes a mean—
> Her height conforms to proper measure.
> Her shoulders seem as if sculpted,
> Her waist is like bundled silk.
> On her long throat and slender neck,
> White flesh is clearly revealed.
> Fragrant oils she does not apply,
> Flower of lead she does not use.
>
> Billowy chignons rise high and tall,
> Long eyebrows are delicately curved,

Scarlet lips shine without,
White teeth gleam within.
Bright eyes do well at casting sidelong glances,
Dimples lie on either cheek.
Her wondrous manner is of uncommon beauty;
Her comportment is quiet, her body relaxed.
With tender feelings and graceful bearing,
She enthralls with her lovely words.
Her wondrous attire is unsurpassed in the world—
Her figure and form accord with the paintings.
She drapes herself in the shimmering glitter of a gossamer gown,
Wears in her ears ornate gems of carnelian and jade,
Bedecks her hair with head ornaments of gold and halcyon plumes,
Adorns herself with shining pearls that illumine her body.
She treads in patterned Distant Roaming slippers,
Trails a light skirt of misty gauze.
Obscured by the fragrant lushness of thoroughwort,
She paces hesitantly in a mountain nook.[6]

After reciting this part, he slapped the table, and unintentionally blurted out, "If I could marry such a handsome woman, what need would I have for endless honors and wealth piled up to the sky? I would be satisfied for the rest of my life."

Although this was just a thoughtless slip of the tongue while he was in his cups, Duan's heart was bursting with flames of anger. She asked bitterly, "How can you, my lord, glorify the beautiful features of a river goddess with such overwhelming praise and belittle me as less than human right to my face? If river goddesses are so great, I'll happily become one when I die." Before she could get all the words out of her mouth, she ran out the door like a puff of smoke.

Boyu thought that would be the end of it and wasn't worried. He didn't expect her to run down to the riverbank, where, with the force of a sparrow hawk in a dive, she plunged into the river and sank into the depths. Boyu was paralyzed, as if his soul had left his body. He wailed loudly and called out for help to drag the river to find his wife, but there was no trace of her at all. Boyu cried for seven whole days, until he was quite hoarse. He stumbled and fell, felt dizzy and fainted.

Then he saw Duan coming toward him from the water. "My lord, since you like river goddesses so much," she said, "I've become one! Someday, when you need to cross here, I'll invite you down so we can grow old together!"

Before she had finished her words, Duan started pulling at Boyu's sleeve as if trying to drag him down into the river. Boyu was so shocked that his soul flew out into the sky. He jerked his sleeve back with great force and suddenly woke up—it was all just a "Southern Bough" dream.[7]

Boyu forced himself to go home. He never expected, though, that Duan's spirit would refuse to disperse. Day after day, she'd cry out at the ferry or appear from nowhere to wait for her husband to cross on the ferry so she could fulfill her threat. She didn't expect Boyu to be so frightened that he'd never cross the river again. From that day onward, all beautiful women who came to the ferry crossing had to change their clothes and make themselves look ugly so that they could get across safely. Otherwise, the winds and waves would kick up, and some incomprehensible misfortune would befall them when they reached the middle of the river.

The two younger men said, "That Duan was really not very understanding. She should only have distrusted her husband. Why should she be jealous of other women, too?"

A different old man spoke up. "This scholar told us a tale about a woman who remained jealous after becoming a ghost. What about that story of a woman who became a deity but remained jealous? Where did that happen?"

A third old gent interjected, "Let me tell that story! Now, in the entire world, there are only two ferry crossings haunted by jealous women. The one you just heard about in Shandong sounds pretty common. Let me tell you about one that was really fierce."

The young men all heard this, and, astonished, they stood up one by one and asked, "Where is that one?"

ANOTHER OLD MAN'S TALE

It was opposite Shandong, in Mian County, Taiyuan Prefecture, in the part of Shanxi that used to be Jin territory. For miles around, people on the road talk endlessly about this and that, but they always get around to things that happened at this ferry crossing, which I didn't believe. On the way to the ferry crossing, I saw many women dressed up in country garb to make themselves look ugly, just like in the other story from Shandong. I didn't think there was anything strange about it until I happened upon a big grove of trees surrounding a fairly large temple. I jumped off my donkey, handed the reins and whip to my driver, adjusted my clothes, and brushed myself off. I walked all the way around the back wall to get to the main walkway. When I looked up, I was given a fright.

On the temple roof were two hornless dragon heads pointing straight up into the sky, surrounded by hawk's talons scraping the clouds and mists. The interlocking tiles on the roof ridge were decorated with eight kinds of jewels that dazzled my eyes. The door knockers were shaped like gluttonous ogres and were cast in turbid gold, which shimmered before my eyes and made my heart pound. On the left stood celestial soldiers mustached in vermilion with shocks of red hair who led chariots with fiery horses and wheels—everyone would guess they were followers of Zhurong, the fire god.[8] On the right were figures who I thought must be the aides-de-camp to the Commander of Pestilence, with their green faces, ferocious fangs, black parasols, and dark banners. In the center of the main altar sat an emerald-eyed, high-cheekboned, sunken-purple-faced woman of middling age, whose red mouth was wide open and as big as a winnowing basket. Holding a short stick of charred wood, she crouched ferociously on the altar. By her side stood a short hunchback who looked like he was in utter misery. He was facing a cabinet on the left, but why was this? I was about to inquire, but my driver signaled to me, saying, "Don't ask—let's go, let's go." I got back on my donkey and continued with my journey.

After we had gone five or six *li*, I quietly asked my driver again and again until he finally spoke.

The Driver's Tale

This goddess's name is Lady Shi You, and the man beside her was her husband, Jie Zhitui. They were from the state of Jin during the time when the different states were fighting one another, before the Qin and Han dynasties.[9] Because Duke Xian doted on a jealous woman, Concubine Li, he caused the death of his son and heir, Shensheng, and nearly brought harm to his second son, Chong'er, as well.[10] Left with no choice, Chong'er fled for his life into exile.

Jie Zhitui was the son of Jie Li, a high minister of state. He had just reached the age of twenty when he married Shi You, the daughter of another high minister named Shi Yu. Both Zhitui and You were romantically inclined and good-looking. They got along like fish in water—it was a Heaven-ordained match between a talented scholar and a gorgeous beauty, a pair without equal. However, because Chong'er had been struck suddenly with a great misfortune, he immediately went into exile. As a member of the heir-son's bodyguard, Zhitui's loyalty demanded that he ignore his own safety and accompany the prince. Zhitui followed Chong'er on horseback, never returning home to explain things to his wife. As he traveled, he kept looking for an acquaintance who could take a message to her.

Chong'er, as the son of the Duke of Jin, had altogether five retainers—one was Wei Chou, one was Hu Yan, one was Dian Jie, one was Zhao Cui, and the last was, of course, Zhitui. All of them left in haste, worried that word would reach the ears of Concubine Li, and that she would talk Duke Xian into sending an army after them, which would have been quite troublesome. That is why they all made superficial changes to their appearance, put on ragged clothes, stopped only for the night, and rose early the next morning, all under great duress.

Lady Shi was at home. How could she know this sequence of events? She could only think, "We were so much in love. How could my husband abandon me without warning? He must have met someone outside and suddenly deserted me for her!" She shouted to the heavens and pounded on the earth. By turns she was bitter, she wailed and cursed, and became obsessed. She wished that she could pull Zhitui up by his hair from midair, drag him before her, and eat him alive—that would be the only thing that would satisfy her. Day by day, and year by year, a lump began growing in her chest that was as hard and compact as a rock. No knife could cut it out, no ax could smash it. It was called jealousy. As the common saying goes, when there is a stone attached to a woman, and no skin to cover the stone, the disease has gone too far and can never be melted away.

How could she know that Zhitui was a loyal subject with a strong sense of moral integrity? He followed Chong'er to all corners of the world, tasting danger and hardship. They once fled deep into the mountains, where they were without fire or food for seven days, and Chong'er fell gravely ill. Although he had five retainers, only Zhitui was willing to cut a piece of flesh from his own thigh to make soup for Chong'er, an act that saved his life. Gradually, before they realized it, nineteen years had slipped by.

Chong'er was finally able to return to his state to be enthroned as Duke Wen, after which he was elevated to become the hegemon over the several states. Thereafter, the four retainers who had followed this royal dragon were all made high ministers and received valuable rewards. Among them, only Zhitui maintained his love for his wife as steadfastly as ever. Once he returned to his country, Zhitui went home to find out where Shi You might be, but she had moved to Mianzhu Mountain more than a decade before. Zhitui then went to the mountain to inquire after news of her. In the meantime, Lady Shi had molded a clay sculpture of her husband so she could scold and beat him from morning to night.

At last they saw each other again. Since they both looked much older, they didn't recognize each other at first. They began discussing their reasons for being there and thus finally recognized each other. Suddenly, Lady Shi let out a wail that shook the heavens and moved the earth. Zhitui explained all that had happened, but Lady Shi could only scold him, "You heartless thief! You dodged me for years and now try to hold me off with your false excuses and evasive explanations." She refused to believe him, but she didn't hesitate to use a woman's oldest methods—she slapped him with her hand, bit him with her mouth, butted him with her head, and kicked him with her feet. Beaten like a wounded soldier in battle, Zhitui hung his head in sorrow and dared not utter a word.

He hoped that if he kept his mouth shut and treated her well, her anger would pass and their affection for each other would return. He could then go back down the mountain and become an official. How could he know that Lady Shi's heart was filled with venom? Back when she had been at home, she had prepared a red silk rope made of nine woven cords that she kept in her clothing case. She brought it out and tied it around Zhitui's neck so he could never leave her side even for a moment, not even to stretch. Lady Shi said, "I don't want gold or silks, prosperity or rank, or to wander to the ends of the earth. My one desire is to be together at home, live a simple life eating only pickles and salt, and make up for all the romantic delights I lost over those nineteen years. Let those with an exalted fate become officials."

Zhitui was trussed up so tightly that he could neither write a memorial to the court to inform the duke nor pen letters to ask someone to come up and help reconcile the couple. Duke Wen of Jin didn't know where Zhitui was either. However, when one of the five retainers who had gone through the hardships with Zhitui didn't see Zhitui descend the mountain and noticed that the court wasn't looking into his disappearance, he conceived a plan by himself, not willing to simply let the matter rest. He wrote a vulgar piece of doggerel in four-character phrases and pasted it to the palace gate. He secretly hoped to move Duke Wen with it. The poem said:

> There was a brave and mighty dragon,
> Who suddenly lost his place.
> There were five snakes who followed him,
> Who wandered without leaving a trace.
>
> When the dragon was starving, with nothing to eat,
> One snake cut some flesh from his thigh.
> Now the dragon has returned to his own deep pool
> And secured his old domain afresh.
>
> Four of the snakes have entered their holes,
> All of whom have some place.
> But there is one snake who has no hole
> And wails out in some desolate space.

The poem quickly spread far and wide from the palace gate. Someone sent it in a memorial that was read to Duke Wen.

Embarrassed, Duke Wen panicked. He summoned Wei Chou to inquire into Zhitui's whereabouts. But Zhitui was all tied up—how could he get away? Wei Chou was a warrior—would he really have the patience to search everywhere for Zhitui? Mianzhu Mountain was some seven or eight hundred *li* around, which made it difficult to track someone. All he had to do was start a fire on all four sides of the mountain. There was no way to know where to look for him, so Wei thought that once the fire began to rage, Zhitui would flee and come out. It was early spring weather, and the brush and trees on the mountain were still quite dry. Wei Chou ordered people to set the fire in the direction of the wind. In an instant, flames rolled across both earth and sky.

Seeing the fire all around him, Zhitui knew it must be Wei Chou looking for him, but he had no way to escape. Like a crab bound with vines or a soft-shelled turtle tied with straw rope, Zhitui couldn't wiggle free. Even if he met Wei Chou, his dignity had been so destroyed that he no longer thought himself capable of becoming an official. All of a sudden, his heart filled with such vehement hatred that he wanted to die immediately!

Taking advantage of Lady Shi still being sound asleep, Zhitui decided to set his own remorseless fire. Although the fire was powerful, at first it produced only a few wisps of curling smoke that mingled with the dim light filtering through the cracks between rocks, not enough to come to the notice of the mountain dwellers. But before long, the fire swept up through the tree branches and leaped forward when it hit the pine pitch and cypress resin. The wind fanned the flames, and their tongues made the wind blow even more wildly. The flames rolled across the sky and plunged back to the ground. In an instant, hundreds of golden snakes were dancing and writhing, thousands of crimson horses shook their manes and neighed. The crackling sound—*bibi baba*—from all four sides was louder than firecrackers during the Lantern Festival. Seething and sparkling flames shot halfway into the sky, like the conflagration that consumed Xianyang for three months.[11] The foxes who tried to escape and the deer with nowhere to run became well-cooked meat and charred skin. The crows and hawks whose cries could not be heard and the peacocks and cranes unable to fly were all burned to a crisp.

Lady Shi had no road into heaven or door into the earth—she could neither run on ahead nor retreat behind. As the fire closed in around her, she clutched Zhitui tightly and said, "I'll never be jealous again." But her regret came too late. Who would have thought that when the fire moved closer, a calm would come over her? She wanted only to hold Zhitui in her arms, there being no more reason for regret or remorse. And so when the fire was at its fiercest, Jie Zhitui and his wife remained relaxed. Before long, they both became a pile of ashes.

When Wei Chou searched the mountainside later, he found the two burned bodies. He realized that Zhitui and his wife had committed suicide. As he was about to gather up their skeletons, he saw within them a lingering flame that had not been extinguished. When Wei Chou examined it carefully, he saw that it was neither black nor red, neither purple nor green, but like a round will-o'-the-wisp, a truly astounding sight. Wei ordered his attendants to poke it with an unburned branch. In the center was a stone the size of a quart measure gently rolling back and forth. The flames gradually died down, but the heart of the stone continued to emit a single strand of black vapor that rose into the sky—not even the wind could blow it away.

Seeing how strange it was, Wei Chou immediately wrote a report and presented this lump of treasure to Duke Wen. The memorial described how

Zhitui, as a principled hermit, refused to become an official and burned himself alive. It also recorded that he died the day before the Qingming Festival.[12] Disconsolate, Duke Wen ordered officials to set an altar where he made offerings to Zhitui from afar in the direction of the sky. He also ordered every household in the state to hang a willow branch over the doorway to commemorate him. On that day, no one was allowed to cook with fire but had to eat cold food left over from the night before. Even today, this is the story behind the tradition of prohibiting fire and eating cold food.[13]

Duke Wen thought that this lump of treasure must be a diamond *śarīra* created through self-cultivation by a living buddha or immortal.[14] He asked his lady and concubines to preserve it carefully in the rear of the palace. Who could have known that the stone would be the embryo of all sorts of trouble? Once the stone entered the inner palace, all the palace women starting bickering with one another, disagreeing about everything. Duke Wen later realized that the stone must be causing all the problems, but he had no way of exorcising it. Finally, he requested that the Hundred-Times-Refined Diamond Hammer, used for subduing demons and smashing jealousy and handed down by the imperial consorts and concubines, be brought from the ancient storehouse of the heavenly kings of the Zhou to hit the stone and smash it to pieces. Specks of its dust filled the heavens and covered the earth. Even today they can be found scattered among the common people, where, from time to time, the black vapor can still be seen rising. But that's a different story, to be told another time.

Let me go back to Lady Shi. As the inferno pressed ever closer, with her bright and heroic soul, she clutched Jie Zhitui and forced her way into the court of the Lord-on-High to loudly give him a piece of her mind. Although the Lord-on-High knew the weight of her sin of jealousy was not light, he also knew she had remained faithful to her husband for nineteen years. Her accumulated hatred could not be dispelled quickly. It just so happened that a group of flower-scattering fairies were at the court. They all pitied this sincerely devoted husband and wife for their helplessness because during their lifetime they had not received the land of Mian promised them by Duke Wen. The Lord-on-High decided to allow them to consume the sacrificial meat offered from the land of Mian.

But Shi's jealous heart was not transformed after all. All women who want to cross the water must not paint their eyebrows, put on face powder, or wear broad-sleeved long gowns—they must all change their clothing. Nor are men who come to the temple allowed to say that Lady Shi You's face has become ugly or mention any of her faults during her lifetime. Instead, anyone who flatters the lady and criticizes Zhitui is sure to have a smooth and peaceful trip.

Just recently, I heard of a country woman who deliberately dressed herself up to look charming and crossed on the ferry—she suffered no retribution. But that was only because Lady Shi happened to be out attending a party. Her guard was down, and she missed the chance to punish the woman. Who would have thought that this woman, all proud of herself, would go into the temple in high spirits to crow about her victory? "Lady Shi is no goddess anymore," she gloated. "I dressed like this but crossed on the ferry untouched." Before the woman could finish her sentence, Lady Shi's jealousy-assisting generals reported these words to her. The next instant, a ferocious gale picked this woman up and threw her into the river, where she drowned.

Based on what I've learned, when the temple was first built, Zhitui and his wife were seated side by side in formal dress. After this incident, Zhitui's statute suddenly shifted so that he was facing left. Local headmen in the area become nervous and rebuilt the statute, but before long it collapsed. From that, the headmen understood the lady's intentions and built it as I described.

Now I ask you, isn't this a story about a woman who remained jealous even after becoming a deity? Even today, the women of that area have an extremely violent temperament, but all the men are law-abiding and never dare act in any kind of unbridled way. People arriving at the ferry crossing see only the Yin winds and the mists of hate casting their pall over the area, a barrier set out by Lady Shi's vicious soul. Someone in the Tang, seeing a friend off at the crossing, wrote a poem with the line "This wine from an old friend, alas, cannot match the power of Shi You's wind."[15] This line should be sufficient evidence, I believe.

The young lads all exclaimed, "Marvelous! Marvelous! The 'green bamboo viper' poem does get it just right."

One of them said, "Today, the bean arbor was like a lecture hall. It's getting late now and time for us to be heading home, but if our respected elders are willing to offer us further instruction, by all means join us early tomorrow. We'll prepare a pot of wine for you that will be far better than the simple tea we had today."

General Comments

The Extensive Records of the Era of Great Peace *says, "Women belong to the metal agent, men belong to the wood agent. Just as metal overcomes wood, men are controlled by women.*"[16] *However, female jealousy and male dread are both endowed by Heaven, not acquired through cultivation or regulation. Even so, if one pursues the reasons behind this according to the laws of production and overcoming, wood produces fire, and fire overcomes metal, metal overcomes water, and water in turn produces wood. The mutual production and overcoming creates the wonderful situation in which men can also control women. Hence, the world is divided by* Qi *life force—half the world is "jealous" and the other half "dreads," making a constant balance between principle and power.*

The Honorable Aina's Idle Talk *devotes its first session to an elaboration on the word "jealousy," which is neither specific to women nor should encourage their existing strengths. Jealousy named ferry crossings, made beautiful women change their appearance, and, concentrated into a lump, caused disharmony in the inner palace. Speaking repeatedly and in detail about these despicable and deplorable situations should cause every reader to grind his teeth with anger and should break his heart with sadness. It echoes the saying in the classics "The inner is the superior man, the outer is the petty man."*[17]

This story is a study of the conduct of the petty, their extreme persecution of others and how they carry on. It is also a study of the conduct of the gentleman, his extreme helpless dependency in such situations. In the end, the spirit of what is Right prevails and perverted inner feelings will be exhausted—it is the same great rectification applied by good historians and former sages. With this knowledge, one may compare the role of this first story about jealous women in Idle Tales *with "Fair, Fair, Cry the Ospreys" in the* Classic of Poetry *or with "Marrying Down" in the* Documents of Antiquity.[18]

Translated by Mei Chun and Lane J. Harris

Fan Li Drowns Xishi
in West Lake

An old saying goes, "A thousand cups of wine are not enough when true friends meet—half a sentence might be too much when they disagree."[1] This is why, when you drink, you should drink with a close friend. Otherwise, even half a cup is hard to swallow. For a good conversation, fear a listener who has different views, for if you find a kindred spirit, he will enjoy it no matter how much you talk. He'll listen happily and be irritated only if you stop after just a few sentences. In general, when outstanding men of great refinement meet, they may discuss philosophies rational and subtle, the conversation going tirelessly back and forth for hours without either one being exhausted. If he were to talk to a fellow who has no ideas, however, it would be as if the words were like chestnuts raining down on his head, with none entering his ears. But what young folks find most to their liking are strange stories from far-flung places and tales about common events from everyday life that they have never heard before.

Even though new shoots with tender leaves are growing up the bean arbor that I set up some days ago, the bean vines have not yet entirely covered the arbor, and beams of sunlight still shine through empty places among the leaves. These spaces are like storytellers who break off at some crucial spot in the middle, leaving gaps that make the audience unhappy. But let's be done with this troublesome talk.

Now about those young lads who came here yesterday—they went home with a bellyful of tales about jealousy and retold them all to their families under the lamplight, both fathers and sons. Some thought that these were made-up stories like those heard from the professionals and would not believe them.[2] But some did believe that such violently jealous wives do exist in real life. And there are others who were half convinced and half doubtful and wanted to ask around to shed some more light on the question. Yesterday's stories so upset several of the young men's hearts that they tossed and turned in their sleep, just waiting for the sun to rise so they could come back to the bean arbor for more old tales.

On this day when the sun was just at its highest, there were not many people out yet. But as the sun slipped westward, sellers returned from the market and field hands took a rest and started to gather under the bean arbor, each finding an empty place to sit. Before long, the old gent walked up with a smile on his face. "My dear brothers, it's good to see you all here so early. I believe we agreed yesterday that I'll tell some more old tales today."

"Dear Uncle, just as we promised yesterday, we prepared some wine and snacks so that we could hear some more of your great tales," the young men said happily. "But please don't tell any more stories about jealous wives. They take the shine right off the faces of young men like us. Tell a story about a woman who is both talented and beautiful and virtuous as well, who reaped her just rewards. This is the kind of story we've got a taste for." The old man tilted his head and spoke.

The Old Man's Tale

Such a person would be too perfect to exist in this world, for "great face, bad fate" has always been the case since ancient times. Beautiful women are not necessarily talented, and talented ones are not necessarily attractive. Those who are both beautiful and talented are not necessarily virtuous. Even if you could find a woman who is talented, beautiful, and virtuous, she wouldn't necessarily come to a good end. There's no way to know about those who lived way back before the Three Sovereigns.[3] And even when the Three Dynasties of Xia, Shang, and Zhou were at their peak, there may have been a few sagely and virtuous empresses, but I've never heard of one who was talented, graceful, virtuous, and beautiful altogether. Instead, whenever a dynasty was in its final decline, some monstrous vixen would appear who was perfect in both talent and beauty.

The young men asked, "Who was it who brought King Yu of the Xia dynasty to his peak?"

Let me think about that. I remember that the father of Yu was Bosun, who married a daughter of the Youshen family called Xiuji. She conceived after seeing a shooting star crossing the Pleiades and gave birth to King Yu at Shiniu Village in the state of Bo.[4] At that time there was a great flood that came halfway up to the sky. King Yu had just taken a Ms. Tushan to wife. They had been married for only four days when King Yao executed Yu's father at Yushan because he failed to quell the flood. The king's successor, Shun, then recommended Yu as the only one capable of bringing that flood under control. So Yu left home, and for thirteen years he never came home to see his wife once, even during the three times when he passed right by their house. Knowing that her husband had a strange and solitary personality, Tushan did not come out to see Yu either. After several years, the flooding was relieved, and King Yao presented Yu with a black jade scepter as a reward for his success. Later, Shun yielded the empire to Yu as well, and Tushan became the queen. Isn't that a woman with both talent and virtue? Yet no one of those times ever mentioned whether she was pretty. So this tells us that the greatness of a woman sage is in her virtue rather than her appearance.

After sixteen or seventeen generations, the crown was passed to Lügui, who became King Jie. Jie had always prized courage. He was strong enough to fight off ten thousand, and he could straighten out iron hooks with his bare hands. But he was greedy, violent, decadent, and lustful, and as a consequence his people lived in misery. He had invaded the lands of all the dukes and marquises. The Youshi clan saw how immoral Jie was but could not think of a way to take revenge on him. All they had was a daughter called Meixi, who was extremely beautiful and very talented as well. She would be able to bewitch the ruler's mind and was therefore a suitable tribute to offer to Jie.

Sure enough, King Jie became obsessed with Meixi at first sight. He did whatever Meixi asked of him and obeyed her every wish. He appropriated all the treasure and property from the people and wasted it like water. He piled up all the rare foods and fancy dishes on the table like a mountain of meat. He poured all the fine wines into such a huge pond that even boats could cross over. The dregs from brewing it piled up on the sides like a dike along a river, and from the top of it, people could see for miles. Whenever he happened to visit, he would have a drum beaten on top of it, and the people down below would get down on their hands and knees to drink wine from the pond. Since they looked like cattle drinking water, people called it "bull-drinking." Meixi would not find it amusing unless there were at least three thousand drinking at one time. Jie's lustful character and insatiable appetites made the people furious. Fortunately, the Shang king Tang the Completer arose to take Jie's place, killed Meixi, and exiled King Jie to Nanchao. What we know today as Chao County in Luzhou Prefecture, Jiangnan, is the place where Jie the tyrant met his end. This is why Meixi was the very first monster among women.

When the realm of the Xia was taken over by the Shang, there were wise queens for many generations, but most of them were quite ordinary, with no exceptional talent or virtue. But then in the twenty-eighth generation of the Shang rulers, King Zhou appeared on the scene. He was intelligent by nature and handled all things quickly and skillfully. He was brave and aggressive and able to fight off fierce beasts. He had a particular way with words that often surprised people. If someone was about to reprimand him, he would know beforehand and would interrupt him before that man could even open his mouth. When he did something wrong, he would gloss over it with endless clever excuses. He spent his days overseeing construction projects, and every one of his chariots and palaces was of the finest workmanship.

Then he fell in love with the daughter of the noble Yousu, named Daji. She monopolized his affections, and he satisfied her every desire. At first he tried to copy even the wine pond and forest with meat hanging from its branches made by that immoral King Jie of Xia. Not only that, he even ordered the maids and servants of the palace to strip naked and do filthy and obscene acts wherever he wished, without a second thought about this offending the Emperor of Heaven. He set up nine markets in the palace where he drank and sang late into the night, getting too drunk to appear for the morning audience—and that, too, produced resentment on all sides. Daji saw how the people hated King Jie and worried that some of them might rebel. So she suggested that he use cruel punishments, forcing people to hold on to red-hot iron bars until their hands were badly burned. Then he erected an iron pillar, heated it red-hot with fire and ash, and then forced people to embrace it, which immediately burned them to a crisp. These were called the "burning punishments." There were other cruel punishments, too, too many for me to tell about. Since King Zhou cared only about what Daji liked, nothing else concerned him. This is why when King Wu raised an army to overthrow him, King Zhou burned himself to death. If Daji had possessed only beauty but no evil talent, she would never have become so powerful. She is yet another example of a monstrous creature who was both talented and beautiful.

King Wen, the father of the Zhou king Wu, was a sage, and King Wu's mother, the queen, was most virtuous. She had talent and was able to help her husband from inside the palace. Because she had not one shred of jealousy in her heart, King Wen had hundreds of sons with his concubines—which is a rare case in history. While some people sang "Ospreys Cry" and "Hooves of the Unicorn" to praise her outstanding virtue, others said sarcastically, "These songs are surely composed by the Duke of Zhou. Auntie Zhou would never sing such songs."[5] This was certainly not to criticize the queen, but to show how unusual it is to find a virtuous queen among the many jealous women in the world. When King You succeeded to the Zhou dynasty throne, another monstrous creature appeared.[6] This one was quite different from Meixi and Daji in the Xia and Shang dynasties, for this woman nearly ended the Zhou dynasty's reign of eight hundred years. This monster was named Baosi. Even though she was King You's queen, her origins could be traced back five or six hundred years to the Xia dynasty.

The young men said, "This monstrous woman sounds strange indeed. How could the seed of a disaster have been planted as far back as the Xia dynasty?"

Baosi's ancestors had the family name Xia, the same as the Xia dynasty. When the Xia dynasty's virtue was exhausted and their end was near, Baosi's ancestors transformed into two dragons. They presented themselves in the royal court and spoke in human speech, "We are the rulers of the Kingdom of Bao." Hearing these words, the King of Xia was furious and ordered the dragons to be killed. The dragons spat out frothy spit and disappeared. One minister was amazed by the dragons' spit and sealed it up in a cask, which was then stored in the treasury. There it stayed until King Li went to the treasury and opened the cask to have a look. The spit rolled across the floor all the way into the palace where it hit a young girl and then disappeared. This girl was only twelve or thirteen years old, but she became pregnant because of it.

At that time, a rumor went around that said, "Woven robes and a mulberry bow will bring an end to the mighty Zhou." Not long afterward, a man with a mountain mulberry bow and a woman carrying a robe woven from grass came to town to sell these things. When people in the market saw that the couple matched the omens, they wanted to report them. The couple ran away to hide, because they were afraid of being caught. Along the way they happened to see the newborn daughter of the young girl who had gotten pregnant abandoned by the side of the road. The couple took pity on the poor baby and took her with them as they fled to the state of Bao. Some time later, the baby girl had grown into a lovely young woman. When the ruler of Bao was charged with a crime and put in jail, he presented her to the King of Zhou in return for his release. Once the King of Zhou saw how beautiful the woman was, he made her his concubine.

The young lady was elegant in all she did, but she never opened her mouth to laugh. Usually when we see a woman who won't laugh, we would think this is because she is especially respectable and virtuous. Who would have guessed that this woman's not laughing could have disastrous consequences? The one time she smiled caused the fall of the state—this is why it would have been better if she had not suddenly shown her teeth. King You had tried thousands of ways to make her smile, but none of them had worked.

At that time, there was a standing order throughout the Zhou Kingdom that whenever there was a threat of invasion, signal fires would be lighted on the beacon towers so that all the nobles could come to the king's assistance. One time, King You lighted the beacon fire for no reason. All the nobles hurried to the rescue, but there was no threat of invasion. Seeing that the nobles had all been tricked and had come in vain, Baosi laughed out loud before she realized what she was doing. Later when the dog barbarians invaded and approached the capital, King You desperately had all the beacons lighted, but the nobles thought the King was tricking them again, so none came to save him. Consequently the dog barbarians killed King You. So isn't this another example of a monster woman who caused the fall of a state? From these examples, we can see that women with both talent and virtue are rare indeed.

At that point, a younger man responded, "Those bewitching women who destroy states, who overthrow kingdoms with their desire for pleasure and wealth—people are still talking about them today, and everyone knows how despicable they were. Yesterday, there were several plays performed in the village, and I watched *Washing Silk*.[7] The story is about Xishi, who lived at the foot of Mount Ningluo. Minister Fan visited her several times and sang the line about how Xishi would be the savior of the Yue Kingdom, 'All the people east of the river depend upon you, dear lady.' Because neither the civilian officials nor the military commanders were able to rebuild the strength of the Yue Kingdom, they had to use that Xishi woman to do it for them. Later, when people saw Xishi and Minister Fan leaving on a boat together, they believed that the couple had become immortals. Isn't this an example of a woman having both beauty and talent, having accomplished great things, and on top of that, who came to a good end?"

Even though the play might tell it that way, people might have seen it in a different light in real life. We see so many successful and famous literati refusing to take the opportunity to resign when the emperor becomes suspicious of their loyalty. Minister Fan Li was one example, because King Goujian killed him in the end, even after Fan Li had helped him restore the Yue Kingdom. This is why they made up the story that he became an immortal. It was merely meant as a strong incentive for those who have wealth and talent to step down once they reach the top. On what basis could he really have become an immortal? What I've read in an unofficial history is considerably different from what you were told.

It says that Xishi was a village farm girl living by the Ruoye Stream. Officials at that time were really tired of looking at women from wealthy families who wore fancy clothing, had fashionable hairstyles, and put on too much makeup. One day, when Fan was taking a walk in the mountains, he happened to see this young, lively girl in simple but elegant clothes and wearing only a little makeup. To Fan she looked exceptionally beautiful, even though in fact she was merely ordinary. And when he caught sight of her in her narrow lane, she was surrounded by many ugly village women. She was the only one who was not too young and not too old, who was elegant in her movements, and who knew how to speak to people. How could Minister Fan's heart not have been moved? Have you ever seen an unmarried young lady from a fine household who would approach a man and talk to him like that? And who would give a man a piece of the silk she was washing as a token of her feelings—just because she enjoyed the flirtation? Or who would even go so far as to say that she would miss him?

Others probably would have forgotten it all after three years of being apart, but Xishi remained unmarried even though Fan Li never came back to marry her. She even suffered from heartache because of him. When they did finally meet again, Fan Li told her that the state was in great danger and needed her assistance. Xishi foolishly went along with Fan Li. Xishi was a girl who had lived in the mountains all her life and had no parents to give her sound advice, so it's no surprise that she would say a few words to men she didn't know and that she would follow a young man who had no home whatsoever. After wandering for a while as bums, they finally arrived at the Yue Kingdom. There she learned how to play musical instruments, to sing, and to dance. She also learned tricks for attracting men before being sent to the Kingdom of Wu.

The King of Wu at that time was just a Suzhou phony who wanted to hear only the sort of flattery that would disgust you. His freeloading attendants could easily talk up ugly maids as gorgeous or halfway-pretty girls into beauties for the ages. When Bopi, as one of the king's courtiers—and because he had accepted no small amount of bribes—said that Xishi was an exceptional beauty, who would dare to contradict him?[8] Since he had no thoughts of his own, the King of Wu believed all the praise he heard about Xishi and fell in love with her at first sight, as if he had been given a precious gift. The old saying goes, "A knight will die for one who appreciates his value, and a woman will make herself beautiful for the one who takes joy in her."[9] Since the King of Wu treated Xishi so well, she should have tried to help ease the tension between Yue and Wu. If she had, she would have supported the King of Wu in his bid to become hegemon over all the nobles by being loyal to Wu without betraying Yue. In that case, we could have said that she was a stalwart woman of the sort you'd see once in a thousand years. Why go to the trouble of promising herself to Fan Li in the first place, and then let herself be presented as a gift like a goose or wine to the King of Wu! On the one hand, being the filthy bitch she was, she made the King of Yue so subservient to the King of Wu that he even tasted his shit.[10] It is said that people from that area still have bad breath even today! On the other hand, it was because of her that the King of Wu ignored his duties as ruler altogether, going hunting today, picking lotuses tomorrow, squandering the people's resources by building towers and digging out pools, not to mention what he spent on constant wars against neighboring states. The people of the Wu region all hated him. When the enemy invaded the capital, the King of Wu saw his chance and made a run for it, while Xishi—his confidant and the beauty who shared his bed and had brought him boundless joy—was thrown away like so much garbage.

Do you know what Xishi had in mind then? She hoped to return to Yue and use her remaining beauty as a middle-aged woman to her advantage. She even thought she could win the heart of the King of Yue and rise above the queen. Who would have thought that Minister Fan's scheme would actually work out? If Fu Chai had been clever enough to listen to the good advice of loyal Wu Zixu instead of the crooked words of Bopi, then he would never have been so totally defeated. What if after all that secret planning, the Yue king Goujian had not lived so long? In that case, even if the "ten years of preparation and ten years of training" had been useful, he would not have achieved such total success. Moreover, the plot was kept so secret that so much could not be told to others—it was cheap and despicable, involving many situations that people would be embarrassed to see.

When the state of Wu finally fell, Minister Fan was quite old. On the one hand, he was worried that if Xishi returned to Yue, she might use her old tricks to destroy the Yue kingdom as she had Wu. On the other hand, he was afraid that if the King of Yue recovered his role as hegemon, Xishi's presence would remind him of his shameful past, which might cause people to laugh at him. Likewise, Fan Li was born in the family of Sanhu at Chu, which nowadays is in Wujiang County but originally was under the jurisdiction of Suzhou.[11] Thus, as a commoner from Wu who had become a loyal minister in Yue and who in turn had plotted against Wu, while remaining loyal to Yue, Fan could be considered a traitor to Wu. When the King of Yue was in exile, he was always conscious of the origins of this minister, nor did he forget to maintain the proper distance between ruler and subjects. But after he returned to Yue and revived his ambition to become hegemon in control of the various states, he really did not care about much else beyond having strong armies and sufficient grain reserves.

All those ministers who had helped him regain the throne harbored their own secret plots. What if they were serving a ruler who did not trust them? What if they offended the king unknowingly, and out of the blue the king decided to charge them with a crime? This could be disastrous to themselves and their families! This caused Fan Li to come up with a plan. He found a boat and left, saying that he'd had enough of the material world and wished to spend time drifting around the Five Lakes region. But since the Five Lakes are only three or four hundred kilometers across, is it possible that he would leave no trace of his whereabouts? Later people would all say that the King of Yue was a long-necked, sharp-mouthed man[12] who was a good companion during bad times but never during good times. And doesn't that description fit Fan Li himself? He stashed away treasure and wealth while serving at court and yet later pretended to become a hermit—he even changed his name to Sir Taozhu, which means "to flee from execution."[13]

In just a few years, Fan Li had accumulated a significant amount of property, mostly obtained while at court. Could it be that he had some magic to turn stone into gold that produced the wealth and silks that accompanied his rise in position? Only Xishi understood Fan Li's obscure schemes. Xishi's only strength was to make herself up as she had done when she was lady of the state of Wu in an effort to entrap him. Yet Minister Fan's feelings for her were not the same as they had been long before. Word that they were together would get around, and the King of Yue would probably come after her. Better that Fan resort to a stratagem he had used as a conniving court official—he invited Xishi to watch the moon on a lake. When Xishi appeared that evening, fully made up, she was ready to lift a wine cup to the moon and to lament lost time. She did not expect that Minister Fan had worked all this out in advance, and at a deserted spot, totally unexpectedly, he pushed Xishi overboard. With a splash, she went straight off to the Crystal Palace.[14] This is what the poet meant when he wrote:

> and now there is only the West River moon,
> which once shone on the lady in the palace of Wu.[15]

"Your story is too far-fetched!" the young men said. "Where is the evidence that Minister Fan did what you said he did in the middle of a lake?"

I wasn't a witness, but I wouldn't wish to accuse him falsely. You can find evidence in "Minister Fan Buries Xishi in the Lake" in *News from the Rustic Boat*, or "Lord Dongting's Complaint on Behalf of Xishi" in *The Du Tuolin Collection*.[16] Now in the Wu region you can find Xishi Bay, the Xishi Shore, Xishi's Sweet Sweat Pool, Xishi's Silken Sails Brook, and Sailing the Moon Slope, while in the lake you can find "Xishi's arms," "Xishi's tongue," and "Xishi's breasts," all of them in the water.[17] Can you say that these are not visible evidence? If she were not buried in the water, why would Minister Fan have changed his name to Master Chi Yi? *Chi* means "owl" and *yi* means "to harm" or "to kill." Since Xishi was also named Yiguang, certainly Fan named himself Chi Yi because he "killed" Xishi. During the Warring States Period, the philosopher Mencius once said that Xishi was so unclean that people would cover their noses when they passed her. Therefore, even if she were buried in the lake, her bad reputation has never been washed clean!

"What you've said is absurd," one man said. "Since ancient times, there has been only praise for Xishi, comparing her beauty with the most magnificent lake in the world—West Lake in Hangzhou—as in one of Su Shi's poems:

The shimmering ripples delight the eye on sunny days;
The dimming hills present a rare view in rainy haze.
West Lake may be compared to Beauty Xishi,
Lightly adorned or thickly made up, lovely both ways.[18]

So are you saying that Su Shi did not know as much about her as you do?"

Old Dongpo considered West Lake so beautiful that he ran out of words of praise and happened to compare it to one of history's most famous beauties. In fact, he did not mean to praise Xishi in particular. There's another meaning underlying the comparison that people have never been able to comprehend. You see, all the lakes in the world are surrounded by plants and grasses, so that the water running down from the surrounding mountains year after year could nurture edible creatures such as fish, shrimp, water caltrops, seaweed, and some herbs for medical use. And so the poor villagers could depend on the lakes for food and basic needs. And yet West Lake is different from other lakes. It is located just outside the walls of Hangzhou, with splendid mountains and clear waters. The twin peaks and three temples of Mount Zhu stretch high into the clouds—inside and out we see six stone arch bridges and the reflections of peach trees and willows. We see numerous small shrines, Buddhist monasteries, and Daoist temples surrounding the lake, perhaps a thousand altogether. There are wineshops and places of entertainment one after the other. Day or night, flutes and drums never cease to be heard from its painted boats. Traveling merchants or officials from other provinces—not one will leave without wasting some money here. And who knows what fortunes are frittered away by local playboys in gambling houses and brothels?

On the surface we see beautiful scenery and glamorous houses in the city of Hangzhou. Yet household after household is empty. The reason is that West Lake is too close to the city. Every day we see men young and old, tall and short, coming to the lake, and every one of them will spend at least several strings of cash. This is why people in the past compared West Lake to Xishi, since West Lake brings no benefit to the city of Hangzhou. Is this not similar to how Xishi brought down the state of Wu by using her overwhelming beauty? People nowadays overestimate Su Shi's poem because of his talent and fame, and consequently they recognize only the beauty of West Lake but don't grasp the full meaning of the reference. However, there was a judicial supervisor called Hu Lai[19] who wrote a couplet on a pillar of the Temple in the Heart of the Lake that reveals the truth:

Joyous song and sound of *sheng* the year round,
Still the poor can only sing laments to the moon at night.
Six bridges, flowers and willows all abound—
For mulberry trees and willows, not a sliver left of ground.[20]

You can find other poems written on the pillars, but since most are by visitors from other parts, they all describe the many beauties of West Lake. They even criticize Judge Hu's poem as too moralistic!

But I have another very short story I wish to tell you. Recently a young gentleman from the Wu region passed through the Yue region on his way to take his post. He made a point of asking about buying a boat and a horse so he could travel to Ningluo Mountain. When he got there, he was so captivated by the beauty of the mountain and its rivers that he didn't want to leave. He even started humming to himself, composing a poem in which he wondered whether Xishi had gone off to take her place in some immortal realm. He went so far as to ask a matchmaker to help him select a girl from the region, hoping to bring a hint of Xishi back with him. While he was asking around, an old villager came to him and said it just right. "You really think that Xishi was the most beautiful woman in the country? In fact she was a local villager's daughter who was just some shopworn goods, an old maid no man wanted to marry. Her fame was a total accident. If she truly had been an exceptional beauty, she wouldn't have ended up marrying an outsider like you!" Having made a fool of himself, the young gentleman promptly left.

The young men all applauded the story and laughed. "This old guy does have the guts to take the high ground! That saves Suzhou people the effort of having to mock their own."

At this point they all got up and were about to put the food and wine out on the table, hoping to enjoy a meal together. Yet when they looked up, they could see dense clouds building in the west. Surely heavy rain would be coming down from the mountains soon. Seeing this, they all hurriedly bid farewell to one another and went home.

People think that the writing of fiction dawned during the Tang dynasty, not realizing that it began as early as Master Zhuang of the Lacquer Garden and the historian of Longmen, Sima Qian. Nine-tenths of The Zhuangzi is fables in which we see animals as big as Kun and Peng and as small as orioles, pigeons, and wrens. A useless tree and a cackling goose are used as allegory to illuminate the cultivation of life—even the butchering of an ox and the fashioning of a wheel are used to convey profound meanings.[21] There are also stories that mock worthies and sages and ridicule emperors and kings. These are the fictional works of the Lacquer Garden. After Sima Qian was castrated, he composed Records of the Grand Historian, which consists of "The Basic Annals," "The Hereditary Houses," "Tables," "Treatises," and "Biographies." These works indeed contain righteous statements that are as bright as stars and enlightening as the sun and grand speeches as magnificent as the rivers and the ocean. Yet they also contain random experiences that are sad or joyful, and not only in the biography of the jesters. For example, chapters such as "The Treatise on Religious Sacrifices," "The Treatise on Weights and Measures," "The Biographies of Cruel Officials," and "The Biographies of Knights-Errant" are either satires or parodies that draw readers into the narratives and engage their minds, yet readers are not aware of their effect. That is because they read these chapters as official history and consequently dare not treat them as fictional tales. Similarly, consider the depiction of the conflicts between Dou and Tian. Is that story any different from romantic tales written during the Tang?[22] Toward the end of the chapter "The Hereditary House of Goujian," there is an additional passage about Taozhu, narrating how Fan Li lost his son, who was killed in the Kingdom of Chu because of Fan Li's friend Zhuang Sheng.[23] That anecdote is obviously fictional. This is why I say fiction writing did not begin with men of the Tang.

The story "Water Burial of Xishi" in the second session of Aina's Idle Talk collection is an extremely rude account of Xishi! We were amused by tales of women in the Xia, Shang, and Zhou dynasties—all stories familiar to anyone who reads history—that are like flower clusters in a vast expanse, told in such a lively manner they seem to be recent events rather than old texts. As for the main Xishi story, it is not told merely as a continuation of the Baosi anecdote but instead was presented as a subtle addition of detail to another person's praise of Xishi's beauty as he recounted the play Washing Silk. He turned this classic beauty into an ordinary village woman and made an exceptional strategist into an experienced schemer. His story's three layers were overturned and jumbled—making wave patterns, not like others who would probably tell a story all at once. He explains the origin of "Chiyi" and "Yiguang," annotates poems about West Lake, and talks about the matchmaking business, all of which are quite extraordinary and *refreshing while yet extremely enlightening and admonitory. The story opens up people's minds and develops their wisdom. Not even Master Zhuang and Sima Qian could do better than this, to say nothing of those Tang dynasty writers!*

Translated by Li Fang-yu

A Court-Appointed Gentleman Squanders His Wealth but Takes Power

The wind and rain suddenly came, and from that day forth the dark clouds did not part. The rain fell in fits and starts, and it was ten or so days before the blue sky, bright and refreshing, was seen again. The fellow who had planted the beans walked over to the arbor to have a look about. He saw that the vines had grown long, with a profusion of leaves and branches, and so he delicately straightened out each of the sprouts and guided them upward along a length of string. Under the leaves were numerous gnats that he picked off one by one.

His neighbors were all outside their gates, calling out, "The weather's cleared up and somebody's under the bean arbor waiting to tell some old tales. Let's go!" Before long they had gathered one after another, but still the old storyteller from before was nowhere to be seen.

The crowd said, "The old man's stock of tales is limited, and he has nothing else to say. Since it's been raining, he likely won't come by today."

There was one among them who said, "I heard quite a fine tale at my relative's place yesterday. But if I tell it today, I'm afraid you'll want me to tell one tomorrow, too—and if I can't tell you one then, what you've said today about the old gent you'll say about me as well."

"Just tell us whatever's in your belly without holding back," the crowd said. "It's like back in the day when the scholar Su Dongpo was at home with nothing to do. If he ran into people, he would ask what was new and have them tell him ghost stories.[1] He took them as so much malarkey, but still he listened. People manage their own minds and moods—it doesn't matter what other people say."

Su Dongpo is precisely the person I was going to mention. He was born during the Renzong period of the Song dynasty and served as an academician in the Dragon Diagram Hall. From the time he was small, he surpassed others in intelligence, and whenever he perused books or histories, old or new, he understood them at a glance. He could see that the affairs of the day were in turmoil—the reins of power were in the hands of corrupt officials like Wang Anshi, with his "Green Sprouts Policy," and from time to time, Su would ridicule him or wrote poetry meant to provoke him.[2] He led with his quick wit and sharp tongue, giving no heed to his own safety and that of his family. It would have been better for him to be a simpleton and just follow the crowd, painting his gourds and following the beaten path. He would have gotten himself a top rank with a promising future and enjoyed smooth sailing to the end of his days.

As you'll see, Su Dongpo was subjected to many trials and tribulations, all because he was not careful about what came out of his mouth. One day at home, when he was feeling terribly frustrated, he inscribed a poem on the wall that read:

> People, when they have a son, want him to be smart;
> I have, by being smart, wasted my whole life.
> All I want is for my son to be stupid and dull;
> So without disaster, without hardship, he'll have the official's art.[3]

This poem ridiculing those high-ranking officials holding the reins of government expresses a long-standing grievance of Old Su's, but no more of that now.

Later on there was another old gentleman who was also unwilling to simply go with the flow in his official career and so was removed from his positions several times. Seeing that the clever and quick-witted can serve as high officials and thereby profit greatly, he, too, wrote four lines of poetry on the wall after the fashion of Su Dongpo:

> Only because I was born being not so smart,
> Have I wasted my whole life in court robe and cap.
> All I want is for my son to be clever and quick,
> So he can take whatever steps it takes to learn the official's art.

This poem appears to overturn Master Dongpo's, and yet because it ridicules those in charge as did Old Su's, it must also be taken in jest.

Surely we can't say it's always a good thing to have clever and quick-witted sons! Then again, there are those who are neither clever nor smart at birth. At first they appear to be nothing more than lumps of mud or chunks of meat, but later, when the time is right, the day finally arrives when they can do deeds that lift heaven and shake the earth. They're promoted to generals and appointed princes. No matter how rare, these things do happen!

For example, during the Three Kingdoms, there was one Kong Wenju who was just ten *sui* when he accompanied his father to Luoyang for an official appointment.[4] At that time, there was a renowned metropolitan commandant named Li Yuanli. When important local officials would go to see him, no matter how highly placed they might be, his gatekeeper would put on airs and throw his weight around, and so it was difficult to reach Li in just a single visit. Wenju was merely a lad of ten *sui* then. With a confident swagger, he brandished a calling card indicating he was a close family friend of long standing, and when he arrived at the gate of the mansion, he said, "I'm a close friend of the Li family."

On seeing that intelligent and handsome child, the gatekeeper promptly announced his arrival. Some time later, Master Li granted him an interview and asked, "How is it that Your Honor and I are related?"

The imperturbable Kong Wenju replied, "Previously, my ancestor Confucius and your esteemed forefather Laozi enjoyed a 'teacher-confidant' friendship. Thus it may be said that a 'venerable and luminous friendship' exists between our two families."

When the numerous guests in attendance heard this, they all declared it extraordinary. At that time, there was one among them named Chen Jian, who was last to come forward. Li Yuanli relayed Kong Wenju's words to Chen Jian, who said, "Just because a person is bright and all-knowing when young does not mean he'll turn out well when he matures."

Kong Wenju answered him, "It looks like you, good sir, were bright and all-knowing when young."

Everyone present broke out laughing and said, "To have a wit like this—who knows how far he may go in days to come?"

How could they have known that this sharp tongue would incur the jealousy and malice of all? Later, a misfortune befell his father's political clique, and as a result his entire family was exterminated, root and branch. So we can see that to be too obviously bright when young really is the worst of all possible things.

Now I'll tell you about one who was muddled and ignorant while young but later achieved great things and had the highest of ranks thrust upon him. Now *this* is *truly* marvelous! This person emerged at the time of the Sui-Tang dynastic transition, when the whole world was seething like a boiling cauldron.[5] His name was Wang Hua. At first, though, he had no proper given name, just the childhood name Xingge. A native of Xin'an Commandery, nowadays called Huizhou Prefecture, he lived in the town of Leyi in Jixi County.[6]

In that place there were a great many wealthy households. In the previous dynasty, there had been several very rich men who had made financial contributions to the military in the amount of one hundred thousand ounces of silver. The court conferred the title Gentleman Official upon them, and so they came to address one another respectfully as "Gentleman."[7]

To resume our story, Wang Hua's father, Wang Yan, was the offspring of several generations of frank and honest common folk. From the time he was fifteen or sixteen *sui*, he learned the business of being an itinerant peddler from some clerks. This was a Huizhou custom—starting out with nothing, people could come and go with nothing more than cotton clothes and grass sandals, traveling on foot with carrying-pole loads on their shoulders. Such people were never ones to give up a copper or to spend one. Wang Yan did this for more than ten years, during which he worked himself to the bone and suffered bitter hardships, gradually accumulating many thousands of ounces of silver in capital.

When he was about fifty, he calculated his total worth. Without realizing it, he had accumulated more than two hundred thousand ounces of silver and over one hundred or so clerks, of various levels. He squared his accounts, and at first he was overjoyed. Raising his cup, he drank until he was half drunk, when suddenly he began to weep. His clerks all asked him why. Wang Yan said, "It's for no other reason than this—I used to have no son, but then the bodhisattva Guanyin of Potalaka Mountain in the Southern Sea blessed me with one, and I named him Xingge. He has a square face, large ears, and a goodly appearance. But he's dull and stupid. At fifteen *sui* he still titters and babbles, points at heaven, and scratches in the earth. He can't make a single clear sentence, just like a deaf-mute. Whenever he comes upon food and drink, it doesn't matter how much there is. It's as though he has a furnace in his belly—he leaves nothing behind. How can he not be the son of a Squire Jiao, the husband of Hu Yong'er?[8] Although I have struggled hard to build up this enormous wealth for my family, it has all been a fool's errand." He finished speaking and wept, whimpering and sobbing.

Among the clerks were some who cared to come forward and comfort him. Some advised him to go to Yangzhou or Suzhou to find a new concubine and have some good children—others plied him with wine and played the finger-guessing game. But we will say no more of this.

Finally, an old, experienced clerk came up to him and said, "You need not be in a hurry, squire. Next year the young master will be sixteen *sui*. It is a tradition in Huizhou that when people reach sixteen they go out into the world and learn to do business on their own. I see that even though the young master is not one for talking, still, he has a nimble mind and his face predicts good luck. Why not withdraw some capital and let me assist him in learning the business on the road? It won't be so hard once he has gained a few years' experience."

The clerk informed Xingge of this, and the lad nodded his head several times. The clerks all said, "The young Gentleman grasps it! It won't be hard, not hard at all!" And then they went their separate ways.

On the first day of the first month of the following year, all the clerks came by en masse to wish their master a grand new year. In the course of drinking, that experienced clerk from before raised the matter of Xingge's going into business. Wang Yan said, "He is young and foolish. For now I shall give him three thousand ounces of silver to go out and open a small pawnshop with. Teach him to sit there and watch how things go. You can set out in the second month."

He had not yet finished speaking when Xingge stood up with aplomb and said very clearly, "You have such a great family fortune, and I'm the only heir. How can you give me only three thousand ounces and send me out on my own? It's simply not enough!"

The crowd was flabbergasted. Even Wang Yan, when he heard it, perked up without his realizing it and said repeatedly, "Marvelous indeed! What he says is clearly right. I think this must be a case of 'being blessed with a nimble mind'!" Everyone present in the hall expressed their admiration.

On the first day of the second lunar month, Xingge prepared his luggage, bade his father and mother farewell, and set out on his journey. Wang Yan cast lots and determined it would be best for Xingge to go to Pingjiang.[9] Pingjiang was a commercial port city. Its market buzzed with excitement, and the smoke from its hearths mingled as one. Many pawnshops had been opened there. How could that three thousand ounces of silver have been enough? Xingge responded by saying, "I'll need ten thousand in silver. Otherwise I'll just sit at home with my lips sealed as before."

Wang Yan said, "That's reasonable . . ." and provided him with the ten thousand ounces of silver.

Xingge prepared the usual dried pickled vegetables, jars of lard, and bottles of roasted peas and merrily departed. The old clerk had already entrusted some people to set up a street-facing shop with a residence in the back. They outfitted it with a signboard and shelves, as well as some other odds and ends, and selected an auspicious day to open for business. They had just hung up the signboard when a person came in carrying ten boxes and said, "Congratulations! I have come to show my admiration for the young Gentleman in opening up his own shop. May the young Gentleman use these ten pairs of 'interest boxes,' which I would pawn for ten ounces, to bring him good luck."[10]

Xingge heard this and merrily said, "I don't want your boxes. I'll give you twenty ounces of silver in thanks for your kindness."

The head clerk said, "Do not listen to him, young Gentleman! This rascal has been loitering in the market all day long and has come by to get something for nothing! All this talk of 'good luck' is nothing but a line—do not give it to him!"

Xingge said, "Please let me spend some money to ensure smooth business in the future."

The clerk shut his mouth. A short while later, he saw a group of fine gentlemen wearing the hats and robes of the gentry approach, bearing in both hands cloth of the kind traditionally given as a gift. He saw on the card of introduction nearly forty names written out in a neat and tidy hand. They said they were neighbors who had heard that a Gentleman had opened a pawnshop, and so each had contributed one ounce of silver as a cash gift as well as an additional five coins to pay for the ritual objects, wine, and cakes. These things they had brought to congratulate him on the opening of his business. The employees had no choice but to invite Xingge to come out and play host. The neighbors each greeted him and offered their congratulations. All sat down according to their roles as host and guests, took tea, and then departed.

Xingge turned around with a merry look and said to the group of clerks, "No wonder my father the senior Gentleman divined that this would be a good place to open a shop. Such thoughtful neighbors truly are hard to come by."

While saying so, he tore open two of the envelopes containing the gifts of cash. The employees all came forward and held back his hand, saying, "This is but a common courtesy. You can't accept it! After a few days, you should put on a theatrical production and a banquet for them. Then you can return the gifts."

Xingge said, "Twenty ounces of silver walked out the gate just now, and here forty have walked in again. This is a good sign of a future return on our investment. Why not reward the fellow who just pawned those boxes?"

He finished speaking and took the cash gifts inside with him, just as he had started to do before. The anxious crowd of clerks was flummoxed but could only grumble. A moment later, he called for a young man in his employ to enter. Xingge opened the cashbox, selected silver ingots weighing ten ounces each, and neatly sealed them into forty parcels. As he did so, he changed clothes, prepared cards of introduction, and walked out of the shop, saying, "I go now to return the courtesy."

The group asked, "Why the forty packets of silver?"

Xingge said, "I am not a local, but still they treat me with such generosity. I prepared these gifts to repay their kindness."

The group of clerks said, "It would be enough to spend twenty ounces on a banquet with wine and a show. Why so much?" They all put out their hands to stop him, saying, "Don't!"

Xingge said, "You see this only from the perspective of poor households. Since I'm opening up a shop in their territory to earn money, I would like to get to know my neighbors, which should make things easier if something comes up in the future. As the ancient saying puts it, 'He respects me one foot, but I respect him ten.' These ten ounces of silver are just how things have been done in the past—truly, it's not all that much."

He finished speaking, went directly out the gate, and delivered the packets of silver to each house one by one. Each and every one of his neighbors was delighted, and they commended him, saying, "This young Gentleman is a man of means." The employees stamped their feet and heaved a collective sigh, but there was nothing to be done, and that was that.

After Xingge had made his visits, he returned to the shop and took a seat. Just then a man led a horse through the gate and said, "I am a horse trader, and I have bought fifty horses for resale valued at one hundred ounces of silver each. I met with a sluggish market, and my horses neigh in hunger. I have come to your fine shop to pawn one for fifty ounces so as to buy feed for the rest. If I can sell the rest of the horses, I'll return your money with interest."

Deep down, Xingge loved fine horses, and at the first glimpse of the animal he began to smile. The employees said, "We do not pawn livestock. Go away, go away!"

Xingge said, "A horse would be useful in the area around the provincial capital. And if I do not let him pawn this horse, the other forty-nine might starve to death. Wouldn't that be a shame?"

Having finished speaking, he went back inside. The clerks refused the horse trader again and again, but for a long while he refused to go and was determined to wait until Xingge came out and gave him an answer. Before long, Xingge emerged bearing two fine silver ingots. He gestured for the horse trader to approach the center gate and handed the silver over. "One ingot would be enough," the horse trader said.

"You suffered much in coming here—you need money for your business," Xingge said. "If you pawn a horse worth one hundred ounces of silver for only fifty, would you not be taking a loss? Be on your way!" The horse peddler fell to his knees and bowed to him four times to thank him for his generosity and departed. The group of clerks was not aware of what had happened.

Again, Xingge went into the shop and sat down. He saw a poor man carrying a steel wok in his hands. A clerk pawned the wok for three qian of silver. As the old man departed, Xingge shook his head and thought to himself, "This poor man had only one wok at home. Now that he has pawned it, how will his wife do the cooking? Are three qian worth all that?" He ran out of the shop carrying the wok, mounted his horse, and shot out the gate like a puff of smoke in pursuit. He eventually found the poor man and returned his wok.

All around the shop, the employees bubbled with agitation as they discussed the business with the horse that had just taken place. They were surprised again when Xingge returned and closed the pawnshop gate in the middle of the day. They followed Xingge into the hall, where they all sat down in their proper order.

The old clerk said, "Young Master, you are making mistakes. You have never once been away from home, and we bear the responsibility for your well-being and prosperity. Although we have ten thousand ounces of silver as our capital, that was after we promised the old Gentleman a return of 30 percent interest! You have been in business for only a day or two, and you have turned everything on its head! Already we have lost a goodly part of that capital. How will we square the accounts in the future?"

Xingge said, "That shouldn't be hard. If you say you must add 30 percent interest, then just withdraw three thousand ounces and leave the remaining capital to me to do with as I will. I know all your old ways of being pawnshop clerks. They're nothing other than replacing the old with the new, exchanging the distant for the close, skimming a bit off the top of daily expenses, opening fake accounts in the course of helping out officials, scraping a bit off the silver when taking in or paying out, claiming lost pawn tickets, pocketing monthly shares, selling pawned goods, demanding extra 'wine money'—I don't aim to allow those tricks of yours! If you want to go, then go, but how can you say that I've lost my way?"

After this scolding the clerks were speechless. The old one said, "We can't let this happen." The clerks wrote up a detailed report and the next day returned to Huizhou, where they submitted it to Wang Yan. Xingge saw the old one go and relaxed a bit.

Before long, word of Xingge's generosity had gotten out among his neighbors, who all laid their traps to catch his money. Some said they had been involved in lawsuits and so needed to hurry off to rescue their mothers and fathers, some said their land taxes were in arrears and they needed to go immediately to help their kin avoid being flogged, some said their parents were sick and facing death and needed to be nursed back to health, and some said they were rebuilding temples or constructing bridges and so their funds had temporarily grown tight. In each case Xingge desired no security for the money but just handed over what his neighbors asked for. Within a month, those ten thousand ounces of silver had been transformed into Zhuang Zhou's butterfly.[11]

He was on the point of seeking out a fellow townsman or relative to write out a cashier's check and give him more cash with which to continue doing business when Wang Yan arrived swift as the wind, entered the gate, and looked all around. Voicing a string of protests, he grabbed Xingge and struck him.

Xingge just laughed merrily and said, "If people didn't disperse their money, then you'd still be living in your little thatched hut with a few pieces of cotton clothes, a few carrying-pole loads of unpolished rice, and a jar of lard—just enough for you to live out your life. Why should you have suffered so many hardships doing business if you were only going to store your wealth away in your cellar and never enjoy yourself with it?"

Wang Yan was exasperated to hear this, but in his old age he only had this one son. What could he do except laugh it off? The following day he packed his luggage and ended the lease on the storefront, and the whole group went home. He shut Xingge up in a room and did not allow him to socialize with others.

Before they knew it, four or five months had flown by and—who knows where he found it?—Xingge had five thousand cash. He had given each of the clerks working in the family business one hundred coppers and every month received two hundred in return. Since they all worked for the family, they just gave him whatever sum he asked for, and in less than half a year, he had amassed some thirty thousand. When the elder Gentleman learned of it, he said, "The boy knows how to earn interest now. This is nothing like he was before." Xingge just acted as though he had not heard this and lent out money in private all day long.

One day Wang Yan said, "Since you know how to make great sums of money through lending, why not head out again with ten thousand?"

Xingge said, "Since I squandered ten thousand last time, I want you to give me even more so that I may work diligently to earn that first ten thousand back."

Wang Yan said, "That sounds reasonable." Then he asked, "Will you open a pawnshop as you did last time?"

Xingge said, "There are too many in the pawnshop business nowadays. I won't do that. I need fifty thousand. Perhaps I'll go to the capital to sell pearls and precious metals, perhaps make stoneware and porcelain in Jiangxi, perhaps buy imports in Fujian, or even set up a Huaiyang salt business. I'll act as opportunities arise and go where life takes me. This won't be like last time, when I went to Pingjiang based on fortune-telling."

Upon hearing this, Wang Yan was delighted and weighed out fifty thousand ounces. He selected eight household servants, who carefully bundled everything up. Altogether there were thirty loads of luggage. As before, Xingge rode his horse, cutting a dashing figure as he left.

On the road Xingge's manager informed him that Mingzhou had a thriving sun-roasted fish industry, and so they set out for Mingzhou. They made their way to Xiatang Street alongside Pontoon Bridge, where several wealthy men managed their businesses and Xingge could find lodgings. They moved into one merchant's house and stowed their luggage there. How could they have known that the sun-roasted fish business doesn't pick up until the middle of the third lunar month and that Xingge had arrived half a month early?

The temporary lodgings were too lonely for him, and so he went with several servants to Mount Potalaka for a few days' relaxation. He aimed to offer incense in the temple and take in the sea, which would be pleasant. That mountain was sacred ground and quite free of vulgar sorts. The following day Xingge went for a solitary stroll under the moon. He absentmindedly walked directly to an outcropping known as "Turtle Fishing Rock" facing the boundless sea, where he sat down and crossed his legs.[12] The moon was at its zenith, bathing all with its light, and the sea air cooled Xingge's sleeves.

Just when he was about to go back, he suddenly saw a man walk out from the shadows of the grove beside the rock. Xingge said, "How strange!" and sat down as before. When he and the man were almost face to face, Xingge finally saw him clearly and leaped in fright. The man truly had a strange and monstrous visage:

> He could see only two protruding eyes,
> A mustache and goatee,
> Two temples in fluffy disarray,
> As if he were Zhong Kui descended to the mortal realm.[13]
> Twin eyebrows hanging down at angles,
> He resembled an arhat come from the West.[14]
> An air heroic, gallant, difficult to restrain,
> Clearly a spirit dragon playing in the sea.
> In spirit depressed, lacking a destination,
> The image of a starving tiger that has lost its woods.

Xingge came forward and was on the point of welcoming him when the man walked away with great strides, not paying him the slightest regard, and finally leaned against that marvelous rocky cliff soaring high in the air, where he called out in a loud voice, "Oh Heaven, can it be that I, Old Liu, am done for? How could I obtain fifty thousand in cash, so that I can finish my one-day enterprise!"

Xingge clearly heard what the man said and was astonished. He came forward and asked, "Good sir, for what do you desire that fifty thousand ounces right here and now?"

The man gave him a sidelong glance and said, "You're not worthy of knowing my business, you milk-breathed stripling!"

Xingge said, "I'm no mere child, but you, sir, are undeniably a country bumpkin if you see fifty thousand ounces of silver as any great challenge."

Hearing these words, the man turned and bowed down, saying, "I'm petty, indeed, and failed to see how you, my lord, could come to my aid. If you can manage to lend me the money, I'll come back on this day of this month next year and meet you at this spot, where I'll return one hundred thousand ounces to you. I won't eat my words."

Xingge said, "My lodgings aren't far from here. I'll help you get it."

They set out together, boarded a boat, met with Xingge's retinue of fifteen or sixteen, and returned directly to his lodgings in Mingzhou. Xingge invited his landlord to come out and called the serving boys to fetch the luggage. Then he handed the fifty thousand ounces of silver to Liu piece by piece.

Liu said, "You, sir, have no particular need for this horse now. Please give it to me to ride along with everything else. I'll return it to you on another day, good sir."

Xingge hurriedly untied the reins and handed them to Liu. The two saluted each other with folded hands, and Liu departed without another word. The landlord and the serving boys looked on from the side. They were dumbstruck and didn't know what had led up to this.

The landlord just said, "This man must be an ocean-faring fisherman, or perhaps he manages the coastal guard." They could only speculate as to the man's relation to the fish-drying business. He asked, "What is this gentleman's name, and where does he live?"

"I don't know that either," Xingge said, and he called the serving boys to put his luggage in order to return home.

A serving boy asked, "Why did you come here, sir?"

Xingge said, "This transaction will net a 100 percent profit. It couldn't be easier!"

The serving boys had no choice but to follow suit, deliver a confused farewell to the landlord, and depart with Xingge, returning home via the same route as before. All in all, before two months had passed, they were already back home.

Wang Yan asked, "What business have you done that you've been able to return so quickly?" But when he saw how light the luggage was, he was taken aback.

"This month next year, we'll get a 100 percent profit without fail," Xingge said.

Wang Yan asked in detail where the money had gone but didn't receive so much as a word in reply. He asked the serving boys, who just pointed and said, "Just go ask him. We don't know a thing." The old Gentleman's heart beat anxiously, but Xingge just blithely pointed toward the front, saying they should build the grand hall there, and pointed toward the rear, saying they should build the garden there, and implacably gave voice to all manner of impractical nonsense.

Wang Yan seized him and went wild hitting him, but Xingge laughed and said, "Don't bother a rich man worth one hundred thousand ounces of silver! Just be patient until this time next year. If the capital and interest still haven't made it home, then it won't be too late to throw a fit." Wang Yan had no choice but to swallow his anger for the moment and think about something else.

Before they knew it, the beginning of the second month of the next year was upon them. Wang Yan started to hasten Xingge on his way, but Xingge simply said, "There's no need to go so early. So long as I arrive on that evening of that day of that month, then I'll be fine."

Sure enough, a few days before the deadline, Xingge packed up and departed. He arrived the day before the appointment and borrowed a monk's cell as a place to rest for the time being. When it got to be evening, he sat on Turtle Fishing Rock alone, just as he had before. It was already past dusk, the second watch was quiet, and it was almost the third when, from out of the shadows of the trees, sure enough, he saw a man approach the rock with big strides.[15] The man called out, "Where are you, my benefactor?"

Xingge came forward and clasped him by the arms, saying, "A trustworthy man, indeed! What of the last year's events?"

The man said, "Thanks to your generous support, I used that fifty thousand in silver to buy grain along the coast and give aid to the righteous army of the Six Commanderies.[16] We are on the eve of a 'no scarf' rebellion.[17] Fortunately I have received protection from Heaven—from the fourth month of last year I raised troops, and wherever we went, we flattened the opposition before us as easily as smashing bamboo. Now, adding them all up, between Min, Yue, and western Zhejiang, we have already taken over thirty commanderies and counties. The bandits who used to occupy the foreign islands near the coast have also submitted to us in 110 locations. I, your 'younger brother,' am known as 'Liu Cong, Son of Heaven of the Eastern Sea.'[18] Last year I secretly ascended Mount Potalaka to get the lay of the land and go to the monks' residence to borrow some alms contributions for my camps, where we were short on grain. But I never expected that so large a temple would be so bleak and desolate. Dare I ask kind Elder Brother's esteemed name?"

Xingge said, "I'm but a humble country rustic and with nothing to show for myself. Why give my name?"

Liu Cong said, "On the weight of a single word, you offered all you had. I'll be forever grateful for the fifty thousand ounces of silver with which you aided me. I could never fully repay your kindness. Why be reticent about your name?"

At last, Xingge revealed his name and place of residence. Who would have expected that Liu Cong's retainers, who were standing to one side, immediately arranged for men to take one hundred thousand ounces of silver to the Wang residence in Huizhou as soon as they heard this. This was all unbeknownst to Xingge, but that's a part of the story I'll tell you later.

To resume, Liu Cong invited Xingge to come with his luggage to the mouth of the river, where he would be entertained on a boat moored there. It wasn't long before they arrived at a great harbor where several dozen boats with colorful prows were assembled, their bright banners flying boldly. Many armor-clad men bearing halberds on their backs neatly encircled it. Liu Cong helped Xingge onto the boat and commanded that the gongs be beaten. The ship embarked, the banners were put in order, and they set out for the ocean.

It was not yet the fifth watch when there appeared on the ocean some tens of thousands of war vessels and large battleships. Their masthead lights and cannon fire shook the earth and startled heaven.[19] When they reached the large ship, palace maids and concubines prostrated themselves and called out "Gracious Master" as one in ringing cries. Xingge, who felt as though he were on a cloud or in a dream, was hardly aware of himself. There was a great feast that took full advantage of all the delicacies of the land and the sea. Meanwhile, battalions presented themselves in ranks, forming stately and fierce arrays. Music from foreign lands was played while one contingent of troops after another vied to be first, and rarities from beyond the seas were presented in a never-ending stream.

Xingge had tarried for more than ten days when he finally wished to take his leave and return. Liu Cong earnestly begged him to stay, devastated by their parting. But deep down he knew that Xingge couldn't stay. Liu Cong had Xingge's vessel prepared for departure and arranged to see him off, accompanying him down one section of the road after another. At the same time, he brought out peerless treasures, which he presented to Xingge as gifts. But Xingge firmly declined them all without a glance.

Liu Cong said, "These are not payment for kind Elder Brother—they express merely a fraction of my esteem. Since you won't take them, I have three brocade sacks for you.[20] If on some day in the future you find yourself in great need, then take a look inside. I can't yet divulge their secrets."

Xingge bowed repeatedly, accepted them, and departed. He returned home directly, not knowing that Liu Cong had already sent one hundred thousand ounces of silver to his home. It goes without saying that Wang Yan was overjoyed.

To resume, Xingge made his way home without a care in the world, as he had before. When Wang Yan heard that Xingge had returned, the whole family welcomed him. All the most important people of the region came out to congratulate him. Even though Xingge already realized what was afoot, his expression didn't show it in the slightest. Employees of many years also came by, having prepared banquets and gifts welcoming him back. Xingge didn't go to any of their houses but just gave each one fifty thousand copper coins in recompense for their company in days gone by.

In the rear garden he erected a hundred-foot-tall tower for watching the stars and observing the ethers. He overheard roadside rumors claiming that the "Son of Heaven of the Eastern Sea" had occupied certain departments and counties and was gradually advancing toward Huizhou. The people were in great turmoil and made plans to flee. Xingge said, "Matters have now become urgent." He opened one of the brocade sacks and saw instructions to do such and such.

At that time the Sui dynasty had already fallen, and the ruler of the Tang had ascended the throne. Xingge prepared a letter of introduction, which he had delivered to Military Commissioner Li Mian's yamen. Xingge requested that Li memorialize the emperor on his behalf. Xingge claimed that he could raise a militia three thousand strong to protect the area. It wouldn't cost the imperial court one copper or a single grain of rice, and only after peace had been restored would Xingge accept a reward from the court. Military Commissioner Li was desperately seeking men of worth at that time, and so when he received the petition, he had it transferred to the emperor forthwith. The Tang emperor declared that Xingge was to be temporarily awarded the position of Military Coordinator of the Southern Route and allowed to act at his own discretion. Xingge recruited his force and put them in order. Then they promptly set out, making their encampment between Wenzhou and Muzhou in Zhejiang.

Those bandits from the islands didn't respect the Chinese calendar, and so when they heard that Xingge's righteous force was first assembling, they promptly mustered their troops and horses and thronged forward, surrounding Xingge's camp with one dense ring after another, as tight as an iron bucket.[21] At that critical moment he looked inside the second brocade sack. Following the instructions therein, he set up a pole a hundred feet tall in the center of the encampment from which was hung a yellow banner bearing the words "Military Coordinator Wang—Thirteenth Route Combined Forces of the Eastern Sea Army and Navy." Those foreign islanders arrayed outside saw the banner, and their numerous leaders immediately waved their banners to the left. The soldiers divided into four divisions and were stationed left, right, fore, and rear.

Not long after, there came from the southwest quarter a unit of cavalry and infantry numbering more than 110 men. They led a white horse, fast as a shooting star, straight ahead. A man called out, "At the command of the Son of Heaven of the Eastern Sea, this white horse is expressly sent to his gracious benefactor Old Master Wang."

The message was delivered to the camp, and a vanguard was ordered to come and receive the letter. Upon careful examination, it turned out that this was the horse Xingge had originally lent to Liu Cong. The horse was snow white from nose to tail, and all along its back and rear were twenty-four black spots. Its name was "Snow Grape." It was truly a dragon horse. Xingge had loved that horse from the time he first saw it at the shop, but he had not known its name. From the time Liu Cong borrowed it, it was happy as a fish in water once it reached the seaside. Liu Cong had ridden it and found success everywhere. Everyone within the East China Sea region recognized it as a dragon that had appeared in the world. Not only did people fear it, but even the ten thousand horses galloped up with manes flowing when they saw it. There was no one who didn't bow in awe before that horse.

Wherever Xingge rode the horse within the coastal region everyone thought that Lord Liu had come leading troops. Everywhere they surrounded him in welcome, offering their earnest affection. Without discharging a single arrow, all came to pledge their allegiance. Initially, Xingge had gathered a righteous brigade of only three thousand, but now, in less than a year, he had already assembled an army of fifty thousand.[22] All had been given advance instructions by Liu Cong, for he wished to give Xingge the ten market towns at Zhangnan as recompense for Xingge's earlier kindness, which had made possible his many victories.

Unexpectedly, a severe drought occurred during the third year of the conflict. The army was stationed in Jiannan, where the price of rice rose wildly, reaching five ounces per bushel. The people were anxious, the soldiers cried out in hunger, and the army teetered on the cusp of rebellion. Xingge was anxious and opened the third brocade sack, which just so happened to provide the solution for this situation. He immediately dispatched orders that all the coastal beacon towers should fly white signal flags. Within a few days Liu Cong was notified of this by the seafaring scouts who had been monitoring Xingge. Liu Cong immediately ordered that five million *shi* of grain be prepared and distributed as material assistance along the coast. Soldiers and civilians alike gave earthshaking cheers. Peace and tranquility were restored, and all throughout the Thirteenth Route, peace reigned.

Infantry and cavalry had already arrived at the Zhangnan post, where they placed a grand banner indicating the establishment of a government office. The newly established border commandery reported one great military success after another, and the emperor time and again rewarded Xingge with promotions and gifts. He was promoted to be the Duke of Wu and issued a dragon-embroidered imperial robe and jade-studded belt. The emperor also issued him a ceremonial sword indicating that he would be empowered to act at his own discretion. He had no less power than the Son of Heaven himself.

One day during these momentous times, Liu Cong appeared, leading a fleet of one thousand battleships, entered a bay of the southern sea, and sought a meeting with the Duke of Wu. Xingge, the newly appointed Duke of Wu, opened the camp and lined up his ranks. The scene was one of extraordinary pomp and circumstance, just like his previous meeting with Liu Cong.

After three rounds of wine, Liu Cong asked, "Since kind Elder Brother emerged from his 'mountain seclusion' that year I haven't yet heard anything about your taking a wife. If you wouldn't reject her, my younger sister is already fifteen years of age, and I wish to deliver her here that she may begin preparations to serve you as your wife."

Having heard this, Xingge dared not accept and so humbly declined. Liu Cong insisted over and over again. "Marriage is a weighty matter," Xingge the duke said. "If I were at home, I would ask my parents' permission. Since I'm abroad, I dare not accept unless we request permission from the imperial court first. But since you and I are to become related by marriage, as your younger brother, I have another proposition. The sagely emperor of Tang has just ascended the throne, and all within the four seas feel his influence and seek his guidance. Rather than residing overseas, wouldn't it be better for you to swear allegiance and pay fealty to the Chinese court?[23] Within the court, you wouldn't lose your moral reputation as a devoted minister, and outside the court, you wouldn't lose the power and prestige you have gained throughout the coastal region. The imperial court harbors no suspicions about you, and the maritime region is at peace thanks to you. This righteous move would establish you in the court and bring you fame."

Liu Cong consented at once. That very day they assembled the camp chiefs on both sides, prepared the grand sacrifices to Heaven, and in the most solemn of ceremonies smeared blood on their mouths and swore mutual devotion. Liu Cong drafted a document of surrender, while Xingge sent a memorial vowing to serve as the guarantor for Liu's surrender. This was the fourth year of the Wude reign period of the Great Tang [621 CE].

When the Son of Heaven inspected the memorial to the throne, his imperial visage was flooded with great joy, and he specially decreed that an official of the Imperial Academy should be sent to the coastal area in order to proclaim the imperial reward widely as proof of the emperor's moral uprightness. He elevated Xingge in rank, conferred upon him the title Prince of Yue, bestowed on him the new name Wang Hua, and commanded the Imperial Bureau of Astronomy to select a date for the wedding. Lady Liu, Wang Hua's bride, was given the title Mistress of Anhai Commandery. An iron plaque with gold script was issued to this lineage that it should be ennobled for five generations with the same title. Liu Cong was granted the title Sea-Pacifying King and was to be permanently stationed in Haidong. From one generation to the next, the Wang and Liu families regularly intermarried through to the end of the Tang. They spared no effort in adhering to the principles of high office. This became an instructive anecdote that has been passed along for more than one thousand springs and autumns.

The crowd said, "Today our friend has told us this story that was much more pleasant to hear than the usual fare. We didn't expect to have added another under the bean arbor who can speak of events both old and new. What an interesting fellow!"

The man said, "I never received an education when I was a lad. This is all just hearsay badly retold. The tale is from long ago, and the name of the dynasty, official titles, places, monikers are all made up off the top of my head. I just wanted to tell something so good that it would leave everyone's ears ringing. If you're all like a country teacher who would refute a story just because he finds a few errors in some difficult words, then tomorrow I won't have the nerve to come by and learn from all of you!"

"Don't be so modest!" the crowd said. "Dear brother, your eloquent speech flows like a waterfall, your words clear as engravings on stone. You must have more strange experiences and hearsay waiting inside you. We'd be honored to hear more." Each thanked him in turn and went on his way.

GENERAL COMMENTS

When reading this session, one must not have a mistaken understanding of foolishness and wit, for that would be to see Wang Xingge as two different people. The reason he was stupid and mute, dispersing ten thousand in gold, was in order to establish the foundation of his great subsequent achievements, with the result that he saved the state and was granted an honorary enfeoffment of the Kingdom of Yue.

All the men of marvelous talents and famed heroes under Heaven have a penetrating discernment of the Ten Thousand Things, and in their minds, all have thoughts that can't be glimpsed. They see men with eyes that see beyond the mundane by one hundredfold. In word, in action, they don't resemble quotidian men in any way, all the more so when compared with those inconsequential slaves to wealth who keep guard over a little cash, or to servants selling vegetables who receive a piddling sum as reward—those in particular are long to be despised and ridiculed.

When, as in the twilight of the Sui, the world is enveloped by the havoc of war, then the course of human events is clear to those great men. If they can't be Emperor Taizong of the Tang, then they can at least be Qian Wusu.[24] To flee across the seas like "Curly Beard" is another clever move in the chess game—certainly he disdained to be merely a minister serving the emperor.[25] Living in this troubled age, if one can't go into hiding but rather appears as a marvelous talent or famed hero, this is not an advantage to one's career but instead tends to invite disaster.

In the Five Dynasties period, Wang Taifu of She County was a man of great learning and a fine writer. When Xu Zhigao took up the post of commander in Jianye, Wang submitted a memorial to the king of the state of Wu outlining the advantages and disadvantages of the appointment.[26] Xu Zhigao thought it marvelous. Song Qiqiu was jealous of his talent and sent someone to lure Wang Taifu to drink to his heart's content, whereupon they pushed him off Toad Cliff at Stone City, and he died.[27] This is the result of not being able to remain "stupid and mute."

This piece describes Xingge's activities as extremely bold, uninhibited, and clever. Even so, it's activities such as these that would cause an ordinary person to be anguished and sigh. Who could know that Lord Wang and his friends had already predicted the future, uncovering the truth of Heaven and Earth as if they had divined it by tortoise shell or it had been illuminated by candles. The twists and turns of the brocade sacks are just devices made up by the author in order to entertain his listeners. This story should be performed as a play, to open the eyes of the blind people of the world. Let's wipe our eyes clean and await that performance!

Translated by Alexander C. Wille

The Commissioner's Son Wastes His Patrimony to Revive the Family

A poem by Tao Yuanming says:

> Growing beans by the southern mountain,
> Weeds rampant and seedlings scarce.
> Tidy up the weeds early in the morning,
> Return home with my hoe when the moon rises.[1]

Whichever type of beans you grow, if you want them to grow well, you first need to reclaim a piece of arable land and then plant the seeds carefully in the earth. Once the seeds absorb the energy from the soil, they will naturally flourish. But if you wish to see them mature, you need to get up early every morning and clear out all the weeds around the bean stems, so that they won't have to compete with the weeds for the nutrients in the soil or for the rain from the sky. In this way, the beans can eventually grow to harvest.

Similarly, an infant in swaddling clothes needs righteous parents to nurture and educate him, so that he won't be misled into emulating any unfilial behavior. When the child grows older, he also needs a righteous brother to guide him, so that he won't be lured by fraudulent behaviors. In this way, he'll naturally go along the upright path every day. If a person is well cultivated from childhood, he'll no doubt establish a family and build a career when he grows up, making his family prominent and bringing fame to himself. If one generation achieves success in this way, the later generations will naturally prosper for long into the future. They won't go through ups and downs and, generation after generation, would be hailed as a virtuous family. Never can one see a child who has lived an immoral life end up well, nor can one see future generations continue to benefit from ancestors who did ill to others in the past.

An old proverb says, "If you plant melons, you get melons—if you plant beans, you get beans."[2] It is obvious that the changes of *Yin* and *Yang*, as well as the creation of Heaven and Earth, all have their roots.[3] You can only benefit from the merit you earn. How could anyone understand this if it's not explained clearly? Today, as we gather here under the bean arbor, the significant meaning behind growing beans should certainly not be overlooked.

One man in the group came up to the old man, saluted him, and said, "Dear brother, the story you told yesterday indeed had a lot of meaning. Today you mentioned beans again, only from a different perspective. Please continue." The old gent at first modestly declined but then began to talk.

The Neighbor's Tale

Today I won't talk about the past but rather tell a story from recent times. You, dear friends, can ask around after you hear my story. Then you'll know that my story isn't what Su Shi called "speaking with reckless words, listening as if it were reckless words."[4] I'll begin by introducing famous sayings by well-known historical figures, so that you'll have a sense of what my story is about.

Do you know whose sayings I'm going to talk about? They are from a chief councilor in the Song dynasty named Sima Guang. He was given the title Duke of Wen, so people called him Duke Sima of Wen. Here are few lines of moral teaching he passed down: "If one accumulates wealth and leaves it for one's descendants, they might not be able to maintain it—if one collects books and passes them down to one's descendants, they might not be able to read them. One should rather accumulate merit in the unseen world, so as to benefit the later generations."[5] These aren't some random words from ordinary people, but wise words based on Duke Sima's broad social experience and acute observations of life. No matter how smart and clever you may be, you can't be exempt from these few principles.

Take the son of a wealthy aristocrat, for example. His family's wealth might overfill the Big Dipper, but if later generations fail to understand the hardships his ancestors had to go through in order to establish their fortune, he might think that every household is as rich as he is. He wouldn't treat money as money. He'd spend it on things that are necessary and squander it on things that aren't worth having. Day by day, the family wealth would be dissipated bit by bit until it's all gone, just like trees fall after lengthy sawing and even stone wears away after the constant drip of water. How would it be possible to maintain the wealth left by his ancestors? This is what the Duke meant by saying "Descendants . . . might not be able to maintain it."

People say that money is easy to fritter away because one is tempted to think about it all the time. Since wealth and fame were in most cases accumulated by families of scholars, why not pass down all the rare and special book collections to their descendants instead? They might study them and become successful like their ancestors, and hence maintain their families' prominence. Compared to saving money, this is a more promising way of securing the family wealth. Who would have thought that wealthy families, perhaps due to their extravagant lifestyle, would raise children with uneven intellectual capacities? While the smart ones can easily understand what is written in the books and make good use of it, the stupid ones not only have a natural distaste for books but being around books is like a nail in the eye that they need to get rid of as soon as possible. Some are even so careless about these precious books that they might lose a few titles of a set or damage a few fascicles of a book. Or they might treat books that none have seen, such as those edited by the Imperial Court Archive or some hand-copied confidential records, as another *Rabbit Garden Texts* or some children's primer, selling books worth ten ounces of silver for two or three and books worth two or three for half an ounce or less.[6] Just like that, the books might be squandered in no time.

It could also happen that freeloaders and hangers-on in the family would take advantage by deliberately tearing apart the bindings of these books and saying to the master, "These are obviously incomplete volumes so they'd better be weighed and sold as scrap paper." Then they would secretly reassemble the bits and parts of the books, bind them together, and sell them for a substantial price. It seems that such offspring not only are illiterate but can't even read a character halfway—half of the word "read" (*du* 讀) is "sell" (*mai* 賣)—if they can't sell the books for a proper price.

This is why Duke Sima of Wen urged people to accumulate hidden merit instead. If you do so, all your merit will be calculated and weighed precisely by ghosts and gods in Heaven and Earth without anyone else ever knowing about it. If the merit you accumulate is so great that you couldn't exhaust it in your lifetime or that of your offspring, it would be carried on to the next generation, and if the merit can't be exhausted in ten generations, then it will continue on generation after generation, age after age, endlessly. It all depends on what good you have done and how much merit you have accumulated in your account. Never will one's merit be left uncounted or attributed to the wrong person. But this is quite hard to explain to most people, since one doesn't always know the consequences of one's own doings. Sometimes retribution occurs in one's own lifetime—sometimes it comes after ten generations have passed. After all, under the law of the universe, everything has a far-reaching destiny, not like "lightning, bubbles, a shadow" that are gone in a moment.[7]

But let's not digress too much. Last year, while I was on my way north on business, I passed a place near Linqu County in Qingzhou Prefecture in Shandong. Given free rein, my mount took me into a village. There I saw, in the midst of a thicket of trees, a mansion with eaves high in the clouds, grand walls as white as snow, ornamented rafters reaching high into the sky, painted beams with detailed decorations, lofty chambers and soaring towers beside clear green ponds, with carved banisters and curving railings—too much for me to take in all at once. Around the mansion there were many acres of fertile land, where I saw herds of cattle in countless numbers. Meanwhile, I was feeling tired due to the heat of the sun on a midsummer day, so I went into a Buddhist monastery that served tea to rest for a while. There I asked a monk, "Whose mansion is that?"

The monk smiled and looked around him. When he saw that no one was around, he said, "This is the mansion of our benefactor Yan the Fool. Everything you see here was earned by Yan the Fool himself."

I said, "How could he have achieved all this if he's a fool?"

The monk said, "It's a long story. If you'd like to know, Layman, please come inside and have a vegetarian meal. While you eat, I'll take the time to tell you the story, which is quite an extraordinary tale."

I then followed the abbot into the dining room, exchanged some greetings, and sat for a while. After having some tea, the monk pointed to the benefactor's donation record in front of the altar and began to speak.

The Abbot's Tale

This is in the name of our respectable donor, Yan Xian. He is fifty-three years old. His father was Yan Guangdou, a metropolitan graduate in the early Wanli period.[8] Obtaining such a high honor at an early age, he was first appointed magistrate of Kunshan County and later promoted to supervising secretary in the Ministry of Personnel.[9] He was intelligent and adept. One could say that he was a fair and impartial magistrate before he was promoted. But after he took the post in the Ministry of Personnel, he got involved in political factions. He became the leading figure of one faction and took the initiative in presenting several accusatory memorials to the emperor, but the emperor only retained them at court without taking any action. Officials at the provincial level were all afraid of him. Whether in court or at home, every day Yan took countless bribes from all the realm's corrupt officials. Later, when his term was over and he was transferred to be provincial administration commissioner of Zhejiang, he embezzled local tax revenue without concern for the law, which resulted in who knows how much funds going into his own pocket every year. Some officials at court couldn't tolerate him and reported him to the emperor. He then retired from his post most happily.

At first he didn't have any children, so he was more flexible with money. But after his half-wit son was born, he realized that he had an heir to inherit his wealth, and he became stricter and more miserly day by day. Every day, he gathered loafers and vagabonds to check on each household and think of ways of taking advantage of his debtors. His henchmen woke up early in the morning and went to check all the farms and lands they could reach. They conducted surveys on the amount of cattle, sheep, and horses each household owned and asked about plans for the land. Sometimes they brought small umbrellas and stood by the major roads. When they saw local gentry or young profligates go past, they would approach them with big smiles and warm greetings and invite them to a casual meal at the commissioner's mansion. During the meal, the guests were asked take out loans from the commissioner or sell land that was close to the commissioner's property. The guests were duped into signing sales contracts but were never paid afterward. Later when the loafers saw their creditors, they would find places to hide as fast as they could. After five or six years, the real estate and production under the name of Commissioner Yan were ten times more than what he had owned before.

One morning after his son turned ten, Commissioner Yan went off to join the immortals. All the properties he left were taken by the retainers, who not only took their share but embezzled the rest. His relatives, all of them having been taken advantage of by Commissioner Yan, stood aside indifferently and looked at the young master with cold eyes, doing nothing to help the boy. Yan's wife hired a tutor to teach the boy to read, hoping he could succeed in his studies and maintain the family property. Who could have known that the son was incompetent in letters and therefore could not pass any civil service examination, not even at the county level? The son knew that this was a matter of family honor and paid someone a few ounces to recommend him as a qualified candidate for the examination. But since his relatives and friends only wanted to cheat him, how would anyone lend him a hand? Without realizing it, Yan had already turned eighteen, and, he, too, was feeling frustrated with himself.

One day the young master changed into simple clothes and went fifty or sixty *li* out of town. He wanted to hear what people had to say about his family. He saw several people sitting under a tree and heard one of them saying, "Such an influential man as Commissioner Yan finally got the payback he deserved!"

Hearing this, the young master also sat down by his side and calmly asked him, "Where did this official Yan live?"

The man replied, "He lived in town."

The young master said, "Since the official is already dead, how could he suffer retribution?"

The man said, "You're too young to know." He then told the young master how Commissioner Yan deceived people and forcibly seized their land and how he swindled them and cheated them in their accounts. The other folks also added their own complaints about Yan. Toward the end, one man even got so upset that he wished he could dig Yan out of the grave and whip his corpse three hundred strokes like Wu Zixu whipped King Ping of Chu, in order to work off his anger.[10]

The young master was shocked dumb and hurried home immediately. He sighed and said, "If my father was the kind of man they said, our family surely will not survive for long!" Having realized this, he gathered the property managers and farm heads and asked them to list all the land, shops, and household names. He inspected all the contracts and matched the names with the properties. Then he called a servant, mounted a lame donkey, and set off to visit each household and return the contracts. All were inexpressibly grateful. Within half a year, the land of the Yan family was reduced to half of what it had been. The lands that had been obtained so long ago that all trace of the original owners had been lost were what remained as the family's property.

Since the young master did not care much for his studies, the hangers-on and freeloaders were keen to notice his interests and eager to flatter him by accompanying him in doing anything he enjoyed. Within a year, more than a hundred hangers-on were living in the Yan household and more than three hundred accompanied him on his hunting trips with falcons and dogs, in hand- and foot-ball games, and at practice with staff and spear.

One day it was raining outside, and Yan had nothing to do, so he called a storyteller to the house. The storyteller kowtowed to the young master and presented him with a mackerel. Yan called his chef to take the fish into the kitchen, but we will speak no more of that. It was approaching midsummer, and mackerel were in season, each worth a thousand copper coins. The storyteller had made a great effort to find one and expected a large gratuity from Yan but found only that Yan couldn't care less about the fish. The storyteller was perturbed, and not long after he started telling the story, he brought the matter up again. "Sir, the fish I just presented to you was something I worked really hard to get. I suggest that you taste it while it is still fresh." Yan did not heed his suggestion, so the storyteller had no choice but to keep on going. After forcing himself to say a few sentences, he tried again, and this time Yan rewarded him with five ounces of silver, told someone to give the storyteller a large box, and asked him to leave. As he went out the gate, he opened the box and saw ten mackerel inside. At that moment he realized that wealthy people's daily expenses are beyond what a humble man could even imagine.

Yan's mother and wife were worried to see Yan spending his money carelessly and repeatedly tried to talk some sense into him. But the young master said, "What I've spent so far is nothing! At the Tomb-Sweeping Festival, it will be my turn to hold the temple fair in the southern manor.[11] Have all the family members mount carriages and follow us men on horses and donkeys to the fair—then you'll see how much I can spend!"

The next day his mother and his wife did indeed go to the southern manor. The young master had already asked people to build ten tall stages and selected twenty troupes of players and reorganized them into ten troupes, one for each stage. Some people favored plays performed to southern music, and some preferred the northern tunes. Some liked to watch lyrical plays, and some liked plays featuring martial arts. People gathered from here and there, around ten thousand altogether. Yan was afraid that people would leave halfway through the plays because they were hungry, so he provided thirty to fifty baskets of copper coins and had them thrown out to the crowd. All the villagers tried to grab as many as possible, people falling over and stepping on each other, shouting and whooping. They took the money to buy food from vendors carrying cooked food on their shoulder poles, and they filled their bellies. This is called *"mai chun."*[12]

The performers exerted themselves onstage. When they played the part that they were most confident about, people threw silk handkerchiefs or luxurious Suzhou-Hangzhou fans onto the stage as a show of admiration. Yan sat on the central terrace that faced all four stages wearing a Daoist "free and easy" hat and a heron-style robe with two young maids standing by, one serving him tea and the other holding his whisk. He never stopped smiling, trying his best to ensure that every one of those ten thousand people had a good time that day. Those who didn't understand the young master said that Commissioner Yan deserved to have such a profligate son. How could they know that the young master hosted this event as a modest offering to the Buddha for all the bad karma created by his father's earlier wrongdoings? His mother and his wife were also upset to see him throwing away the family fortune like that, so they took the opportunity to hide their jewelry and finery elsewhere whenever they could, as savings for the future.

One morning young Yan ordered the servants to carry his felt traveling bag and hold his name card,[13] while he himself stepped into his fine painted sedan to go visiting. It was then that he saw a man hiding behind the front gate, hesitating to come forward. Yan asked, "Who is that man there outside the door?"

He sent a servant to go see, and the servant observed that the man was a scholar wearing a folded hat, a shabby robe, and a pair of worn-down straw sandals.[14] He was skeletal, with a sallow complexion, breathing heavily as if he might fall down dead at any moment. The young master quickly stepped down from his palanquin and had people help the man into the mansion. He took a close look at the man and instinctively felt great respect for him. He offered his formal greetings and with one hand guided the man to the main hall. He bowed to the man in a leisurely manner, and the two sat down, seated arranged as guest and host.

The young master then asked, "What is your honorable name, sir, and how may I be of service?"

The man responded slowly, "My family name is Liu. I am twenty-three years old, and I am a government student from Yidu County near the capital of the prefecture." Slowly he groped for his name card in his sleeve and presented it to Yan. It read "Sincere greetings from your humble younger brother Liu Fan."

The young master received it, saying, "I dare not accept such a great honor!"

Liu Fan said, "After I failed the civil service examination, I contracted a disease, which is why I look so feeble. I have a mother at home, but I can't provide even porridge or gruel for her, and so I dragged myself here today to ask for your help. I've heard that you, sir, are benevolent and generous, and I'd like to offer my services to you as your secretary. I don't dare harbor extravagant hopes—I'll follow along behind your other guests and complete any small task you might ask of me. I don't ask for much in return, just three proper meals for my mother would be enough."

The young master said, "The guests at my humble household are all vegetable peddlers and butchers. To be one of them would be an insult to you, sir. Since you have come this far in such a feeble condition, please stay and rest for a couple of days in my disorderly study. As for your mother's support, I'll take care of it."

He then ordered servants to clean up the study for Liu as best they could and to see to Liu's needs most conscientiously. Liu Fan certainly had a turn of luck at this time, yet this wouldn't have happened if Young Master Yan had not been able to see Liu's stalwart qualities beneath his shabby appearance.

Yan further ordered his senior accountant, "Prepare five hundred ounces of silver, three hundred as a birthday gift for Liu's mother and two hundred for Liu Fan to find a suitable match." In less than two months, Liu Fan had become fat and healthy. Everyone said that Yan was such a good judge of character that Liu Fan should at least be awarded one of the top three places in the palace examination!

But let us speak no more of how the young master showed Liu great respect during his stay. Rather, let us tell how one day, someone from South Village came to Yan and said, "Last night around midnight, thirty to fifty bandits carrying torches brought staves and broke down the gate of the manor. They took a hundred or so bundles of cloth from traveling merchants who were staying for the night. When the farmhands found out, they chased the bandits with their weapons. The bandits abandoned half their loot and got away, all except for the one who was bringing up the rear. He is tall, big, and stronger than most, but he was caught because he got lost in the dark and fell into an old well. They ganged up on him to bring him here, waiting for you, Young Master, to send him to the court for trial."

Those tenants who had risked their lives to catch the bandit all came to the young master for rewards. The young master called them in one by one and inquired carefully about what had happened. Then he wrote out a slip for each of them and asked the foreman to distribute the retrieved goods accordingly. He also exempted each of them from five hundredweight of grain owed him in rent for their personal land. The process continued until dusk.

Afterward, the captured bandit was brought in and a light was shined on him. "Untie him immediately," the young master said hastily. "And bring some clothes for him to wear. Also get some wine and food and invite him to join me on the back porch."

The man was deeply ashamed and said repeatedly, "I don't deserve your kindness."

The young master said, "A good man like you came to the village, yet I failed to accommodate you and thus have driven you and the others to commit such a bad deed. The fault is all mine! You look like a decent man—it is only a matter of time before you find wealth and honor. Why so impatient?"

Then Yan took out three hundred ounces of fine silver and gave it to the man. The man was so apprehensive and ashamed that he got down on his knees and did not dare to lift his head. The young master thought to himself, "He might be afraid to accept the gift because there are so many people around who might recognize him later if he lifts his face." So he sent the others away and said earnestly to the man, "Be a good person from now on and don't spend time with that crowd anymore."

Without even asking the man's name, he instead wrote a sincere letter in which he identified the man as his close relative named Zhao Wanbi and recommended him for the post of security guard serving under Li Rusong, who was the regional military commander of Tieling District at Liaoyang.[15] That night, Yan prepared some clothes, asked him to take the money, and secretly sent him off. None of the other guests at the manor knew about this until the next day. It was when everyone started to wonder what had happened to the man that they realized Yan had released him out of charity. Everyone was so impressed that they couldn't stop talking about it.

Now let's return to Liu Fan. After the young master took him in and gave him so much for travel expenses, he was able to improve his living conditions significantly. In early autumn of that year, the provincial examiners made the test results public, and Liu Fan was designated "Classics

Master" among the highest graduates.[16] Upon hearing the good news, Liu and his mother went to Yan's mansion to show their gratitude. Who would have thought that this was also the day when Yan's fortunes took a turn for the worse? His bedroom suddenly went up in flames, the smoke filled up the house quickly, and Zhurong turned the entire mansion into ashes.[17] Because many lands and houses had been destroyed by flood, there was no harvest, and so Yan was unable to collect any grain taxes or rents from the villagers. His mother and his wife blamed him for his frivolous expenditures previously and distanced themselves from him, showing no regret or sympathy for him.

His relatives and friends also treated him as an ill-fated pauper and even avoided looking at him when they saw him. At first he sold off his horses and donkeys, cattle and sheep. Then he started selling what furniture that remained, and after that he passed his household servants on to other masters and got some compensation. His life became more difficult day by day. At first he thought that being poor meant only that he had to endure having bad food and shabby clothes. How could he have known that he could not afford even shabby clothes and bad food? He could no longer even afford a place to roost. Totally destitute, the young master walked around town one morning with tears streaming down his face, trying to find old friends from former times. He didn't expect to draw a blank nine out of ten times, and many even pointed fingers at him behind his back, saying that he deserved such hardships. The young master had no choice but to pretend he hadn't heard them.

He was desperate to find a place to stay, and then someone pointed out to him, "There is a dirt cellar ten *li* outside of town. It would shield you from wind and rain, and you can easily walk to town to get food and drink."

Yan could only do as he said, and so he settled down in the cellar. On days when he had a little luck, he would bump into a friend he had known well in the past. Seeing him in such poor condition, he would give Yan whatever he had in his purse at the moment, sometimes more than 110 ounces of silver. With this small fortune, he would go back to his old place, rent a big house, buy some household necessities, and get several of his house servants back to take care of him. The hangers-on would gather around him like they had before and exhaust his fortune within a few months. Then they would suddenly leave him as poor as before, and Yan would have to return to his cave to "enjoy" it as before. But no more of this.

Let us again return to Liu Fan. That day he and his mother went to Yan's mansion to thank him after he got the title of provincial graduate, but he wasn't able to see Yan because of the fire, so they returned home disappointed. After he got home, he packed up his belongings and set out for the capital to take the metropolitan examinations. Unexpectedly, he passed one examination after another and became a metropolitan graduate. He was assigned the post of judge of Daming Prefecture. The following month, he obtained his appointment certificate and left the capital for his new post. He arrived shortly thereafter.

There were nine county magistrates under the jurisdiction of the Daming Prefecture Judicial Bureau. With Liu, they were referred to as the "Ten Kings of Hell."[18] They made money and grains easy to raise, and legal cases easy to resolve. Since all the judges and magistrates there were efficient in their duties, many were promoted to posts back in the central government, either in Offices of Scrutiny or as circuit officials. Liu Fan had started out as a poor scholar, and consequently he could sympathize with the sufferings of the common people and put great effort into punishing the evil and the cruel. Within a month his supervisors were impressed with him and respected him greatly.

He then gave some travel money to yamen runners and ordered them to escort his mother to his office from his hometown, and his mother set off immediately after they arrived. But as she neared the vicinity of Daming Prefecture, she refused to enter and asked the runner to find an inn where she could stay. When he heard about this, Liu Fan was anxious, for he didn't understand what his mother was thinking. So he hastily mounted a fast horse and hurried out of town to welcome her. There, he knelt down on the ground and asked why she hadn't entered the prefecture and what her wishes were.

His mother said, "Now that you, my son, have become a judge and glorified our family, I can't help but think about the time two years ago before we met Master Yan, our benefactor. We'd be lying dead in a ditch were it not for him! Have you learned about his condition recently? He's now living in a cellar on the verge of death, a situation even worse than ours at the time when you begged for Lord Yan's help."

Upon hearing this, Liu Fan apologized repeatedly to his mother and asked her to come to the court with him, so that he might send men to hasten to his benefactor's rescue. It was only then that his mother was willing to get into the carriage. The moment he arrived at the court, Liu Fan prepared a gift of ten thousand ounces of silver, some of which he borrowed from the county magistrates, and dispatched a man to Lingqu County to invite Master Yan.

Now the locals at Lingqu didn't know that Yan was living in a cave. There was only one friend who used to have a good relationship with him but had kept his distance after several failed attempts to caution Yan about his profligate habits. When he heard that someone was looking for Yan, he sought out the yamen runner and said, "I know Master Yan's whereabouts. But once you give him a thousand ounces, he'll squander it all immediately. Let me go to the cave first. I'll give him a hint and test his reaction. Let me see if he can be tricked."

The man went there, found Master Yan in no time, and said to him, "An old friend of yours is looking for you. He offers a hundred ounces of silver to thank you for old times' sake. If I direct him to you here, how would you reward me?"

The young master said, "In my present condition, a penny is worth tens of thousands of ounces. If what you said is true, I should thank you with half of the money I receive!"

The man said, "Your old habit of squandering money hasn't changed at all. You have about as much potential to become an immortal as Du Zichun![19] When you were suffering hard times, I wasn't able to help you. How could I accept your generosity now!"

So the man took the yamen runner to see Yan and also purchased clothing for him. Within a few days, Yan's spirits began to rise, and eventually they arrived at the judicial offices of Daming Prefecture. Liu Fan, his mother, and his wife all came out to bow to Yan. Lord Yan returned the courtesy, and all were delighted.

In less than three years, Liu Fan made a name for himself in the prefecture and was promoted to the Ministry of Personnel headquarters in the capital. Lord Yan accompanied him to the capital. At that time, the promotion regulations were quite loose. Therefore, during the recruitment sessions, which were held six times a year, whoever wished to seek favorable treatment had to go through Lord Yan. As a result, his purse accumulated no less than fifty or sixty thousand ounces of silver. Later, when a new position opened up at the Ministry of Revenue and Ministry of Works, Lord Yan paid three thousand taels and was promoted to clerk in the Grand Secretariat. After three years of excellent evaluations, he was promoted to assistant prefect of Changde Prefecture in Huguang. It happened that during that time Zhang Juzheng's political reform failed, and the emperor ordered the confiscation of all of Zhang's property. Yan's supervisor sent him to oversee the process, and he was able to collect innumerable amounts of valuables. He then filed for early retirement because of illness and returned home. There he reacquired all his former lands and properties at reasonable prices. His farm laborers and hangers-on clustered like rain and clouds around him just as before, and he treated them all with his usual generosity.

But then another, yet stranger, event occurred that no one could explain. During the White Lotus bandit uprising, the six prefectures of Shandong were all under attack, and towns and cities were wiped out wherever the bandit army and cavalry passed by—with only one exception. The chief commander of the Qingzhou prefectural troops stationed at the central encampment served under the Earl of Ningyuan at Liaodong. His name was Zhao Wanbi. He had personally commanded a thousand good men who went to guard the area of the Yan mansion. For that reason, no one dared to touch even a blade of grass or a single tree there. This is why every village and town in every department and county in the surrounding areas were desolate and deserted, all except for this mansion, magnificent as ever. If it hadn't been for the young master's turning over a new leaf, the family estate accumulated by his father would have been nothing but ashes.

By now Master Yan is fifty-three years old. He has four sons, and all are studying for their second degree. Their prospects for wealth and rank have risen and will continue to rise. If you are willing to stay for the night, Layman, I'll go with you to pay our respects to Master Yan. It will be interesting to meet him in person, for he doesn't have a trace of bureaucratic airs like others.

I said, "A traveler such as I dare not present myself presumptuously to such a prominent man as Lord Yan. I am happy that you were willing to tell me this story, Your Reverence, so that it could serve as topic of conversation and be passed on for the enjoyment of others!" Then I prepared a donation of three qian of silver to thank the monk for the food, then bowed to him and bade him farewell. You see, I didn't get such a story for free—I had to pay for it!

The crowd said, "It would be petty to mention any payment for these stories we tell under the bean arbor."

The man said, "I didn't tell you this story for your money. As long as you learn from the ones worth learning from and heed the cautionary tales so as not to waste a fine story, that would be good enough for me."

The crowd responded with gratitude, "Well said, sir. Well said."

GENERAL COMMENTS

When a person writes a story, he wants it to enter into people's hearts as well as to surprise them at the same time with unexpected turns of events—just as the clouds arise at the end of river, the peak appears as we round the trees.[20] The most marvelous stories can make readers turn the pages busily but then close the book and think, not knowing what route the story would take. For example, the part where Yan the Fool returns the contracts and the fields to people after he heard complaints about his father is something within readers' expectations. Yan's subsequent great downfall is something that one could hardly have predicted. When Yan kindly befriends Liu and Zhao and receives their ordinary gratitude—that is something that readers might expect. Yet when we follow Yan's drastic changes—from a person who lives in a cave after his house burns down to being a clerk in the Grand Secretariat and later the assistant prefect, with his house intact during the rebellion—this is something that we could not have anticipated. Money all squandered and yet money accumulated enough for one to enjoy, having no education and yet obtaining a higher administrative rank than the educated, not relying on the merits of father and grandfather and yet able to accumulate merit for one's descendants—Yan advanced higher than what was taught by Duke Sima of Wen! Now we know that if you're a fool to an extreme, great wisdom might come from this—when you are poor to an extreme, great wealth and fortune might appear as a result. The painful education of a great man resides between the tip of the pen and the tip of the tongue. Truly, Aina can forge great transformations.

Translated by Li Fang-yu

The Little Beggar
Who Was Truly Filial

In this world, every sentence a person says, every sentence he hears, inevitably affects his fate, for good or ill. All a person needs to do is to recognize the truth, speak it, and accept it, and then he won't go far wrong. As the old saying goes, "Living with the virtuous is like entering a room full of orchids—you gradually stop noticing the fragrance because you've become one with it. Living with the unvirtuous is like entering a fish market—you gradually stop noticing the stink, because you've become one with it."[1]

Think of a man standing at the gate of a prefectural or county court. He hears all the bickering and squabbling, the rights and the wrongs. He can't help but be influenced to scheme against people in countless ways. Slowly learning the form day by day, even someone who doesn't read a single word will acquire the skill to draft complaints for others. Then, if he spends a whole day without provoking some argument, his mind will get intolerably itchy. And the day will come when his original sense of goodness and virtue will turn into a nest of poisonous snakes. But think of another man who walks into a temple or a shrine. He hears the lectures on Buddhist sutras and practice. He chants the name of the Buddha and abstains from meat—surely he will become a bit remorseful over his usual wayward acts and evil ways. Slowly getting better day by day, his violent character and unruly behavior will disappear, unbeknownst to himself, and turn into a land of purity.

According to the *Documents of Antiquity*,[2] at the time of the sage-kings Yao and Shun, kings and ministers were always on harmonious terms with each other. When he saw a deed of appropriate nature, the king would say "Approbate," which means he commended it as virtuous. To this, his ministers would respond with "Indubitably," which meant they agreed with the king on the appropriateness of the action. When he saw an inappropriate deed, the king would say "Disapprobate," which indicated his disapproval of its execution. To this, his ministers would respond with "Negatory," following the king's opinion and showing their judgment of the action as inappropriate. Naturally, this harmony across the court and between the kings and their ministers, between high and low, produced a world of happiness and a time of peace.

Later, during the Warring States Period, Crown Prince Dan of Yan humbled himself and went out of his way in an effort to persuade Jing Ke to assassinate the King of Qin. That was an act of heroism to last for the ages. But why was it that the prince and his followers went to see Jing Ke off, all dressed in plain white robes and hats? And why was it that when they arrived at the Yi River, they suddenly played the mournful *bianzhi* mode? Why, too, did Jing Ke join in the sad song, starting with the line "Brave men never come home again"? At that moment, a white rainbow appeared in the sky, stretching through the white sun, prefiguring the fall of a state and the ruin of a family.[3] Thus we can see that the words we speak can have effects at most on the fate of a state and at least on a man's life!

Today, sitting under this bean arbor, we shouldn't see it merely as a bean arbor. Instead, we can imagine ourselves sitting in the Western Paradise, the Pure Land of ultimate bliss. Amid the hubbub of the day, while leisurely fanning away, we should feel uninhibited either by pride or by shame and bare our hearts to one another.

A breeze has suddenly arisen. The fragrance of bean flowers is wafting across our foreheads, cooling our bodies, preparing us for some idle talk of worldly affairs past and present. But we shouldn't misunderstand the word "idle" here. It's only during moments of idleness that our better nature can assert itself and we can utter the most sincere words that can move us most deeply.

Now in these turbulent times, men's hearts have become unfathomable. Those who are intelligent and clever study the classics only to learn how to be better swindlers. They will lose their childlike innocence entirely once they achieve official position and reach high status,[4] when they will say things that baffle ghosts and spirits and do things that transgress all moral principles. It is rather the villagers, rustic and unschooled, with both feet on solid earth, who keep faith in Heaven with their whole hearts. They live in their own dreams and know nothing about the Duke of Zhou or Confucius, yet they're earnest at heart and honest in all they do, as if they're the ones who truly embody the uprightness of the Three Dynasties and "cling to the customs" of antiquity here in our own generation.[5] If we compare these cases carefully, those who get the title of hero by kicking the air and manipulating the shadows are even worse than worms in a cesspit.

Today, please allow me to be so daring as to tell you, my dear friends, a story about a man of the most humble, most despised origins who was yet able to accomplish far more than the ordinary man. My story may befoul your ears for now, but it will have a good aftertaste when you recall it later.

You may ask, "Who do you mean by the world's most humble?" I don't mean vegetable vendors or barmen, butchers or gravediggers, but a little beggar from an almshouse. My dear friends, are all beggars born as beggars? How could it be that they inherit their profession from their ancestors? No—this one came from a family of prominence.

Our man hailed from Jiangling County in Jingzhou Prefecture, in Huguang.[6] He had the surname Wu and the given name Ding (Unwavering). His grandfather, named Wu Li, was a scholar recommended for the National Academy. Peaceful by disposition, Wu Li was always ready to edify his fellow townspeople with the virtues of forgiveness and tolerance. Everyone in his town followed his teaching, calling him "Mr. Peacemaker."[7]

Among his five sons, the first four all passed the examinations to enter the ranks of scholars, making studying their living. The youngest one, named Wu Xian, was different from the others. Xian's mother was originally a maid, and his father, in his dotage, made her his concubine, allured by her youthful charm. As early as six or seven years of age, Wu Xian showed his peculiarities, expressing little interest in emulating his four elder brothers. In his teens, when their father passed away, his brothers divided the property and went to live separately. Wu Xian moved with his mother into their own house. His mother hired a private tutor to teach Wu Xian the classics, preparing him for the expected academic career. However, by the time he was seventeen or eighteen, Xian had failed to pass even the county-level examinations.

One day he suddenly looked up to the heavens, sighed, and said something that shocked everyone who heard it: "Living in this world, if I can't be as high as the Jade Emperor, I'd rather be a beggar in an almshouse. What's the value of a life that neither sinks nor soars, of being a person the world could easily do without? I'd rather die and return to the Underworld, where I can start over briskly in my next reincarnation!"

Wu Xian was clearly upset and spoke without thinking. But who could have known that the Jade Emperor was passing by at that moment, only three feet above Xian's roof? His celestial ministers heard Xian's lament and immediately reported it to him. The Jade Emperor then summoned to court his judges of the living, of the dead, and of the official positions, to check Wu Xian's predestined life span and official career. Inspecting their record books, the judges found an entry on a Wu Xian from Jingzhou. It noted that he was ambitious yet unlucky, held grudges with little reason, and should be apprehended and dispatched to an almshouse. Nevertheless, since he harbored not one deceitful thought all his life, he was fated to maintain his lofty moral stature despite his assignment to a lowly status. But these matters are handled in the realm of shadows, so I'll say no more about that here.

Instead I'll tell about how Wu Xian, having made this absurd remark at home, a few days later abruptly reached the end of his predestined life span! His wife was pregnant when he died, and when she reached full term, she gave birth to an infant she called Ding'er and later formally named Wu Ding.

This boy was quite good-looking. While he was growing up, his family's fortunes gradually declined. How could this boy manage to prop up his family when he was destined to be a beggar himself? In his twenties a weakling whose shoulders couldn't bear a carrying pole and whose arms couldn't lift things, he had no choice but to move with his mother to another prefecture. But who could have known that his mother would soon lose the sight of both eyes! Holding his mother by the arm, Wu Ding went along the road begging. None of his uncles, young or old, were at all involved with them. His relatives knew him as proud and disdainful but had no idea that he was getting by like this somewhere else.

Morning and evening Wu Ding brought home wine and food he got from begging and wouldn't start eating until his mother had eaten her fill. One day he suddenly realized that the fifteenth day of the eighth month would be his mother's fortieth birthday. Ding'er was anxious to celebrate it but didn't have the wherewithal to do so. Agonizing about it day and night, he didn't know how he could arrange a celebration for his mother's birthday. But we'll return to this later.

Let me now tell you about an eminent man from Chu, a high official of the second rank who, with the emperor's permission, had just returned to his hometown along the courier routes. As it happened, this gentleman was going to celebrate his fiftieth birthday in midsummer at the beginning of the sixth month, while his mother would have her seventieth birthday in late autumn toward the end of the ninth month. Like flowers added to a piece of brocade, these anniversaries only enhanced their wealth and reputation. Celebrations started as early as half a year beforehand. His relatives swarmed in for Buddhist ceremonies and numerous feasts graced with all kinds of rare delicacies, keeping his house extremely busy. "How dare I receive good wishes while my mother hasn't been congratulated for her longevity yet?" thought the eminent man. "Not to mention that I'm now retired and should generally restrain myself on such matters. I had better retreat to the mountains, stay in a monastery, and abstain from wine and meat, bowing to the Buddhist scriptures and repenting my faults. Although I won't ask for any blessings, cultivating my body and mind will suffice as a virtuous practice."

It happened that one day, as he went for a quiet stroll with his walking staff, all of sudden the sound of a small drum came from the edge of the woods. Startled, the eminent man wondered, "My relatives and friends know that I'm here. They must be setting up a banquet and preparing the music to celebrate my birthday." He was most curious to see.

Rounding the foot of the hill, he saw a blind old woman sitting on a big rock under the sparse branches of old trees. A young beggar, holding a brown dog by a leash with one hand and a food basket in the other, was taking a broken gourd ladle, a clay bowl, and other bits and pieces of throwaways out of the basket. He laid them out one by one in front of the old woman. Then he picked up a hand drum and began to play it. Following the rhythm, the dog started to dance. The beggar then went down on his knees. Holding a pot high above his head and intoning some unrecognized song, he moved respectfully toward the old lady, making every effort to please her.

After watching a long while, the eminent man was still unable to comprehend the scenario. So he walked up to the beggar and asked, "How is this old lady related to you?"

"Please don't interrupt, sir," replied Ding'er, saluting. "Today is my mother's birthday, so please don't disturb her!"

"But these are 'plums eaten by larvae,' melons gnawed by mice, leftovers from the bottom of a gruel pot, and wine dregs," laughed the eminent man. "How could they be sufficient for celebrating your mother's longevity?"[8]

"How mistaken you are!" replied Ding'er. "I may not have had much schooling, but I've learned sayings by sages and virtuous men of ancient times. Confucius had a disciple called Master Zeng Shen, and this is how he took care of his father, Zeng Xi. For each of the three meals every day he presented to his father both wine and meat. Already full and tipsy, his father would still ask, 'Is there any more?' To this, Master Zeng would reply, 'Yes, yes.' He would respond with the same 'yes' even when nothing was left. If his father wanted to invite guests, he set up the feast immediately. This is what we call being filial by fulfilling the parents' wishes. However, Zeng Yuan, Master Zeng's son, didn't understand the meaning behind this. He, too, served his parents three meals a day, and there was no shortage of wine and meat. Yet if his parents asked, 'Is there any more?' he would respond by saying 'No more'—not because he was out of food but because he was trying to save some to serve for the next meal. We can call this only 'filling the body.' How could it qualify as filial?

"Although people like me can afford only broken gourd ladles and clay bowls, how do these differ from gold-plated ivory chopsticks and jewel-embedded jade cups? And what is the difference between our wine lees and leftover broth and those exotic delicacies from mountains and seas? My bringing along this brown dog, my rattling the hand drum, my singing of the songs, and my dancing won't pale in comparison to either Sage-King Shun, who orchestrated the dancing of a hundred beasts, or to Lao Lai, who put on colorful clothes and performed babyish antics for his parents."[9]

"Indeed! Indeed!" The eminent man applauded Ding'er's speech.

"Who is that applauding?" said the blind old lady loudly. "Hurry and invite him over and give him a large goblet of wine!"

Respecting his mother's command, Ding'er invited the eminent man over. Too moved by his filial respect for his own mother to decline, the eminent man came over and cheerfully finished the drink in one gulp. Turning to Ding'er, he said, "I appreciate your utmost sincerity and purest filiality. Why not accompany me to my mansion, where you won't need to worry about food or clothing and can take good care of your mother in her remaining years? This will relieve you from the pain of this daily scramble and toil."

"No, no, I will not," said Ding'er, waving his hand. "Even after my mother's hundred years are complete, I'll still be begging from door to door by day and sleeping in a thatched hut by her tomb by night. I won't part from her for a single day, as if she were still alive. Suppose we were to move into your mansion now. Even if you, my lord, would treat me with exceptional favor, what would prevent your arrogant servants and shrewish maids from bullying my mother?

"I've seen that sons from wealthy and privileged families have to leave their parents as soon as they're appointed to a new position. Filled with longing yet separated by rivers and passes, they can do nothing beyond gazing at the white clouds and lamenting in vain. If by misfortune the parent happens to pass away, even though they're able to hold a ceremonious funeral and have their fellow officials join the procession, display silken banners and scrolls, and receive paper offerings and other generous condolences from the imperial court, they can only make pretenses and be busy around the grave. When the offerings are done and the sweeping of the grave mound finished, the children return home and resume their jokes by lamplight, leaving the grave to foxes wailing at the moon.[10] How many filial sons have there been since ancient times who have planted pine and cypress trees, who have stayed in thatched mourning huts, and who have patted the grave upon hearing a clap of thunder? Not one drop of sacrificial wine ever reaches the Underworld. Even if my lord has hundreds of thousands of ounces of gold, how could you ever buy a smile from my mother as when she was still alive?"

Like being frozen in ice and snow from the bottom of his feet to the top of his head, the eminent man found that his passion had been cooled by Ding'er's words. He hung his head and sighed, still fumbling for words.

"My mother is drunk," said Ding'er. And away he went, carrying the blind old lady on his back. Crestfallen, the eminent man went back to where he was staying, but we will say no more of him.

Let us now tell how Ding'er carried his mother back to where they usually stayed and continued his daily routine. More than a year later, his mother passed away. His fellow beggars all came to offer condolences. Singing the song "Dew on the Shallots,"[11] they buried her in an empty piece of open land, planted a few pine and cypress trees to left and right in front of the grave, and built a thatched hut where Ding'er could rest. During daylight hours Ding'er went out begging as usual and presented three meals each day at the grave.

Every day went by like this for the next three years. Everyone in the nearby villages and from the market, across the town and over the bridge, had become respectful of him, all knowing him to be a filial son. Moreover, in years of good harvests, the local people who donated and provided for him vied to feed Ding'er as well as possible, treating him ten times better than those migrant monks who took their meditation mats from one household to another. So content was Ding'er that he had no further aspirations.

On the anniversary of his mother's death, Ding'er got up early, prepared some incense and candles, collected some meat and vegetable dishes from other families, and went directly to the grave. There he laid out the dishes, lit the incense and candles, and began to rattle the hand drum and sing a number of songs, just as he had done when she was alive. Then, after some sorrowful wailing, he finished the drinks he had poured out for the dead. His eyes unable to focus as the alcohol made him drowsy, he tripped and fell asleep by the grave. The sun was setting in the west when he woke up. As soon as he opened his eyes, he stood up and went for a stroll.

In no more than half a *li* he came to a "beheaded brook."[12] He took off his worn-out shoes and stepped down on the sandy bottom. As he approached the opposite shore, he suddenly stubbed his toes against something so hard and that hurt so much he assumed it was a stone. Afraid it would hurt other people as well, he ignored his pain to bend down and feel for it, thinking to throw it out on the roadside. But it wasn't a rock at all—what he pulled up was a big black cloth bundle. He carried it to the shore and unwrapped it in the shade of a tree. Inside was quite a pile of shiny pieces of fine-quality silver.

"Who has lost this money?" thought Ding'er, nodding his head. "How upset he must be now, since he had nowhere to look for it. I fear that this loss might even cost him his life!" He rewrapped the money and, seeing it was getting late, carefully buried the bundle under a dead tree. That night, he took shelter in the corridor of a nearby temple.

The next morning, after asking for some breakfast from the monks, he went nowhere but straight back to sit in the cool shade by the beheaded brook, facing the clear water without moving, waiting for the owner to show up and afraid to close his eyes for even a moment. The path was little used, and few travelers passed by. Then around midday, a man came from the other side of the river. His hair all undone, his shirt open, he was clearly distracted. Barefooted, he crossed the stream.

"He must be the one," Ding'er said. He stood up and walked toward the man, asking him where he was going. Recognizing Ding'er as a beggar, the man didn't answer and hurried on, fearing that the beggar would keep him there for a while asking for money.

Ding'er said, "My brother, you look so anxious. Could it be that you have lost something?"

Hearing this, the man turned and asked, "Could you have found something?"

"Tell me what you have lost," said Ding'er.

"I have been away from home for three years and suffered many hardships," said the man, "and I made some money. Recently I heard that my mother has fallen sick. I was in such a hurry that I somehow lost the money along the way. If you, noble brother, have found it and if you are of noble mind, please take pity on my humble self. I'm willing to give you half the money as a reward."

"Do you know how it was wrapped?" asked Ding'er.

"It is in a double-layer black cloth bag. It took a lot of sewing to make," the man said.

"Yes! So it is!" Ding'er said. "Please come with me."

They walked over to the dead tree, where Ding'er dug out the bundle, intact, and gave it to the man with both hands. The man opened the bundle, divided the money into two halves, and gave one half to Ding'er.

"If I had wanted half of your money, why didn't I just hide it all away?" said Ding'er, firmly declining the reward.

The man knelt and thanked him again and again. By this time, a little knot of travelers had gathered around them, watching them push the money back and forth between them, but Ding'er's mind was unchanged.

"How about giving him two ounces for wine?" suggested the crowd. "Surely you would be willing to accept this?"

Seeing this suggestion as reasonable, Ding'er reluctantly accepted the reward, which he put in a pocket of his shirt.

At this, everyone applauded. "How rare it is! He is a humble beggar, and yet his generosity is as lofty as the sky!"

Thereafter, Ding'er enjoyed even more respect from people far and near.

One day, Ding'er heard that a consecration ceremony was going to be held for a new gold statue in the Shrine to the White-Robed Guanyin at the foot of North Hill, which had been cast using funds collected by a monk. Numerous laymen and laywomen would go there to pay homage to the Buddha and repent their sins. Ding'er not only wanted to see the grand mass, but he was also in a rush to enjoy a few days of the vegetarian meals they'd give away during the ceremonies.

Halfway there, Ding'er took a break to rest his feet in the dense woods. Suddenly, he heard someone moaning in a bamboo grove. When he drew closer, he saw a very young woman as thin as a dead branch and near death. Shocked, Ding'er thought to himself, "How could she have gotten to this deserted place? Could she be some mountain spirit or tree monster come to tempt me in disguise in order to take my life?" Then he thought again, "But if she were trying to trick me, why would she appear so thin and weak? She must be human and is surely not a ghost. There must be something behind this." When Ding'er went back to check her closely, he found that she was still able to speak. "Who are you?" asked Ding'er. "Tell me clearly so that I can help you."

Slowly, the woman said, "I'm a daughter of a family in Macheng, Huangzhou. To my everlasting shame, a faithless man seduced me and talked me into eloping with him. We didn't expect to use up all our money for clothes and travel so quickly. Worse still, I fell ill on the road and had to stay at an inn for quite a while, accumulating charges that we had no way of paying. Last night that heartless man carried me here on his back and left, abandoning me in this wilderness. If you, kind sir, are willing to help me, I'd be grateful even after I die!"

Ding'er believed what she said was true. He lifted her up by the arm, put her on his back, and took her to an old temple nearby, where he gently laid her down. Then, to make her more comfortable while she was sleeping, he found some soft grasses and made a mat on the ground. He found a half-broken clay brazier, gathered some firewood and bamboo sticks, and warmed some water and a little food to relieve her hunger and thirst. Having brought her food and drink, Ding'er found a place to rest outside, treating her as his guest.

Within half a month, the woman had gained some weight and was even able to walk a bit. So grateful was she that she offered to marry Ding'er.

"Madam, you misunderstand me," Ding'er said. "Although you're a dishonored woman, all I wanted was to help you. If I were to seek personal advantage from your hour of direst need, that would be unjust! If I were to make selfish demands for repayment, that would be inhumane! The image you have of me is absolutely wrong. You should focus on your recovery and put away all thoughts of some predestined marriage between us. Since your parents don't live far away, how about making inquiries and finding out how to get you home?"

Within a few days, they reached Macheng and, by making inquiries, found where her parents lived. The old couple had no choice but to quietly welcome their daughter in. So grateful were they to Ding'er that they wanted to give him two ounces of silver for his return travel expenses. Ding'er refused to accept the money, but the old couple were so persistent that he had to take it. Hiding the money in his shirt, Ding'er left, begging along the way.

One day he happened to come to the Huangmei County market, where he saw an old man, his brow furrowed with worry, holding a ten- or eleven-year-old boy with a strand of straw stuck in his hair to show that he was for sale. The old man said he was a total of five ounces in arrears in rent to a wealthy man and would have to sell his son so that he could pay it off. They had been walking around in the market, but no one seemed interested.

After observing them closely for a long while, Ding'er sighed and said, "Why would a rich family care about a debt as small as five ounces? How can they bear to see him end up selling his son in order to pay them back!" So he took out the silver from his shirt and said to the old man, "I'll go and plead on behalf of your son." Together they went to see the rich man.

The doorman reported them, and the rich man said, "Just call the accountant to see whether he has enough to cover principal and interest and then return the original contract to him. Why does he need to see me?"

"There's also a beggar waiting outside to see you," the doorman said.

Hearing the doorkeeper's report, the rich man said, "They must have come here to kick up a row with me by getting a beggar involved!"

"But I've heard that the beggar has some money and wants to pay his debt for him," said the doorkeeper. Finding it hard to believe, the rich man went out of the hall and saw his debtor standing with Ding'er at the bottom of the steps.

The debtor said to him, "We're grateful for the money my lord loaned us and should repay it with interest. But I'm sick, we're poor, and indeed we have nothing worth pawning. I came to plead for my lord's sympathy and ask for a little more time."

"You've been saying this for a long time! You've already promised to sell your son to pay me back. Why must you come to see me with the same story again today!" said the rich man.

Upon hearing this, Ding'er stepped forward and addressed the rich man. "My lord, your house is like that of Yidun, and you're as rich as Taozhu.[13] For you, the sum of five ounces must be like one tiny grain in a big storehouse! Why do you need to force him to sell his son for it? I can't bear to see this. I'm just a street beggar, but I've saved up four ounces here, which I'd like to give to pay off his debt. Please be generous enough to waive the last ounce. If you absolutely refuse to forgo it, I'm willing to stay and beg in your honored county and pay it back little by little."

Infuriated by Ding'er's words, the rich man said, "It is clear that this man used the four ounces to get the beggar here to make a fool of me! How detestable it is! Yet if he is just a beggar, how could he have accumulated so much as four ounces? I've heard that a thief stole four ounces of rice money from one of my farmhands the night before last. This must be it! Quick—write up a complaint and submit it to the Huangmei County court, accusing this old debtor of concealing the booty. I won't be appeased until the stolen money is reclaimed, justice is carried out, and the criminals are tattooed and banished to some other place!" Hearing their master's command, his retainers on both flanks instantly drafted a complaint, trussed up the two of them with the same rope, like chickens, and rushed them to the court.

The magistrate's name was Bao Da. A newly appointed metropolitan graduate, he was both extraordinarily smart and insightful and never sacrificed justice for private feelings, thereby becoming known as "Yanluo's Rival" among the local people.[14] The magistrate ascended the bench in court immediately upon receiving the complaint. During the hearing, he learned from one side that a father had tried to pay off his debt by selling his son and a man had altruistically tried to pay on behalf of the former, and from the other side that a thief and a debtor had been captured and brought to court. While hesitating over his judgment, the magistrate saw a group of respected local elders, around thirty or forty of them, lined up like a string of fish, all kneeling at the gate. He had them summoned inside.

Without waiting for the magistrate to utter a word, these kneeling elders shouted out, "He is a righteous man! He is a righteous man! We can all act as his witnesses. He must not be harmed by that cruel rich man!"

"I won't believe this simply because it comes from a multitude of you," said Magistrate Bao. "Withdraw at once and wait until I've questioned them one by one." First, he asked the old debtor to explain the reasons for his indebtedness and for his plan to sell his son. Then he asked Ding'er to explain the circumstances behind his generous decision to pay the debt and how he had offended the landlord by his words.

Magistrate Bao carefully considered the information. "The only 'silver' begging brings you is grain husks and broken rice, and a few fragments of money," he said. "How is it possible you have saved as much as four full ounces of silver?"

He was just about to use torture on him, when the crowd of elders swarmed in again and encircled Ding'er. Then they told the magistrate the true story of how the beggar once returned a lost bag of money to its owner and also returned a lost woman to her parents.

"That is still hard to credit," said the magistrate. "But the places where he returned the lost money and the lost woman aren't that far from here."

Two official letters were dispatched to the two places, bringing all involved to his court within a few days. Both the man who had lost his money and the man who had lost his daughter retold their stories convincingly. In order to test them, the magistrate first presented them with four random ounces, which they didn't recognize. Then he showed them the beggar's four ounces, at which they came forward, saying, "Yes, yes!" Last, the magistrate divided the pile of broken silver into two halves and put each on a scale. They both weighed exactly two ounces, no more and no less.

The magistrate immediately had the rich man placed in the heaviest cangue, flogged forty times, and imprisoned for making false accusations. The rich man kowtowed repeatedly to the magistrate, pleading for leniency. Appeased, the magistrate changed his sentence and demanded instead that the rich man pay a fine of three hundred ounces, which he gave to Ding'er as his reward. The woman, still unmarried, he also married to Ding'er. Later she gave birth to three sons, who continued the scholarly tradition of the family. Even now, they're a prominent family in Huangzhou.

Respected brothers, do you believe now that the matters of the nether world aren't fabrications at all? At the beginning, I mentioned that in their rosters the underworld judges recorded Wu Xian as someone who was born with low status but who had superior moral standards. Every word turned out to be true in retrospect. It is all because of his unthinking expression of arrogance that he experienced this kind of reincarnation. And so we see the importance of being cautious when speaking. Today's tales of retribution are all intended to benefit our bodies and minds and to enhance our knowledge. As we gather under the bean arbor, we can't know whether the King of Heaven, the Jade Emperor, is passing overhead. Inevitably, we would be punished without mercy in the nether world if we were to tell tales that are obscene or deviant.[15]

At this, they all closed their palms and replied, "Even Buddha's words of truth wouldn't surpass this." Bowing respectfully, they bid one another good-bye and returned home.

GENERAL COMMENTS

The teachings of the various Confucian schools share the same gist of cultivating one's moral conscience and making one's actions sincere. This story tells us about the mutual responses between Heaven and man, about benevolence and material things, about generosity and greed, chastity and lasciviousness. Although the narrator began with sage thinkers and Confucian scholars, by taking the lecturer's tiger-skin-draped seat and by collecting disciples around him, tirelessly discoursing on the Way and pondering the Mysteries, he never got beyond moral conscience and filial piety, the differences between humans and beasts.

Then why did the narrator choose a beggar as an example? Because he'd save Sage-King Shun, King Wen of Zhou, Zeng Can, and Min Ziqian for extrapolating for a higher-class audience.[16] When speaking to lower-class people, he would want to use a protagonist as humble as the beggar yet so capable of performing filial deeds and doing righteous things that everyone from a beggar up should be equally capable of doing the same. In other words, those who neither practice filial piety nor act righteously would be less worthy than a beggar.

Like cold water pouring down the back and hot fire flaming in the heart, this keeps me weeping with excitement and talking endlessly even in my sleep, while my sense of filial piety arises spontaneously and grows unstoppably. I particularly like the ten-odd lines Ding'er said to the eminent man, which are subtle yet earnest. I've seen people abandoning their families when posted to official positions, and then they return home in silken robes. Surely it is true that this glorifies their parents and makes their names known. But how can it compare to the joy—so much that your hands should dance and your feet should tap—of staying at your parents' knee, providing them with wine and food?[17] *Moreover, there are many men throughout this world who lament having been deprived of a way to prove their respect for their aging parents. When they read this session, how can they help but slap their chests and sigh aloud!*

Translated by Zhang Jing

The Exalted Monks Who Faked Transcendence

On this day it was bright and the air was clear. Cool breezes came one after another.[1] Between the bean flowers that covered the bean arbor were a few stems that had begun to show many small pods. Children saw the pods and shouted, "Look! There are beans up there already."

Hearing this, some people raised their heads, craned their necks, and tried to reach the beans. "Baby bean pods are hard to come by," exclaimed everyone.

"Wait for me to pick some," said the host. "I'll boil them as a treat for anybody who can tell a good story today."

"Good idea, good idea." Everyone applauded.

A chair was set up under the arbor. A young man stepped up and said, "Let me sit in this chair today. I'll tell you a most unacceptable story about our world. Once you have heard it, whenever it occurs to you, you'll feel the same disgust again."

THE YOUNG MAN'S STORY

As I see it, there is only one moon and one sun in the heavens, rising in the east and setting in the west, and therefore there has been eternal light for all the ages. All living things on the earth each have only one seed and one true root, and therefore they will regenerate themselves forever. As for the humans here between Heaven and Earth, they alone have managed to come up with numerous names and categories in this world—the rulers are to rule the world, the ministers are to assist the rulers, and the common people are to cultivate the fields and to feed the multitudes. This is why they say that if there were no men of authority, there would be no one to rule the country people, and if there were no country people, there would be none to support the men of authority.[2] This is why the sages and virtuous men of ancient times have established the teachings of Confucianism, which are of cardinal importance.

It's entirely thanks to Confucian teachings that we know how to distinguish the principles of Heaven and Earth, Yin and Yang, how to rectify and illuminate the norms of human relations, how to civilize and enlighten, and how to regulate a family, govern a state, and bring peace to all.[3] This is the principal vein of True Qi in this world that is inconceivable and beyond discussion.[4] There are also the teachings of Daoism. But members of this school spend their time discussing the mysterious, cultivating body and mind, extending their life spans, and enhancing their health. There aren't that many sects in this school, so we don't need to discuss it now.

But Buddhism is much different. It has developed a rather confusing variety of approaches to its doctrines. It was introduced to China in the twelfth year of Emperor Ming's reign during the Han (69 CE), when people said holy men came from the West. It takes up the word "emptiness" as the foundation of its theory, which did no more than exhort people to see the empty nature of the mundane world and to keep their six roots of sensations pure and clean, so that their minds could grow limpid as jade and free from any attachment and obstruction. Such teachings originally included no ideas about retribution and reincarnation. Only because later people gave strained interpretations without a basis and made up a lot of stories about Hell and Heaven did they come up with texts about such ideas so that they could cheat people. I'll come back to this later.

For now, I want to talk just about the monks. I used to believe that it was a matter of greatest importance that they took their vows and started the practice, a smart deal that only men of superior wisdom would make. How could I know that no matter whether they are wise or stupid, good or evil, no matter which crime they have committed—adultery, theft, blackmail, or counterfeiting—every one of them was going down a dead-end path in their secular lives?

When Heaven could not tolerate them and Earth would no longer carry them and they were at their wits' end, they shaved off the few remaining hairs on their heads, hung strings of prayer beads around their necks, draped thin robes over their shoulders, and, carrying wooden fish drums, they call themselves monks. They just did this so people would then partially forgive them for the evil deeds they had done in the past. Seeing how broad this gate is, hoodlums hide themselves away there, and before anyone realizes it, they increase in number day by day.

People who have no way of feeding and clothing themselves can cut a bamboo walking stick, get a bronze bell, buy a length of chain, and, starting out before daylight when even peddlers aren't out yet, roam through cities and villages, binging and banging until your head aches and shouting until you go deaf. Pointing this way and that, they carry on about building temples or erecting bell towers, gilding statues or printing Buddhist sutras—all nonsense made up to swindle people out of money and rice.

If they were content with their fates and stayed in their place, they would not provoke people to detest them. Who can tell whether hidden among them are the extremely violent and wicked able to topple the sky and overturn the earth? People can't recognize such a man in advance. Instead, they might even see him as a buddha or bodhisattva and support him with the utmost piety. Later, when he has committed some crime that causes others to lose their lives or possessions, people lose faith in even the good monks. People like this are a distortion and a corruption of the Buddhists—this goes without saying.

Yet how could all monks be bad? Among them are also golden immortals who can bring salvation to the world and buddhas manifested in this life who preach the sermons and explain the scriptures to save the sinking and enlighten the confused. Like Bodhidharma, who arrived from the West, or Master Zhudaosheng, who was manifested in this world, such monks are enlightened to the Truths and can convert the people of our world.[5] There have been very few of them since ancient times. The few lines of verses they utter and the few famous words they leave behind surpass anything said for a thousand years and are indeed what people need.

No one ever saw the whisk that Śākyamuni Buddha once used in his teaching being passed on lightly to any of his disciples. Nevertheless, the foul spawn of today make up a new situation. They find a few volumes of collected sayings in some monastery and purchase a few commentaries. No matter whether they understand them or not, as long as they can make out a few characters, they'll take them and sit by the altar and practice chanting them. They pretend to be erudite, befriend a few fellow monks—for mutual flattery—and acknowledge a few preachers as their teachers. They may even set up their own sect, claiming that some Exalted Monk from a certain monastery a few years ago had handed them his whisk.

They sneak off to other counties in distant prefectures. There, upon catching sight of a dilapidated temple in an abandoned place, they get in touch with the few prominent local monks and nuns, who will spread the word that a spiritual adviser has arrived at a certain temple, recognizing that it is time for its revival. Meanwhile, they may bury some old stone stelae, only to dig them out seemingly by chance. Or they may pretend that they are deities from a local temple who have come to manifest their spirituality in this place. Or they may sprinkle around some sugary water, saying that it is sweet dew.[6] There are hundreds and thousands of such ways of deceiving the people.

Within half a month, foolish men and gullible women from all around will be worked up over these tall tales. Once they have saved up a few pennies or some food, they decide, "Let us prepare a ceremony for welcoming the Exalted Monk." After preparations are complete, this awkward-looking "monk" marshals a bunch of temple hangers-on and assistants to take his show to the public, copying services from temples elsewhere. Then they may ask people for endorsements from the local police agency or make friends with village gentry known for their support of Buddhism. They copy down large numbers of religious verses and learn the Chan School teaching methods of beating and shouting, post a few sheets of regulations in the corridors or write out long spiritual instructions for the front of the dining hall.

Those who come and go scratch their heads and conclude, "This Exalted Monk's learning is too deep for me—I can't get any enlightenment out of it!" Clearly he has hoodwinked them in broad daylight, which these foolish people will go to their graves never having figured out.

There is yet something else about monks that people don't know. As it usually happens, when an Exalted Monk comes to a new temple to start preaching, the Chan monks, who usually stay in their separate meditation chambers, will get together and make a big fuss distributing the daily work in the monastery. For their interest they give themselves fancy titles such as Head of the Abbot's Hall, Rector, Principal Lecturer, Entertainer of the Crowds, Recorder, Capital Preacher, Head of the Hall, Attendant, Inspector's Office, Prefect of Guests, Prefect of the Bath, Chief of Conversions, Assigner of Seats, Assistant Abbot, Stores Attendant, Visitors' Lodge Head, Temple Caretaker, Annual Evaluator, Task Evaluator, Incense and Candle Manager, Lower Hall Manager, Prefect of the Canon, Prefect of the Followers, Purchaser for the Hall, Head of Patrol and Oversight, General Manager, Capital Manager, Prefect of Crowds, Keeper of the Main Gate, Stores Manager, Head of Vegetables, Head of Bells, Head of Rice Fields, Head Cook,

Head of Tea, Head of Grounds, Head of Fire, Head of Water, and Head of Latrines. Once they have assigned these titles among themselves, they write them down as a public announcement and post it in the tearoom, where it makes a good impression.

When it is time for the Exalted Monk to present his teachings, pipes and bells are softly played. Monks line up on both sides, holding incense, flowers, lamps, and candles, kowtowing and bowing to him with every bit of reverence they can muster. But when the Exalted Monk gives his Dharma sermon, he merely reads aloud from his previous compilation of segments of others' sermons. And who could understand and be enlightened by that? He will have invited his friends—including several degraded village gentry, provincial graduates who feign elevated conduct, and former officials who have retired due to age—who will be spread out among the crowd to play the role of coming forward and sign up as donors protecting the Dharma. Having appeared before these believers to solicit their contributions, the Exalted Monk and his creatures then retreat to divide up the donations. This brings out even greater piety in these village rustics.

If there are wandering monks from elsewhere and a sharp one among them tries to advance to the platform and argue with the master on his interpretation of the doctrines, the master's attendants will encircle this monk and take him out and beat him half to death. Then they'll send out a warning with a detailed description of the challenger to all the local temples. This monk not only won't be able to find a temple that will accept him as a resident—he won't even be able to beg a bowl of rice in that region.

There is one more rule—only the donations recorded in the book of donors in the main hall and the alms collected outside belong to the permanent residents of the monastery. Offerings for rites from officials, pious laymen, and the old ladies are all received and kept by the Exalted Monk and his followers. When the service is over, on the following day they divide up the proceeds among themselves. Each taking his share, they vanish without a trace, hurrying away to enjoy the gains. None of them care if the permanent residents of the monastery don't have the money to pay for firewood, oil and salt, or rice—they'll just have to manage on their own. Hearing that teachings are about to start at another temple, they hurry there to carry on the same business. Don't you think these monks are three times more ruthless than a gang of robbers?

I've traced the origins of the title Exalted Monk. It first appeared during Shi Le's reign,[7] during the Jin dynasty, when a man called Fotucheng called himself that. Truly he was a saintly monk, who regarded Emperor Shi Le as no more than a seagull on the ocean. He had great spiritual power and was able to know both past and future. As stately as Dīpamkara, the Buddha of Light in antiquity, his presence naturally evoked people's admiration. If you ask the monks of today about the Flower Garland Sutra, they haven't even read it—all they care about is how to cheat people. How can they be so presumptuous as to call themselves "Exalted Monks"?

Recently there has been a joke going around that makes fun of "exalted monks" like them. A young gentleman took a boat to visit an Exalted Monk. He presented himself at the abbot's room, where he chatted with the Exalted Monk over tea. Then he stood up to bid him good-bye. To see him off, the Exalted Monk accompanied him to the dock, where the gentleman boarded the small boat. The sunlight was slanting down from the west, so the gentleman took off his skirt and hung it up as a curtain. "This humble monk doesn't dare return to the temple until he sees your boat appear to be as small as a leaf of the *ruo* bamboo," said the Exalted Monk.

Seated inside the hold, the young gentleman pulled back his skirt-curtain so that he could continue to see the monk. As the boat moved ever farther away, the boatman said to him, "The monk standing at the dock looks only seven or eight inches tall from here now, sir. Please put down your skirt." This was to make fun of the monk, because he made himself sound so exalted. This is just a joke.

I have yet another bit of idle gossip, but this one is absolutely true. It happened in Yingshan County of De'an Prefecture in Huguang, at the border with Xinyang Prefecture in Henan. This region is called the "Pass of Agony," because there is a precipitous mountain covered by dense woods. Although it has a major road, travelers who pass through are few and far between. There is an old temple on top of the mountain ridge. It was built with offerings by the end of the Tang or Song and named "Universal Brightness" according to the local gazetteers. It has only twenty or thirty monks, who are all *rakshasas* who eat meat and drink wine.[8] Over the past fifteen or sixteen years, for unknown reasons, ten-odd high monks had died in the sitting meditation position there. The rumor among the locals is that the feng shui of the temple makes it a holy site, and that is why the Chan masters and Buddhist patriarchs often manifest their presence there. Every year the temple manages to survive on donations from various sources.

One day, however, a healer seeking medicinal herbs arrived and asked for a night's lodging, but the monks flatly rejected him. The herbalist had no choice but to walk on in the moonlight. When he was already ten or twenty *li* away, it suddenly occurred to him that he had left his hoe in the stela pavilion outside the main temple gate. Fearing that someone would take it, all he could do was turn around and walk back to the pavilion.

He was looking for his hoe there when he suddenly heard someone crying out in great pain on the other side of the wall. "My lords, please allow me to live for a few more days before you put me on the seat," the person kept pleading.

Finding it quite odd, the healer climbed onto the wall, where, holding onto a tree branch, he took a good look. There, in front of the hall and in the lamplight, a few baldheads had tied up an old monk and were lifting him onto a kind of elevated seat that was too dark to see clearly.[9] For a few seconds the old monk squealed like a stuck pig, and then he went silent. The healer waited there the whole night, hoping to find out what they were up to the next day.

At daybreak, he heard bells and drums sounding in the hall, while the monks' chanting of Buddha's name was loud enough to shake the heavens. A monk came out and announced, "Last night Chan Master Perfect Enlightenment died while meditating in a sitting position."

Notices announcing a vegetarian feast were distributed in all directions, and a lot of head monks arrived in preparation for a grand ceremony. The healer went in and looked at the body carefully. What he saw was a grievous sight—the skin on the dead monk's face as pale as dried vegetable leaves, not even a hint of the color of blood left. When no one was watching, the healer reached out his hand and touched under the seat. His hand came back covered in blood. He felt a rootlike thing protruding from the body's rectum. The healer immediately went to the court of Xinyang Prefecture to report this situation in minute detail.

As it happened, the prefect of Xinyang had dreamed the previous night that he saw an old monk, covered in blood, crying out incessantly in pain. Recognizing its meaning, the prefect at once mounted a fast horse and led his local militia to the temple, which they surrounded.

After he went inside, the prefect summoned the abbot to a meeting. The abbot refused to be called out, relying on his title as an Exalted Monk. Instead he sent a housekeeper to greet the prefect.

"I've heard that another Chan master died sitting in meditation here last night," said the prefect, "so I came to prostrate myself at his feet. Then I'd like to have him placed in a vessel and have a pagoda built to house it."[10] The housekeeper kowtowed in thanks to the prefect. "How many monks are there in this temple?' the prefect added. "I'd like to call the roll in order to give each of you a small donation."

Like wolves and tigers ready for their prey, the monks all came out, their heads bowed and their hands at their sides, waiting for their names to be called. The prefect had his militia watch every one of them. Then he asked his attendants to lift up the dead monk to see how his arms and legs looked. Two soldiers went up and pushed on the body, but it didn't move. Then they tried harder to lift it up. A two-foot-long iron rod suddenly fell out of the dead monk's rectum. Underneath was an earthen pot full of blood, already congealed.

The prefect had all these monks tied up one by one and was about to have them taken to the court, but as his militia broke through one after another of the doors to the monks' rooms, about ten women ran out, crying out for justice. The prefect asked his lictors to bring them up one by one. "How long have you women been here?" he asked.

The women testified one after another. "Some of us have been here for three to five years, and some came this year. These monks ganged up with some troublemakers who pretended to be merchants from distant places.[11] They said they didn't mind how much it would cost, as long as they could find someone to marry and take home, where we could make a living together. Who could have known that after they had tricked us into coming to this county, one day they suddenly used the excuse of taking us to visit our families to bring us directly here, hiding us behind many walls and in the depths of secret chambers, and prevented us from getting even a glimpse of the sun in the sky? There are also a few young girls who are only about ten years old. They are daughters from nearby villages who were kidnapped when they were playing outside and nobody was watching. They have been hidden here ever since, waiting to be used when they turn twelve or thirteen."

"Why has no one ever brought a complaint about this to the county or prefecture court all these years?" asked the prefect.

The women said, "Their underlings were all former murderers or thieves. When they had no place else to hide, they all hid out here. They took care of their daily needs by cheating people out of money or food, which they shared evenly among themselves. They also often gave some small bribes to villagers nearby. That is why no one, inside or out, wanted to get in their way. If anyone among them had raised any objections, the rest would have taken care of him on the spot. This is why they united as one man, and no one discovered anything until today."

"But why have so many of them died in a sitting meditation posture over the years?" asked the prefect.

"They were all merchants who traveled by themselves," the women explained. "They were trapped and brought inside, not allowed to get away. First, they made them take a sleeping potion, then they took off the net, tied them up, and left them in the sun. When their faces and temples became tanned, they shaved off their hair and eyebrows, making them look like mendicants.[12] Or they tied them up sitting in the lotus position and let them starve for three or five days until their skulls turned soft. Then they poured sulfur and saltpeter into their sleeves and seated them up on the altar in the cremation tower. They called up former head monks of this area and asked them to spread the news. People would come from all directions for this spectacle, bringing money to set up offerings, build pagodas, and read sutras. Who knows how much money was swindled from them, which was all divided up evenly among these fake monks in accordance with their custom? Once they had used up the money, they started scheming about the next Living Buddha."

While the prefect was carrying on his investigation, an attendant came to report, "A large number of women's foot bones were dug up in the bamboo garden!"

"Why are these only women's foot bones?" he asked.

"When a man dies, his dry bones are useless," a woman said. "Only the fresh corpse of a woman retains its blood and energy in the leg bones. When you saw them into thin pieces and polish them carefully with water, they look like ivory chopsticks. Nobody can tell them from the real thing, and they can be sold for a large profit. When the monks of this temple had no other way to get money, they often asked around to see if there was a local woman who had recently died. If there was, they stole the body for this dirty business. They used the leg bones, so only foot bones are left."

Having investigated all these atrocities, the magistrate sentenced each monk to a beating of fifty strokes followed by a nail punched into the heart, taking their lives instantly. He prepared a detailed report for his superiors, then eliminated all traces of their evil, even burning the Temple of Universal Light down to the ground, to rid the place of this great scourge. This is a story about recent Exalted Monks.

I have yet one more story, which I also heard from others. It took place during the Kaiyuan reign of the Tang dynasty,[13] in Henei County of Huaiqing Prefecture in Henan. In the Kaiyuan Temple, there was a monk whose

Dharma name was Sihui (Dead Ashes), a rather strange name to begin with. Dead Ashes was born with extraordinarily odd features, his bearing both lofty and imposing. He read the classics widely and thoroughly and was fully familiar with the Hundred Schools of thought. He also studied cosmology and geography and was able to know the past and tell the future, as well as to predict a man's life span. He knew how to compose some poetry, how to do calligraphy in several scripts, and how to paint in several styles, his works surpassing those of famous masters within the seas and shaming those "fancy visitors" from all directions.

Admirers came to visit him from far and wide, bringing unusual local produce to offer him. They would send it into the meditation hall, register in the guests' book, and have to wait for three days before he'd come out from his abbot's chamber to meet with them. Attended by a crowd of monks, he'd mount the steps and take the elevated seat. On both flanks were attendants carrying incense burners and fly whisks and holding walking staffs and flower vases. Floral displays and candelabra sets were arranged in front of him. In the center was a censer in which incense of sandalwood and rosewood was being burned. The fragrant puffs, swirling like strokes of seal-script characters inside and outside the censers, wove together an imperial canopy. What a sight it all made!

Only after three beats on the cloud board were visitors who had questions allowed to move forward in order and kneel down, when they finally got to ask them one by one. Sitting high above, the monk would deliver a few lines of his vague, applicable-everywhere "teachings" and then ask the visitor to withdraw. If the visitor tried to say more, he'd get a blow on his head from the staff and collapse to the ground, muddled, where he was left to guess at how to find salvation on his own. Then it was the next visitor's turn to come up, and the same thing would happen. The monk either gave him a logical puzzle to meditate on or left him with a few lines of verse, which quite often met the person's needs. Sometimes a sick person would come and explain the origins of his condition and ask for a prescription. With his command of the secrets of pulse diagnosis from the *Classic of Difficulties* and of the medical properties of herbs from the *Materia Medica*, he'd write out a prescription for some drugs, which, when taken by the patient, would prove to have uncanny efficacy.[14]

Within a short time, people everywhere were talking about him, as if he were a dragon that had appeared in the flesh. The monk gave up his own disbelief, claiming in public that he was the incarnation of a buddha. As a result, money and grain came to him in great amounts from all directions, like gathering clouds and thickening fog, for rebuilding the monastery and constructing layers of halls and gates in the front and the back. The Kaiyuan Temple became very famous, second only to the four great Buddhist mountains.[15]

But who could know that Pugu Huai'en would rebel that year?[16] The court deployed troops and dispatched cavalry, ready to quell the rebels. A frontier defense commandery was set up in Hebei, a strategic region, and Li Baozhen was appointed the commander. This gentleman was extraordinarily muscular, resourceful, and wise. He and his fifty thousand soldiers and cavalry set up camp in Hebei. He imposed strict discipline, forbidding his soldiers to disturb the civilians' lives in the slightest. The army and civilians got along well, and the local people were as grateful to Li as if Li were their parent. Li gave training sessions to his soldiers every three days and held reviews every five days, not allowing them to go an inch outside the camp.

Commander Li had heard about the abbot. Three days into his posting, he prepared generous donations and, following the etiquette of a disciple, paid a visit to him. At the meeting, seeing that the commander showed him so much respect, the abbot began to put on airs, attempting to imitate Fotucheng's treatment of Shi Le and behaving quite arrogantly. By that time Commander Li had already perceived that the monk was relying wholly on his natural gifts and realized that he had no true accomplishments at all. But that isn't part of this story.

Yet who would have known that the monk was soon to run out of luck? That year the Hebei region seemed cursed. Farmers there didn't harvest a single grain. The troops' monthly subsidy from the imperial court had been delayed for seven or eight months, and no relief was provided. Soldiers had become increasingly discontented and restless, secretly spreading the rumor that they'd end up like the eight thousand Chu soldiers who packed up and went home when they heard Chu songs everywhere.[17]

At his wits' end, Commander Li had no choice but visit the temple. There, he praised the Exalted Monk for his great skills in handling crises. Then he folded his palms and knelt in front of the monk, expressing his sincerity and humility in seeking his advice. The abbot was usually more than capable of hoodwinking petty men. However, confronted with this urgency that the troops might rebel at any minute, and realizing that putting together enough money and food to distribute was the only solution, he was cornered and embarrassed, unable to come up with any strategy for the commander.

In fact, Commander Li already had prepared a plan on his own. All he had to do was take his time presenting the situation and delude the monk by flattering him with "my Exalted Monk this" and "my Exalted Monk that" until the cleric fell into his trap, never suspecting anything. That was the beauty of his plan.

Commander Li deliberately knitted his eyebrows, looking worried. Then, after a moment, he resumed by asking, "How about your supplies of grain and money for this temple's permanent residents? Can you loan me enough to help out my soldiers for the next month or two?"

The monk's heart was like that of the monastery's guardian bodhisattva, pleased when offerings came in and concerned about any outlay. He replied, "Recently our supplies haven't been enough to support us for ten days. Fortunately, this humble monk does have some share of happiness allotted by fate. Whenever we suffer or lack anything, the people hurry to provide. This is how we have been getting through these times. If you ask me how much we have in stock, in fact we have nothing."

"Then I can't borrow from the monastery's supplies," continued Commander Li. "However, I have a plan, for which I ask my Exalted Monk only for some of your share of 'predestined happiness.' With this, your disciple will find a way to survive."

Hearing that he wasn't borrowing money or food but only some luck, the abbot turned ten times more animated and asked, "What do you have in mind?"

"Your disciple," answered Commander Li, "has taken my cavalry and infantry to fight south and north. We have been to many other places. None of them seem to have so many people who love virtue as you do here. Now your disciple has a rough idea, which relies on your 'predestined happiness,' Your Eminence. Let us post an announcement in front of the temple tomorrow, saying that your disciple invited the Exalted Monk to give a lecture on the Dharma treasure of the Flower Garland Sutra and to perform the Peacock Sutra. We'll draw in some laymen and laywomen among the faithful and ask for offerings, some of which can be used to cope with my current emergency."

"A service such as this won't motivate the people," the abbot said. "I fear that not many will come. How can we get enough?"

"Your disciple has another plan," Commander Li said, and then he lowered his voice and whispered so and so to the monk. The monk gave a laugh, nodding repeatedly.

In no time, in an open space within the temple, a high seven-layer lotus platform was constructed and covered with multiple covers. The monks got some pine kindling from outside and piled it up around the platform. They also dug a narrow tunnel underneath that would allow one person to pass through.

On the first day of the services, after concluding his lecture, the Exalted Monk remarked, "My audience, you must concentrate and quickly comprehend these teachings, because I won't be with you for long. As soon as I complete this forty-nine-day service, I'll pass away and return to the West."

Upon hearing that the Exalted Monk was going to "transcend" soon, his pious audience was amazed. The news created an instant sensation and spread far and wide. Donations came in large amounts, heaped up like hills, enough to fill the sea. Commander Li secretly arranged for a few senior monks to register all the donations and store them carefully.

The day of the completion was approaching, and visitors would not disperse either day or night. Even more kindling was piled around the platform. People gathered around it like spectators in a theater, waiting single-mindedly for the monk to ascend the platform, wondering what spiritual power of a Living Buddha or what evidence of a saintly monk the Exalted Monk would manifest.

Meanwhile, the abbot was thinking to himself, "I have that underground passage underneath the platform. The moment they announce the lighting of the fire, I'll make myself disappear and escape through the tunnel. By following the commander after this, even to the ends of the earth, I'll have more than enough to enjoy."

But who could have known that all the while the commander himself had been scheming against the monk? When it came time to light the fire, he had already sealed up the tunnel exit. Only then did the old monk finally realize that the commander had tricked him. What else could he do but toughen himself to endure the calamity? In no time he turned into ashes.

The commander bowed with utmost sincerity. By this time someone had already made up a story: "I saw with my own eyes the Exalted Monk. Wearing a crimson cassock, surrounded by five-colored auspicious clouds, and with many hanging banners and celestial canopies, he set off for the West."

The next day, the commander put some fine white pebbles in the remains of the fire, and everyone said they had found many *śarīra* cremation relics. The commander collected these relics and immediately built a pagoda for the Dead Ash Patriarch. This corresponded perfectly with the prediction written into the monk's ominous Dharma name. The locals, men and women, all came to give alms. Within a month they had collected more than three hundred thousand. The commander took all of it to provide for his soldiers, of which no one was aware.

So I've told another story of how an Exalted Monk "transcended." If this old monk had concentrated on practicing asceticism, burning incense, and meditating, and had not put on all that pretense, Commander Li would not have carried out such a cold-hearted act. Later, when the real story of this monk came to be known, everyone applauded. If this Exalted Monk really had known how to tell the past and the future, how could he have been so deceived and come to such an end? This proves that all "exalted monks" are fakes. People delude themselves and let themselves be cheated out of money earned by their sweat and blood.

His audience commented, "Nowadays we have Exalted Monks jostling around and bumping into one another, truly too many of them! How is it possible that every one of them is able to ascend the lecture platform and preach the Dharma? Yet people have also become somewhat disgusted with them recently, no longer entirely willing to support them. When they come together but have no midday meal to eat, they have no choice but go out, treading on each other's heels. Like the stinky rats from the corners of a house, following each other in a long line, they each carry a chime, hold an alms-bowl, and beg for food along the streets, following the model of Śākyamuni Buddha begging in the city of Śrāvastī. This is how they end up when they claim to be Exalted Monks!"

The bean arbor host remarked, "My dear brother, these stories you've told have been delightful. Now that the beans are boiled, may I invite you to try some?"

GENERAL COMMENTS

The whole world fawns on Buddhism. Who can be the rock in the current that resists the wild waves? Men of discernment have been deeply concerned about this. His Literary Eminence Han wrote the "Memorial on the Buddha's Bone" in opposition to this trend, although it nearly cost him his life.[18] Despite this effort, the event could not be stopped, but his writing has been passed on. After all these ages his moral integrity is still tangible and awe-inspiring. When he assumed the position of administrative head of the capital region, his armies did not dare violate any law and referred to him as "the one who would have burned the Buddha's bone." Ah, the staunch spirit with which he opposed Buddhism can also be formidable! There are no more men like Han Changli in today's world. We can only rely on those in power to reason against it rationally and restrict it legally. Even this is not enough to suppress vulgar practices. How could they, instead, add more fuel to such flames? Perhaps they believe that they can repent for their sins by paying lip service to giving alms.

It goes without saying that as a matter of course, if the ruler likes something, the ruled will like it even more. Even if they can't go so far as the emperor of Northern Wei, who destroyed Buddhist temples by the tens of thousands, nor follow Emperor Wuzong of Tang, who forced the shaved heads to grow out their hair, still, if they could slightly curtail belief in it and rectify its customs, they could bring peace to the people and quiet the heresies.[19]

This session took up Li Baozhen punishing Dead Ashes as an example of the authorities' strategic handling of a crisis, although Li didn't have to be so callous and cruel. As the saying goes, when you attempt to copy the best, you'll only hit the mean.[20] Replacing a display of wrath toward Buddhists is none other than his display of compassion. Likewise, although these foreign deities may look violent and strange, they properly bow their heads and hang their hands. The reader shouldn't hastily conclude that this is an attack against Exalted Monks. You should compare it to Changli's essay "The Origins of Dao." It would also be appropriate if you compare it to his "Proclamation on Driving Off the Crocodiles."[21]

Translated by Zhang Jing

On Shouyang Mountain, Shuqi Becomes a Turncoat

Yesterday our young friend's account of the detestable acts of the "exalted monks" was so thoroughly satisfying that our host boiled some beans for him and arranged for the young fellow to join us again the next day to delight us once more with his tales. He also prepared some additional refreshments. The next day, sure enough, the young fellow arrived early under the bean arbor.

One of our listeners said, "There are too many 'exalted monks,' and loathsome they can be, my dear friend, but your mouth is too bitter, your tongue is too sharp, and your stories are too tart. We're vegetarians and read sutras all day, we invite others to Buddhist ceremonies, and we urge them to give alms. We now find it quite difficult to even mention such matters anymore. Even if we make it sound like flowers are falling from Heaven, no one will believe us. Rather than have you tell us another tale about the ways of the world, we have a test for you. Yesterday, our host boiled some beans as your reward for telling those stories. Today why not tell us a little tale about boiling beans? You can show us the depth of your talents without repeating idle talk and gossip about the ways of the world."

The young fellow glanced up into the sky, thought for a moment, and began.

THE YOUNG MAN'S TALE

Well, that's easy enough. There's an ancient poem that says:

> Boiling beans, burning their stalks,
> The beans in the pot cry out,
> "Born we are of the selfsame root,
> Why do you boil us so hard?"[1]

This is a poem by Cao Zijian. Zijian was the son of Cao Cao, the king of Wei during the Three Kingdoms period.[2] There were three brothers in the Cao family, all sons of the same mother. The eldest brother was Cao Pi, who styled himself Ziheng, the middle brother was Cao Zhang, known as Ziwen, and the youngest brother was Cao Zhi, called Zijian.[3] Early on, Cao Zhang was poisoned by Cao Pi and died. Zijian was so talented that Cao Pi, jealous of his brother's abilities, concocted rumors that his brother's poems were prewritten, memorized, and then presented as if composed on the spot.

One day, when they happened to be eating beans, Cao Pi asked Cao Zhi to recite a poem on the topic. Within the time it took to take seven steps, Zijian declaimed a poem on boiling beans. The four five-character lines, altogether just twenty characters, fully explored the theme of brotherly jealousy and sibling rivalry. Seeing how quick-witted his brother really was, Cao Pi became even more jealous.

Yet who could expect that someone as talented and knowledgeable as Zijian would be destined only for a poor fate and die soon thereafter? Cao Pi, on the other hand, inherited the empire. Talent and blessings, it seems, are all predetermined. As it turned out, there was no need for Cao Pi's cruelty and jealousy, which simply hurt their brotherly affection. All this happened during the time of the Three Kingdoms. Finding ourselves under a bean arbor about ready to boil some beans, I've told a tale about beans and brothers. Now that I think about it, far fewer brothers have harmonious relationships than are estranged from each other.

Long before the Three Kingdoms, there was a dynasty called Zhou. The son of King Wen and the younger brother of King Wu of Zhou was the Duke of Zhou, called Dan. He was a great sage. When King Wu left this world, the duke assisted the young King Cheng in ruling the empire. Everyone acknowledged that the duke was sincerely helping King Cheng, except the duke's older brother Guan Shu, who, though born of the same parents, had a heart distant from his brother. The Duke of Zhou believed in his brother and assigned him to guard the descendants of Yin.[4] Instead of performing his duties properly, Guan Shu took advantage of the fact that he was guarding Yin and, along with his other brothers, Cai Shu and Hou Shu, concocted rumors about the duke such as "With all authority under his control, the Duke of Zhou will soon betray his duties, and the child King Cheng will be in great peril."

When the Duke of Zhou heard these evil rumors, his sleeping and eating became disturbed. His mind wandered in a state between dreaming and sleeping soundly, and he no longer dared to serve as a minister at court. All this happened shortly after the end of the Shang dynasty, when every corner of the world was in chaos.[5] East of the capital an army arose, a righteous army in the estimation of the Shang, but a band of diehards to the Zhou. With the eastern expedition as his excuse, the Duke of Zhou rode off with his men to secure the eastern frontier, there to escape any further rumors.

But by then the rumors had spread in the four directions. No one knew who started them, but the Duke of Zhou couldn't bear to harbor suspicions about Guan Shu. Only later, when King Cheng discovered that Guan Shu, Cai Shu, and Hou Shu were in league with Wu Geng of Shang did he realize that those traitors were behind the rumors. King Cheng had the metal-bound casket opened and found that when his father, King Wu, was gravely ill, it was the Duke of Zhou who placed a bamboo tablet inside the casket praying that Heaven would take him as a substitute for King Wu. Only then did King Cheng know that the Duke of Zhou's heart was purity itself—like the bright sun in a blue sky, he had nothing to hide.

Some time earlier, while the Duke of Zhou was in the east, there was a great storm of wind and rain that whirled rocks and sand and that toppled and uprooted great trees throughout the countryside. When King Cheng greeted the duke on his return to the capital, the uprooted trees righted themselves. Therein lay proof that Heaven, earth, spirits, and deities were all moved by his integrity. Had the duke died before the rumors stopped, no one would have believed in him, even a thousand years later. As you can see, even a sage can be implicated without proof by his evil brothers. Let me tell you another story about two brothers in the Zhou.

This next story can't be found in the classics or histories but only glimpsed in the jottings and unofficial histories that escaped the fires of the First Emperor of Qin.[6] It's a rather marvelous thing that happened before the Zhou established its control and the Shang reached its demise, when two brothers, born of the same parents but of different minds, started off by coming together but ended by separating. The older brother was called Boyi, the younger brother was known as Shuqi.[7] They were princes of a Shang vassal state. Their ancestral name was Motai, and their father was the Lord of Guzhu. They were born of the same mother and, initially, quite congenial. They were unsurpassed in their friendship and mutual respect.

Boyi was born with an aloof disposition and showed no interest in governing. His father thought he was unreasonable and intolerant, that he was unsuitable as heir and lord of the realm. On his deathbed the father ordered that Shuqi, wise about the world and understanding of the feelings of the people, should be the next ruler. This was the father's command, but Shuqi said, "In establishing a state, the one cardinal principle of the world is to enthrone the eldest. Although Father has expressed his dying command, the specter of approaching death must have confused his mind." For this reason Shuqi ceded his inheritance to Boyi in accordance with the practices of old.

Boyi responded, "How can you just change our father's dying wish?" The two brothers politely deferred to each other for a while but, in the end, decided to run away. Well, these two brothers abandoned the throne of a ruler just like throwing away an old pair of worn-out sandals. They wanted to abide by the lofty morals and standards of behavior that had survived since ancient times.

Suddenly, because King Zhou of the Shang was ruling in a depraved fashion, King Wu raised an expedition against him.[8] As the cavalry led by Lü Wang, the Grand Duke of Qi, sallied forth, the people all laid down their swords and pledged allegiance to his cause. Many welcomed him with food and drink.[9] Without need for spears or swords, the world quickly returned to peace. Boyi and Shuqi realized that both the Mandate of Heaven and the people's hearts had already abandoned the Shang. They thought about summoning people from bygone days to form a righteous army to restore the Shang, but no one would have responded. Finding it no more possible than clapping with one hand, they decided to resign themselves to fate.

When King Wu raised his army, King Wen had passed away but hadn't yet been buried. Boyi and Shuqi discussed it between themselves. "He was an official of the Shang family. If we look at it from the perspective of justice, he committed regicide and seized the world belonging to his superiors. When a father dies, a peaceful burial is of the utmost importance. He could seize the world but didn't even think about burying his father? This is the extreme of unfiliality! Let's castigate him with this moral argument and see whether he can deny it!"

While they were discussing this, the Zhou cavalry swept in with the speed of a great wind. Boyi and Shuqi saw their opportunity. They blocked the road and, clutching the reins of King Wu's horse, remonstrated with him. "Is it filial to wage war when your father lies dead and unburied? Is it humane for a subject to kill his lord?"

Hearing these words, King Wu clamped his lips shut. When his attendants saw King Wu's face change color, they were about to hack down the two brothers with their swords. Luckily for them, the grand duke was riding next to the king.

Because King Wu had raised the army to comfort the people and punish the tyrant, the grand duke quickly stopped the attendants. In his heart he knew it was Boyi and Shuqi but found it inconvenient to explain. He said only, "These are righteous men. Do not harm them."

The duke asked his followers to help them up. Boyi's and Shuqi's words were of no use, but they had explained the ethics governing the world for everyone to hear so that all human hearts that knew righteousness would be inspired. King Zhou of Shang, however, was guilty of the most heinous crimes, and the people's hearts had deserted him. Their few words remained irrelevant, like putting frozen ice and burning charcoal in the same stove. Boyi and Shuqi also realized that everywhere—in the capital, cities, towns, and countryside—the Zhou troops were on guard. There was nowhere to take refuge. Rather than die for no particular reason, they decided it would be better to cover their tracks and go into hiding. Perhaps a time would come when they could act again. The brothers gave it some careful thought, called up their spirit of righteousness, and slipped out of the capital to find shelter on a mountain in the countryside.

The mountain was called "Shouyang," and it was in the area of Puzhou.[10] It was seventy or eighty *li* across with thousands of layers of rocky crags and surrounded by four or five hundred *li* of great wilderness. There were few trees on the mountain and no dwellings. There were, however, pleasing hidden caves that could provide shelter. At the top of the mountain, in cracks in the rock, grew fiddlehead ferns with clean, fragrant, tender stems that allayed the brothers' hunger. At the bottoms of the ravines and in hard-to-reach places ran clear, deep, and cold springs that quenched their thirst. Boyi and Shuqi resigned themselves to living on the mountain.

At first, when the brothers lived all alone, it was a pure and carefree life. But people in the cities and the markets began to hear about Boyi and Shuqi remonstrating while clutching the reins. Their stern and righteous words excited many people, either active and retired Shang officials or half-baked literati and phony moralists who liked to talk about purity and act immorally. At first, such people hid themselves in remote areas so as to prolong their lives, afraid that others might find them. Later, when they heard that such-and-such a person had switched his loyalties and that some other person had come out of the mountains, they hid their fear and envy and started expressing their lofty views and making caustic comments. As time passed, they began to fear the new dynasty's edicts because they were tainted by their past associations. So they began to talk about Boyi's and Shuqi's escape to West Mountain, passed on what they heard, and soon put out a call to the like-minded to get together. They flowed toward the mountain like a spring tide, like a fish on a string, like pilgrims with their incense in the second month of spring.[11]

Although there were few trees on the mountain, there were quite a few wolves and jackals, as well as tigers and leopards. When these wild beasts saw traces of humans, they bared their teeth and sharpened their claws behind the thick foliage and among the dense trees. Putting on a ferocious show, they hoped to make a tasty feast of some unlucky human. But as the number of people heading up the mountain increased, the foul creatures became suspicious, thinking it must be a hunting party coming to catch them. But they didn't see any nets or spears.

Just as they were deliberating uneasily, they saw an old man standing on a steep and precipitous peak. Only two or three feet tall, with broad eyebrows, white teeth, and gray hair and whiskers, he was bidding them to come over. "Dear foul creatures, come over and hear my commands," he called. "Boyi and Shuqi, two virtuous gentlemen, recently came to the mountain. They're not low, common folks. They came to demonstrate their personal integrity to the ages, because the court has a new ruler and they refused to submit. You savage lot should pull back your claws and tuck in your teeth, hide yourselves, and avoid doing anything rash."

The world, the animals suddenly realized, was no longer named Shang. They thought, "Even though we're just animals, we also have an innate nature and consciousness. If humans belonged to the old Shang, so did we. We walked on Shang territory and ate Shang flesh. Why is it that only Boyi and Shuqi are said to be naturally endowed with integrity? Why are we said to be unfeeling and unaware?"

The tigers and leopards shook their tails and, along with the badgers, dogs, and foxes, charged up the mountain one after the other, their righteous spirits aroused, to search for the place where Boyi and Shuqi were living. They wanted to bow and pay their respects to them. They bowed their heads and drew their paws together, and just like a dog guarding a home, they slept in the ravines and caves. It was now beneath them to pounce on rabbits, track sheep, or chase deer of any kind.

Later, the people who appeared at the bottom of the mountain said strange things and wore weird clothing, appearing more and more odd and peculiar, their numbers increasing every day. But Boyi was determined, as solid as a rock. He wandered day in and day out, whistling freely and proudly.

Leaning on his walking stick, he'd pick some ferns to eat and never talked about hunger. Eventually such hordes of people came that they bumped elbows on Shouyang Mountain. Rather than an empty peak, it started to look like a crowded market.

Boyi observed, "There are many in the world who value righteousness. This is a great focal point for the power of the Shang."

Shuqi, however, was irritated by what he saw and frustrated by the emptiness of his rumbling belly. One day a realization suddenly came to him. "What a mistake I made by coming here! My elder brother, Boyi, should have succeeded as the lord of our fief. He should have inherited because of the ethical principles upheld since ancient times and because of the ancestral instructions of the Shang. The Viscount of Wei ran off, Bi Gan remonstrated and died, and the Viscount of Ji acted crazy. Those people have already been written up in the best texts.[12] Over many generations we were enfeoffed by the Shang as a permanent state that shared weal and woe with our liege lord, so we couldn't just follow the hordes and submit to the Zhou. Even so, I'm the *second* son of the Lord of Guzhu, quite different from my elder brother, and I have a little wiggle room.

"The other day when we came across the great army, having a high opinion of myself, I joined my brother in shouting out some ludicrous things and nearly lost my life for it. Fortunately for me, Grand Duke Jiang was traveling with the army. He is a distant relative of ours—we dwelled on the coast of the Northern Sea and he on the coast of the Eastern Sea. He called us righteous men, but it was only because he escorted us to the side of the road that we were spared. Otherwise we might have tossed away our lives on that desperate throw of the dice. Now that the great army is gone, I can see that the Shang is shattered beyond repair. I was careless and impetuous when I came up the mountain. I thought that there would be only two of us and that we'd be ranked as the first and second paragons of virtue for all time.

"Who could have guessed that so many would want to pump up their pride by making a similar reputation for themselves and act like hermits in the hope of being invited to court? The ferns didn't need to be cultivated or have to be taxed, but this crowd gets up early to pick them clean. I'm so hungry I feel like a thin-skinned, dried-up vegetable leaf. My ribs are bent in like the window frames of a ramshackle house. A few days ago, I could straighten my chest, show off my arms, and go wherever I wanted to, but now my legs are weak and I can't bear the emptiness of my belly. I just can't go on.

"It finally dawned on me that men in this world pursue only two ideas—fame and profit. Some people will praise my older brother for being a sage, a saint, pure, the most virtuous, austere, and nothing less than a great man and a hero. But if anyone mentions my name alongside his, it would only be in passing. By attaching myself to his fame and following in his footsteps, even if I made a name for myself, it would only be as a hungry ghost, a hanger-on. Just suppose we started a righteous rebellion this morning and raised a great army tomorrow. If we somehow bungled it, *I* would be the one branded the ringleader of the troublemakers.

"Thinking about it this way, I see it's like a length of sugar cane. The more I chew on it, the more tasteless it becomes. As I look back, I'm glad it's not too late to act. As the ancients said, 'Better a cup of warm wine while alive than empty fame after you're gone.' My brother's resolve is like metal or stone—he won't waver. If I were to tell him that I'm leaving, he'd never let me go. However, today I can take advantage of his being around the back of the mountain picking ferns. I'll just take my bamboo staff, pick up my woven basket, and sneak around to the front of the mountain. I'll wait and see. If there's an opportunity, I'll walk down off this mountain."

Boyi was already faint from hunger and not on guard against Shuqi. With his mind set on switching sides for many days, Shuqi had prepared some clothes for leaving his refuge. Once he was down the mountain, he threw away his bamboo staff and discarded his woven basket. He put on his purple formal robe, wound a sackcloth mourning scarf around his head, and shod himself in eight-eared hempen sandals—an outfit never seen before on the mountain or anywhere else in the wider world. If anyone along the road questioned him about his clothing, he could say it was meant to represent both filial piety and loyalty.

Let's set aside the story of Shuqi going down the mountain and return to the jackals and wolves, tigers and panthers who had followed Boyi and Shuqi up the mountain. The beasts faithfully guarded the mountain single-mindedly.

Now among the beasts was a certain kind of fox. He was good at flattery, inclined to suspicion, and awfully hungry. He suddenly came to a realization. "Who knew that when the Shang was replaced by the Zhou there would be so many people charging up the mountain to profess their loyalty? But who among them won't have second thoughts about it? My only fear is that they're trying to ride two horses at the same time or have a foot in two boats at once, waiting for their chance to make trouble."

The fox called together several roe deer, chamois, apes, and rabbits to go out in every direction as scouts and listen for rumors. If they heard of any activity, they were to report it at once to the tiger, the king of the mountain. The tiger said, "If you find a turncoat, try provoking him with words. If you get him to reveal his change of heart, we can have full bellies for a day."

After discussing the matter thoroughly, they all went their separate ways to investigate. On the front of the mountain they saw someone hiding in the shade of the trees. Having spied him, the scouts quickly moved to one side. When the man came forward, they saw his face, and despite his different clothing, his appearance had not changed—it could be none other than the younger of the brothers who had led the migration up the mountain, the honorable Shuqi! Startled, the pack of animals grabbed him. Speaking in human language, they said, "Shuqi, honorable sir, you have dressed strangely today. Might you be thinking about changing sides?"

Shuqi said, "I dare not hide the truth from you. I've held out until today, but I can no longer uphold my old position."

The animals asked, "But where is your elder brother?"

"My elder brother would rather die nine deaths before changing his mind," Shuqi answered, "but I have my own humble ideas. Just yesterday I was going to seek out your master and explain my reasoning so that we might go down the mountain together. I didn't think we'd have this opportunity to meet. Please sit down on the rocks on the slope here, and I'll explain it to your hearts' content. Then may I trouble you to explain it to the king of the mountain? It will do us all good."

Hearing Shuqi speak so persuasively, the animals all felt relieved in their hearts and let go of his clothes. "Yes, please," they said, "enlighten us."

Shuqi began, "We are descendants of the Shang royal family. My elder brother was supposed to inherit the title of ruler, so he should die with his kingdom. Now, because of his boundless righteousness, it's only right that he should retreat to the mountains and refuse to eat Zhou grain, upholding the cardinal principle of obligation between vassal and king. I, however, am the *second* son—our obligations are totally different. My priority should be carrying on the family line. Although I followed my brother into the mountains, it was just a way of helping him into exile. I always intended to come right back down again. He follows his ambitions, and I mind my own business. Needless to say, I regret having stayed this long.

"You and the descendants of the king of the mountain aren't like humans. You aren't bound by ethical principles. Heaven bestowed life on you, allowing you to be cruel and vicious, to drink blood and eat flesh. You were originally man-eaters. During this time of dynastic change, there are many past wrongs and long-standing sins in the human world. The time is right for you to use the power of your strong claws and sharp teeth to gulp and bite, to let loose your heaven-and-earth-shattering force. This is called 'rising when destiny allows and acting when the time is right.' Why follow the humans of today, with their fake dispositions, who speak like sages and saints but who act like Bandit Zhi?[13] Half awake and half asleep, as if dreaming or drunk, you've put up with empty bellies and relish this simple life. This is dead wrong. Hurry away to the king of the mountain and explain my ideas to him, and he'll clearly see the light. And to repay me for these earnest words of mine, if by chance we meet along the road again, you'll bow to me in gratitude!"

The animals were overjoyed when they heard Shuqi's words. They lifted their heads high, bared their teeth, raised the fur on their backs, and bounced up and down to express their joy. Shuqi stood up and saluted them, saying, "Now go tell the king of the mountain."

The animals jumped up and bounded off like a spreading fire or shooting stars. Shuqi looked all around and thought, "How fortunate I am. Without my able tongue and flowery words, these dried-up bones of mine would have been chomped and swallowed down, and they'd be complaining about the smell of my shriveled-up lice."

Relieved, and quite pleased with himself, Shuqi trudged down the mountain for twenty or thirty *li*. Arriving at a bustling market town, he saw incense and flowers, lamps and candles, on all the front doors. On every door was written "We Surrender." He saw people riding horses and mules, people being carried in sedan chairs, and even people carrying luggage on poles. They were all in high spirits. But why? Shuqi made careful inquiries of bystanders and discovered that they were all off to the Western Capital for an audience with the new emperor. Some had jotted down a few strategies to present, some wanted reinstatement to their courtly positions, some had written mediocre essays in the hope of employment, and some held papers recommending them for their integrity and virtues. The people were all rushing along in an endless stream.

Seeing such activity, Shuqi quite unconsciously thought, "These people hurry about in high spirits, hoping to have their turn to raise their eyebrows and blurt out their thoughts for the instruction of the ruler and the benefit of the people, but I don't think they have the right credentials or standing and will likely fail. I, however, was an honored official in the Shang. All the officials who changed sides are my relatives of one degree or another. Of course, I did present a few words of idle talk with my brother in the past, but I don't think the new emperor will bear a grudge over such a trivial matter. And when my older brother lived on the coast of the Northern Sea, he was once the recipient of an honorary ceremony for elders held by King Wen. If I'm at court, I can bear the weight of the high expectations of the people. I'm a sure sight better than all these pretenders from humble families who don't even have a title and are trying to swindle their way into officialdom."

While walking along the road, Shuqi ruminated like this. He soon felt reinvigorated by his imagination. Before long, when he raised his head, he could see the imperial capital barely discernible behind auspicious multi-colored clouds. Knowing the capital was close, Shuqi found a place to stay for a while where he could prepare for his comeback. He dared not act until everything was planned just right. He settled down at the inn for a long night of thinking.

The next day Shuqi headed into the capital to look for old friends and relatives who might give him some money for living expenses. But before he had walked even a *li* or two, he saw a black cloud building up in the north-west. In a few moments, it had darkened half the sky. From a fierce rumbling in the distance, with a mighty roar like thunder and lightning, it rolled across the land on a ferocious wind. Shuqi thought it was a thunderstorm that had arisen suddenly and headed for a dense spot in the woods to take shelter. But suddenly he saw in front of him a squad of infantry and cavalry. They carried black flags and banners, and all were wearing black helmets and black armor. Most of the generals and soldiers wore black robes and had blackened faces as well. When he saw them, Shuqi was scared out of his wits. He never thought that those in front would yell in his face, "We've caught a big traitor!" Before Shuqi could explain, they tied him up like a hawk wraps its talons around a rabbit's neck. Surrounded by soldiers carrying swords and axes, Shuqi was taken to their camp.

Thinking that they were soldiers of the Zhou, Shuqi cried out, "I just came down the mountain to surrender and offer you my services!"

He heard an order passed down. "Since he surrenders and offers his services, loosen the rope for now."

Shuqi gathered his wits and realized that these were dead and wounded Shang troops. All of them had serious burns on their heads and foreheads, had hands but no feet, or had necks but no heads. One of the dead soldiers said, "Since you've come to surrender and offer your services, just what can you do?"

Aware of his precarious position, Shuqi blurted out, "I lived on a mountain for a long time, so I know the medicinal uses of all the plants. Whatever the illness, I can snatch people back from the jaws of death."

The many war-wounded, who were in excruciating pain, heard these words and demanded, "If you have some medicine, bring it right out and cure the lot of us. You can have whatever official position you want."

Before he had finished speaking, a man from the troop of sword- and ax-bearing soldiers on the left stepped forward and snatched off Shuqi's mourning headscarf. "If you want to be an official," he said, "why wear such an ill-omened rag? If you become an official, everyone will blame you for hiding your parents' deaths and being unfilial."

Out from the troops on the right stepped another man, who took a close look at Shuqi's face. "This is the son of the Lord of Guzhu, Boyi's younger brother. His name is Shuqi," he cried. "His face is so gaunt I hardly recognized him."

The rest came forward, and all said, "That's right, that's right. If he's of the noble line of the Shang house, he has the same heart and will as the rest of us. But this outfit makes it look like he's not in the same line of business as his brother. There must be a reason for this."

Someone seated in the middle said, "Nowadays, people's hearts are cunning and crafty. Who knows what they're hiding inside? Don't let him use that glib tongue to escape." He ordered the soldiers to take Shuqi away for more careful interrogation so they could get the truth out of him.

Shuqi finally realized that these were the holdouts from the city of Luo.[14] He didn't realize it, but his limbs began to shake, and even as he was still trying to find the words to get himself out of this mess, a memorial of surrender written in his own hand slipped out of his sleeve. The troops picked it up and read it aloud from beginning to end. Fists started to fall like rain on Shuqi, smashing his face to a pulp.

The officer in the middle cursed him, saying, "For generations your family enjoyed high rank and a hefty salary from the Shang. We might say the Shang treated you pretty well. How can you put on a shameless face and let your heart turn so wicked that you'd come down the mountain to seek officialdom? Even if you had become an official, you'd sit there facing south and feel so ashamed. With the new dynasty's regulations and your two empty hands, how could you hope to become an official? People like you need to be taken out to the crossroads in the market and beheaded in front of the people." The crowd tied up Shuqi once again and were just about to take him out to be decapitated. But wait—this story isn't over yet.

As we said, on the day they heard Shuqi's story, the animals had charged up to report to the king of the mountain. The Lord of the Mountain considered it, then said, "That makes sense, that makes sense! We have borne our hunger in order to guard the mountain, but by doing so, we rebelled against Heaven's will." They all sharpened their claws, honed their teeth, and raised the hackles on their necks to show their might. Rocking the heavens and rattling the earth, rank after rank, they went charging down the slope. At the bottom of the mountain they ran right into the encampment of holdouts where Shuqi was being taken, all tied up, out to the execution grounds.

Just as the troops were about to carry out the sentence, the fox and rabbit, who had been acting as scouts, reported to the king of the mountain, "That Shuqi who advised us to come down the mountain is in trouble."

At once the king of the mountain ordered the animals to save him, but they were held back by the bows and arrows, swords and spears of the holdouts.

"Greetings to your leader!" the animals said. "Shuqi is our benefactor. If you'd like to behead him, you'd better clear it with the king of the mountain first. Otherwise, we'll combine forces to do battle, and it won't go well for you!"

Soon the leader of the holdouts and the king of the mountain came forward. They saluted and made polite inquiries of each other. After that, the king of the mountain said, "His Excellency Shuqi is our benefactor. He pulled the scales from our eyes. Today he follows the commands of Heaven to bring salvation to the world, to bring tranquility to the people, to eradicate villainy, pacify the seas, and spread peace. How can you harm him?"

The leader of the holdouts responded, "There are never two suns in the sky, and the people can't have two kings. Shuqi is from a family long honored by the Shang, but he has deceived his king and father above and turned his back on his elder brother below. He harbors disloyalty in his heart. We've upheld righteousness and raised an army. Although gray Heaven hasn't blessed us and we have nowhere to turn, our heartfelt loyalty and sincerity are as clear as the light of day. The hot blood pulsing in our chests won't dry up for a thousand years. Today we were fortunate enough to bump into this traitor on a narrow road. If we don't destroy this villain and he becomes an official dressed in purple and belted in gold, how will this serve divine justice? How will it accord with laws and rules established by the king?"

Both sides spoke reasonably, and yet neither would yield.

In the midst of this battle of sharpened tongues, auspicious clouds started drifting in from the southeast on the gusts of a fragrant breeze accompanied by a symphony of celestial music. Rare birds and animals flew and scampered along in front of the clouds, while jeweled canopies and beautiful pennants fluttered through the air. Deities and celestial generals clustered around dragon carts and phoenix carriages. An order rang out, "You wild beasts and hungry ghosts, step back!"

The holdouts and wild beasts understood that the deity who had just arrived was the most senior of the Jade Emperor's court, the Master of Making Things Equal, also known as the Buddha Who Confirms the Age.[15] His office specializes in the rise and fall of dynasties, the fortunes and wealth of living people, and the resolution of unsettled injustices and debts among humans. Now this time of transition between two dynasties old and new is the proper time to settle old scores. Seeing him, the diehards, wild beasts, and Shuqi all knelt down and presented their arguments.

The Master of Making Things Equal carefully weighed the speeches of both sides and said, "All see the difference between Shang and Zhou as between old and new. As I perceive it, a rise and a fall is like having a new son in a human family. What is the difference? When the flowers of spring and summer wither, those of fall and winter bloom. As long as they accord with the seasons, they don't oppose heavenly principles. From the holdouts' point of view, the world has belonged to Shang from its very beginning. If after Shang there ought not to be a Zhou, then before Shang there ought not to have been a Xia. With no understanding of celestial time, you've come up with preposterous ideas. Rebelling in the east and raising armies in the west bring no benefit to the Shang king—that only harms the people! Worse yet, you've done things both foul and petty, but nothing from a sincere desire to carry out the Way on behalf of Heaven. In the end, what good does it do? Focusing only on your misbehavior, however, will also erase the age-old loyalty between sovereign and subject, which isn't right. Should you be unwilling to relinquish your lingering resentment, I'll cultivate your strengths. When the world is at peace again, you shall be its founding ministers."[16]

The holdouts responded, "Even though our mission hasn't been successful, we did get to air some of the grievances of the Shang royal family. It's still despicable that Shuqi betrayed his benefactor and chooses to serve the enemy. How can such a disloyal and unfilial person be tolerated?"

The Master of Making Things Equal said, "When the Way is in the ascendant, it ascends—when the Way is muddled, it is muddled. Throughout the ages, aren't the new ministers of dynasties always descendants of the preceding one? The time has come for him to descend from the mountains and, with the wild beasts, to create and destroy with wind and rain, lightning and thunder. This is responding to Heaven and according with humanity, nor does it ever lose track of 'leaving the dark to seek clarity.'"[17]

The holdouts replied, "But the world is wallowing in dust and ashes. Can Heaven really desire such destruction?"

"Creation and destruction are of the same principle," the Master of Making Things Equal said. "In creation lies the mechanism for destruction—destruction completes the mechanism for creation. You're living in the midst of it and have not understood!" Upon hearing this explanation, the holdouts all nodded their heads.

Suddenly, the tigers and leopards scattered, and a great *boom* erupted from the camp of the holdouts, as if the sky had burst and the earth had cracked. The black clouds and fog turned yellow and drifted away in all directions. Thousands of green lotuses, which seemed to appear from midair, littered the ground.

As Shuqi stood up, he realized that it had all been a "Southern Bough" dream.[18] He thought about the argument of the side taken by the Master of Making Things Equal and was confident in his decision to come down the mountain. "When I acquire position and fame, I'll return to West Mountain and bury my brother's dried-up bones, which will be just fine."

The audience said, "No wonder there's a reference to Boyi and Shuqi at the beginning of the Four Books, but when you reach the section on the 'remnant people,' only Boyi is mentioned.[19] There's something behind this story—it's not something you made up out of thin air. Dear sir, you have our admiration!"

GENERAL COMMENTS

Sarcastic humor heavily laden with fury! Its portraits of phony moralists and their dog-like behavior are written with layer after layer of indirect detail. There are exhaustive descriptions and others that leave room for the imagination. Both show the marvelous perception of a detached viewer expressing himself spontaneously.

Only a rotten Confucian, though, would compare the debunking of Shuqi with the rudeness shown to Xi Shi.[20] We must look with favor on the reality in his fantasies and the fantasies in reality. Clearly the story encourages loyalty and righteousness and also provides insights into current customs. But if we're concerned about how tigers and leopards can speak and a celestial deity can appear, wouldn't this all just be a dream told to a fool?[21]

Translated by Mei Chun and Lane J. Harris

With a Transparent Stone, Master Wei Opens Blind Eyes

Among the followers of the great sage Confucius was a man named Fan Chi, who once asked the Master to instruct him on gardening. Why did he want to study menial work like gardening, which is best suited to villagers or country folk? He was gently teasing the Master in order to make a point. Fan Chi had seen him wander the world at his wits' end because he couldn't find a reception for his teachings. Fan Chi thought it wiser to find a hilly acre and there to cultivate vegetables such as melons or eggplants, for then he at least would have a harvest to show for all his labor.

When it comes to harvests, the most bountiful and profitable crop of all, apart from melons and green vegetables, comes from the goat's-eye runner bean. All other vegetables grow precisely where they're planted and would account for nothing if they should be trampled underfoot. You plant these in the ground, and they sprout. When they reach three or four inches, you must construct an arbor to let them send their tendrils up as they please—only then will they yield a fine harvest. Should you just haphazardly scatter them along the ground, they'll struggle on for a time, but once they reach a few feet in length, they'll wither and die.

Similarly (provided you're not one of those people who has entered this world as inferior goods), if you're nurtured from childhood, you'll naturally surpass the common lot and accomplish noteworthy achievements. But what of those who find themselves in unfavorable circumstances? Though they're born with all the gifts of nature, they'll be neither clothed nor well fed, their parents won't make them feel comforted or secure, and they won't enjoy good health. How can they be successful thus? This situation is no different from that of the beans and their arbor.

Yesterday the host of the bean arbor gatherings collected some bean pods

117

and went to the market to exchange them for dainty morsels that he could give to the storytellers beneath the arbor. How was he to know that all those people were rustics? When they heard the invitation to eat, they worried that they might be expected to host dinners in return, and so most of them fled. Ten or so people of taste and refinement remained seated, but none had any real experience in storytelling.

There was, however, one young fellow who at least looked to be semiliterate. The host invited him over to have a seat, and he did, whereupon everybody approached the host, saying, "Don't let those yokels sweep away the fine mood you're in today." Pointing to the youth, they said, "Since we have nobody else, we're counting on our esteemed younger brother here to embellish a story for us!"

"Looking as I do," said the youth, "people say I'm from an official family and must know a thing or two. In truth, I've been spoiled since I was a lad, and even though I may seem bright, I can't read a word. Every day I squeeze in with the crowds to listen to the storytellers and have picked up a few lines here and there, but I'm only good enough to stumble my way through as a nonprofessional. I wouldn't dare get up there to tell you a proper story."

"As long your story is lively and good to listen to, it doesn't matter what dynasty it comes from or whether it's true or false," said the group.

The youth replied, "Yesterday my better half told me to help pick a lucky day for something, but I grabbed the calendar upside down and was made a laughingstock. If I should tell some half-baked tale and everybody on the sidelines smirks and turns up his nose at me or winks and makes faces or can't stop laughing when I miss a few words here and there, then in times to come I'll be too embarrassed even to sit in this cool spot. Still, I think there's no one here who's that flippant, so if you want me to speak after all, then I think that in truth I have no choice but to go ahead and make myself a fool. But, as I say, this is what I've heard straight from the mouths of others—if there is any fault, you should chide them for a dull tale."

"So long as your story has twists and turns and keeps things interesting, it will be fine," said everyone.

"Last year," said the youth, "I was amusing myself at the Northern Pagoda in Suzhou when I heard a monk banging a pair of cymbals together. This is what he said."

Since Heaven and Earth first separated, generation after generation of emperors have in fact been respected arhats who descended to the world of mortals to take charge of affairs. The times of Yao and Shun saw willing abdications, and the times of Tang and Wu saw the overthrow of tyrants. Later, when the Warring States were at odds, Qin and Han gobbled them all up. There were those who attained their kingdoms through benevolence and righteousness, those who attained their kingdoms through ambitious scheming, and countless variations thereon, but in every case there was an arhat secretly guiding affairs. This was demanding employment, but each arhat took his turn without exception.

When the dynastic transition first became uncertain, Heaven had to select an arhat to descend to the mortal realm. In this case there were two candidates—one known as the Venerable Lightning (Dianguang) and one known as the Venerable Free-and-Easy (Zizai). Neither knew the filth of this mortal life, and so both were eager to go. They went to see the Ancient Buddha Dīpaṃkara and asked him to decide who would receive the task.[1]

The Ancient Buddha said, "Descending to the mortal realm is inevitable—it's only a question of whether you do it sooner or later. Still, I have no better way of choosing between you. Each of you will take one of the two iron trees before me and plant it on the east or west face of this mountain. Whoever has the first tree to flower will go." They received their orders, and each went on his way.

Lightning was impetuous and planted his tree in a shady spot he had seen on the western slope that seemed well suited for growing plants. The demonic *rakshasas* in his retinue said to him, "Iron trees must be forged in flames. Only then will they flower." In a moment they moved it over the fires of a bottomless blaze, and a favorable wind whipped around it. Flowers immediately burst forth on the tree, but they were unreal things, and in a flash they vanished before his eyes.

Free-and-Easy was calm at heart. Seeing that the eastern side of the mountain was fecund and full of life, he planted his tree there and waited for it to grow and bloom of its own accord. After a long time it finally bore a few buds that produced several flowers for him.

The Ancient Buddha saw this and said, "Lightning, you're lacking in understanding and pursue only what comes quickly to hand, not what lasts. Still, your tree did flower first, so you shall be the first to go. Free-and-Easy, you were somewhat slower. In time you will follow."

The Venerable Lightning descended to the mortal world, where he was born on our West Aparagodānīya Continent and given the name Jiao Xin (Burned Firewood).[2] With his fiery disposition he took to his corner of the world with thunder and lightning, creating a vast conflagration that stretched from east to west. For the common folk this was like being boiled alive in a crucible, and before long they were all suffering greatly. The cataclysm was fated to be so, and I'll say no more on the matter.

Instead, let me now tell about the Venerable Free-and-Easy, who was calm and composed. After a little while he descended from his place high in the clouds to be born on the East Pūrvavideha Continent, where he had the name Wei Lan (Blue).[3] By disposition he was completely free of delusion from birth onward.

One day he was in the mountains performing breathing exercises and cultivating himself spiritually. Little did he know that Jiao Xin's government at that time was ruthless and cruel. This was unbearable to the people in every quarter, who grew so angry that their complaints piled all the way to Heaven. The God on High was incensed at them and so summoned all the divine generals—the Baron of Wind, the General of Rain, the Duke of Thunder, the Goddess of Lightning, the Fire Wheels, and all the other fire spirits. A great trumpet blast sounded from within the void, and immediately mountains collapsed and the earth split open, wrenching trees from the ground and sending sand flying. Even the "Pillar of Heaven," Mount Kunlun, was split in two. The intense shaking blew half of all the people and beasts into the air, where they were reduced to dust and disappeared without a trace.

Back in the mountains, Wei Lan was scared senseless to see the world plunged into chaos seemingly for no reason, and he fled from the mountains to try to save himself. Suddenly he saw five explosions burst in the sky as if a tall mountain were collapsing, and it looked as though half a mountain had come toppling down. He was utterly terrified but had nowhere to seek refuge. He forced himself to look at the ground beneath his feet and followed the path downhill. There, on the ground, he saw a round stone big enough to hold a gallon suffused throughout with a lovely green light.

Wei Lan was born with heavenly wisdom and knew this was called an "Empty Green Stone."[4] In earlier times when the goddess Nüwa had smelted stones to mend Heaven, who knew how many ovens had been required for the forging?[5] Surely Heaven shedding this stone must have been an event fated since antiquity. Wei Lan knew that by administering a drop of the pure liquid contained within the transparent stone with an acupuncture needle he could cure the blindness of the world. He hugged the stone tightly to his breast, vowing to cure the world of its blindness and return it to the light so that the stone could fulfill its destiny.[6]

He wandered aimlessly, finding his way in time to the old central province, Henan. On the way he rubbed an opening little by little into the Empty Green Stone. With just one drop of the liquid inside, he hoped, all could be made clear, and he would be able to offer humanity salvation from the dark hell in which it was imprisoned. Within two days great numbers of the blind had come from every corner of the Earth to get a drop of that mysterious liquid when, without warning, a deity clad in golden armor emerged from a place high in the clouds.

He addressed Master Wei in a booming voice, saying, "You have violated the Will of Heaven!" Wei Lan dropped to his knees and asked what he had done.

The armored man said, "The present age is in the calamitous phase of a five-hundred-year cycle of divine retribution—not even the immortals of the Upper Eight Caves can escape. The blind of this world did great wrong in their previous lives and deserve their fate. By curing all of them of their blindness, you prevent the stipulations of divine punishment from being applied. Hide the stone away for now. In time you'll get the chance to use it. Don't apply it recklessly!" Having said this, the armored man's cloud faded away by degrees until it was gone.

The Immortal Wei Lan understood the will of Heaven and carefully put the stone away. He visited Mount Hua in Shaanxi, one of the world's most picturesque spots. There the aged Patriarch Chen Tuan had been sleeping for a thousand years when he suddenly awoke, knowing all things past and future and with the ability to instruct the foolish concerning luck good and ill and give advance warning of fortune and disaster.[7] He answered all those who bowed before him. Knowing this, Wei Lan decided to go to Mount Hua, where he could find a quiet cell for his rituals and learn Daoist practice. Of this, our tale tells no more.

Let me tell instead about how in Henan, where the locals had a habit of referring to the blind as *xian'er*, there was one such man with the name Chi Xian, meaning 'Slow-but-Ahead." Someone asked why he had this name, and the blind man replied, "The *xian* in my name doesn't mean the same thing that it does in *xian'er*. Mind you, people these days are highly skilled, with quick eyes and deft hands and feet. When they run into one of life's little problems, they surge ahead without any extra effort, like ships with a tailwind. Unlike those who can't carry on in the face of myriad untold hardships, they move with great haste, striding ahead of those who are suffering, taking advantage of every passing opportunity. Little do they know that Heaven has a heart and doesn't play favorites. It's the fleet of foot who tend to get tripped up on level ground and fall on their faces, only to find that once down and out, they can't struggle up again. I think it's better to take the measure of things slowly and go forward in a smooth and steady way. People see me slogging along and pay me no heed. Nobody knows that I'm ahead of them all, which is why I'm known as Slow-but-Ahead."

His interlocutor said, "How bitter it must be for you to sit at home, smiling like a fool with your eyes shut. On a fine sunny day like today, why not go to the market, get together a few coppers, and buy some wine to drink?"

Chi Xian said, "In truth, I *do* feel bored. Yesterday I was sleeping alone on my cold bed of straw when I heard the swallows and orioles chirping their sweet songs on the branches of the peach and willow trees outside my eaves. I heard flower sellers to the east and wine vendors to the west. Boys and girls were laughing and having fun. People were getting together and forming groups, visiting graves and going on spring outings, everyone noisy and lively. I hate myself for whatever sin I committed in a previous life that led me to lose my eyes in this one. I can't move forward and I can't go back—it's like being stuck in a pitch-black shadow with no notion of how to kick my way out of it. Yesterday somebody said there was a roaming Daoist in the market who carries with him an Empty Green Stone that has cured the blindness of many, but fate is against me. I've been rushing about looking for him but don't know where he went. I've asked around and searched in every direction today, but why should anyone who can see take my arm and guide me on my way? That's why I came up with this idea—I'll stand at this crossroads and wait for a fellow blind man to pass by. Then I'll run into him on purpose, and while he's still dazed, I'll talk him into taking me along as his companion."

Even before Chi Xian had finished speaking, he heard the sound of a tapping cane heralding the approach of another blind man coming from an alley to the west. Chi Xian bent his head to one side and carefully cocked his ear to listen before suddenly thrusting his left arm forward, striking the other man a powerful blow squarely in the face. The man was knocked, half unconscious, onto his back and latched onto Chi Xian's left leg with a death grip. Little by little, the man regained consciousness and bit Chi Xian twice on the leg, cursing, "Who do you think you are, running into things just like I do?" He emitted a rapid stream of curses, like pearls on a string.

Chi Xian promptly said, "The fault is mine—I'm sorry!"

The fellow felt Chi Xian with his other hand and realized this was a fellow traveler. Angrily, he said, "You, too, share my hell of darkness! What's so important that you're careening about so rudely?"

Chi Xian said, "I'm afraid to tell you, for fear that you might become rude and rush off as well. Don't you know that in the market there's an immortal with an Empty Green Stone that has cured many of the blind? That's why I'm so agitated."

"Amazing!" the blind fellow said. "Yesterday I heard of a Chen Tuan on Mount Hua who woke from a thousand-year sleep and can tell men's fortunes and misfortunes past, present, and future. There's a steady stream of people going to him with questions. That's why I set out, looking for a buddy to go with me. Seeing as you and I share the same affliction, why don't we form a partnership? How about we swear an oath right here, that with hearts and minds as one we will help each other find this immortal who can open our eyes and climb the mountain to pay homage to Chen Tuan?[8] That way we'll be killing two birds with one stone!"

Chi Xian said, "Excellent!"

The blind fellow asked, "What might your name be, Elder Brother?"

Chi Xian explained about his name, and the other fellow praised it, saying, "Putting *chi* and *xian* together like that is very clever indeed."

Chi Xian asked, "May I also ask what your name is, Elder Brother?"

The blind fellow said, "Your humble brother's name is Kong Ming."

Chi Xian asked, "How did you happen to steal the name of a military counselor of First Ruler Liu of the Eastern Han?"[9]

Kong Ming said, "I'm not that Three Kingdoms Kongming. I found my name elsewhere. Nowadays people who can make out a couple lines in books or read a few words think they're scholars! When it comes to how they act, some people are nasty and degraded, and some violate the primary relations among family—they pay lip service to the imperial institution and the laws of the land, but deep down they don't fear the spirits of Heaven and Earth. When all's said and done, they're the same as dumb beasts. Meanwhile, those of us who can't read a word but simply follow our human hearts and the Principles of Heaven can understand and explain better what's right and what's wrong, no matter whether in regard to the sayings of sages or to historical events. We say and know these things with more understanding than

Confucius, and so I call myself 'Kong Ming' (Brighter-Than-Confucius)."

Chi Xian said, "It's fortunate that we're so like-minded. But when companions travel together, the days on the road are long. We truly must try to think ahead and be prepared. For example, when we're dealing with shopkeepers, we'll want to keep an eye on our money. Now that we're setting out on this matter, we'll need to get by with nothing but our talents and bare hands, but we don't know what skills we have between us. Why don't we find some empty place where we can show each other what we can do? Then later on, we won't have any disputes about who will do what and won't look like fools and be ridiculed."

Kong Ming said, "Right you are. Let's find someplace more secluded."

The two pressed through the crowd for half a day until they came across a cold and lonely temple. They entered, set down their walking sticks, and called out to the spirits there to make their presence known, sitting down one after the other.

Chi Xian said, "I have lots of talents. I have a poem to the tune of 'The Moon over the West River' that I'll let you hear—'I carry water and tote mud to make tile, / Fan the furnace, grind the powder, haul salt. / I read horoscopes like an immortal; / Everyone commends my silver tongue.'"

Kong Ming said, "My talents are a little better than that. I also have a poem to that tune—'Blow the pipe, pluck the string, beat the drum; / Telling stories, singing songs, I can do it all. / Pray to spirits to ensure good fortune and avert calamity; / The patterns for cards, the classics of chess, I've mastered them all.'"

Chi Xian said, "We've teamed up to travel together. Come high or low, good or ill, you can rely on me. Have no fear that there won't be anyplace to find something to eat on the road ahead. Each of us is going to have to let go of his selfish desires in order to get along with each other. We need to share in each other's fortune, the bitter and the sweet, start to finish, without any second thoughts. Let's each put something up right now. We can burn some spirit money in this holy spot and swear a pact of brotherhood. That way we'll truly be able to believe in each other."

Kong Ming said, "Wonderful!"

They asked each other their days, months, and years of birth and found that Kong Ming was older than Chi Xian by one *sui*, so he was recognized as the elder brother. He went first and withdrew ten cash from his undershirt, six of which paid for a piece of bean curd and four of which bought them a candle. Chi Xian also produced ten coppers and bought them a bottle of rice wine and a coil of incense. These they set out formally, and each prayed, swearing an oath and bowing four times.

Kong Ming then quietly stuck out his hand, feeling for the wine bottle to take a furtive swig, just as Chi Xian reached for the bean curd. Each felt the hand of the other, and a duet of anxious voices immediately rose up from them. One said, "You stole a bite," and the other said, "You drank first." How absurd that these sworn brothers should turn on each other in a moment, yelling and about ready to start pummeling each other.

They attracted the attention of two local troublemakers, one called "You-lihua" (Oily) and the other one called "Hualiyou" (Slippery), who stood on the side watching for a long time before saying, "I don't know where those two blind fools came from, but they met on the street and became sworn brothers. But then the first time one sounds a false note in the conversation, they start a ruckus—what a hoot! We can use this argument to our advantage. One of us can play at being an official and the other a yamen runner, and call them forward to explain themselves. Won't that be fun?"

Oily pretended to be a yamen runner and called out, "Stop yelling!"

Slippery said, "Who's making this commotion? Quick—bring them here!"

Chi Xian and Kong Ming thought the two were for real and fell to their knees, explaining the whole matter.

The "magistrate" said, "This little matter has disturbed even this high official. My first thought is to treat you to twenty strokes, charge you with a crime, and fine you several ounces of silver. But I'll spare you, since you're such pitiful wretches. All you have to do is put on a show for me."

Chi Xian asked for the eight characters that made up the astrological signs of the "official" and the "runner" and spent a long time calculating their horoscopes. For his part, Kong Ming also spent half a day chanting the text of the popular story he had compiled, 'Li the Dashing Takes the Capital.'[10] They chanted until their tongues were dry and their lips chapped and kowtowed many times before they were set free.

Chi Xian asked, "How is it that this place has such a fine magistrate? If we had gone through a different yamen, who knows when this case would have ended? They didn't torture or interrogate us but just took care of us without delay. That's not something you see often. If this were a big county in a big prefecture, such an honest and upright official would surely have inspired a shrine in his honor."

Kong Ming said, "You and I should be good to each other as before.

Brothers have run-ins with the law all the time. If it hadn't been for this dispute, we wouldn't have seen each other's true colors. From now on, if we can cleanse our hearts of ill intentions, then all will be well."

After that, the two regarded each other with respect and love. During each stage of their journey they relied on their skills to provide them with food.

Before they knew it, they had journeyed all the way to the foot of Mount Hua but had not yet found the Daoist who was dispensing the Empty Green Stone cure for blindness. They entered the main gate of the mountain and, bowing with each step, made their way toward the peak. On the summit was a place where Daoist immortals hid themselves away to practice asceticism. There were flowers and fruit trees, apes, cranes, birds, and fishes, all quite unlike anything in the human realm. Immortal servant boys carefully tended the medicine stoves and elixir furnaces. Although those seeking immortals to ask for blessings were many, all were calm and expectant. These seekers waited patiently until Chen Tuan gave a sermon and only then would go ask him questions. Chi and Kong, who had reverently traveled so far, had hoped to return with an answer immediately—how could they wait?—and so broke into loud weeping.

The Old Patriarch Chen Tuan saw that the two were sincere, and so he instructed an immortal servant boy to dress up as a fellow collecting firewood and give them a little trouble, saying, "If you wish to visit an immortal here, you must first go to the foot of the mountain and cleanse yourself of all your former thoughts and feelings. Only then may you ask your questions.[11] How could you have been so rash and thoughtless as to just come here and start sobbing?"

Knowing that they had not been sincere, Chi Xian and Kong Ming pleaded with the "wood gatherer" to lead the way down the mountain to a pool, where they scooped up handfuls of water and washed out their mouths.

The "wood gatherer" said, "Here's how to cleanse your thoughts and feelings. I have several small white stones for you to swallow. Wait for them to grind around, and that will clean you out from the inside."

They swallowed the stones as instructed. Before long they spat them up again along with great quantities of filthy flesh and blood and immediately felt they had been purified. The "wood gatherer" also fed them each a jujube, after which they felt no hunger.

Just then an immortal youth standing at the crest of the mountain summit called out to them, "Quickly, you two mortals, come up to the mountaintop to receive your instructions!" They prostrated themselves as before and ascended according to the youth's instructions.

Kowtowing before Chen Tuan's platform, they spoke loudly, saying, "We have been grievously sinful and incurred the anger of Heaven, which deprived us of our sight, condemning us to live our lives in bewilderment. We've heard that you, Patriarch who has slept a full thousand years, can see times past as well as those yet to come. We, your disciples, sincerely ask, what evils did we do in our past lives that we should have set the Five Agents against us and now are encompassed in darkness without one crack of light and have to bear the bitterness of stumbling about and falling down?"

Chen Tuan said, "You two have come far to make your inquiry. A bright ray of honesty shines forth from your natural disposition and consciousness.[12] How were you to know that you've committed extraordinary sins worse than all others? Everyone's suffering is different, but no matter what it is, whether being deaf, lame, crippled, or afflicted with a tumor, such suffering won't last more than two generations. Take those who are harsh by nature, who take trivial advantage of others, who say 'yes' when they mean 'no,' or who obstruct the good deeds of others—they haven't yet violated the major principles and therefore would be able to resolve such trivial debts in this lifetime or, at most, in the one to come. But if you close your eyes and sink into the vilest degradation in broad daylight, then the karmic retribution will be all the heavier.

"Now, this world is vaster than your pair of feet can ever cover, its treasures more than your two hands can ever hold, its flavors more exquisite than your stinking bellies can ever enjoy. It's only because the people of this world are so cutthroat that, from the very moment they emerge from their mothers' wombs, they want to read all the poems and books in the world if they're smart and seek to overwhelm the good men of the world if they're strong. When riches come into their hands, they want to be high officials, and when high positions come into their hands, they want to be emperors. Say one word against them, and they'll suddenly shoot you in the dark. If you have a little power, they're willing to sell out their own wives and children to flatter you. Hence, prestige always stands on a foundation of riches, frightful words are just so much hot air, and behind every noble enterprise is a pack of schemers.

"These you see before you who have any discernment have come here to leave their bodies behind and leap beyond the circle of life and death. Meanwhile, the lesser sorts are shit that is riddled with maggots. You were so blind in your past life. How could you see clearly in this one? If you acknowledge in this life that you have sinned deeply and quickly set out to perfect yourselves, your sight will be restored in your next life. But if you remain misguided and refuse to repent, then not only will Heaven take your sight but you'll be condemned to endless suffering in Hell."

The Old Patriarch's words cut the two to the quick. They both looked toward the sky, wailing loudly, thinking that they would never see the world of light in this lifetime. They decided to discard their bodies by finding a steep cliff and leaping off.

Chen Tuan said, "Talk of 'discarding the body' is just a call for fools to stop clinging to desires. It isn't literally jumping off a cliff. It's not that hard if you two want to have your eyes opened and see the world of light. I have a Daoist friend, an immortal by the name of Wei Lan, who lives in a thatched hut on the mountain to the west. You can seek him out, and that should be that." As for how Chi Xian and Kong Ming courteously thanked him and left, no more need be said.

To resume our story, from the time he had arrived at Mount Hua, Wei Lan the Immortal spent each day in discussion with Chen Tuan. He saw that the world was in total disarray from east to west, with no place that was undisturbed. He observed the stars in the heavens and realized that the time had come for him to emerge from the mountains. Throughout his journey, all those dutiful sons, obedient grandsons, righteous husbands, and faithful wives were already listed in the Book of Transmigration, waiting for their fated return to earth, one after another, in accordance with these records. He sealed up his Empty Green Stone and kept it hidden beneath his pillow all day.

Suddenly he saw Chi and Kong, with the immortal boy leading them, coming from the east mountain, bowing with every step. They arrived before him, and, just as before, Chi and Kong broke into loud sobs.

Wei Lan looked at them, and felt a burst of compassion in his heart. He said, "Since you've been sent to see me by the Old Patriarch, I can have no objections. It's only the Empty Green Stone beneath my pillow that can heal you." He then went to the place where he slept and retrieved the stone, opened the seal, and placed a drop on the pupils of the two men.

Their four eyes cleared, and they immediately kowtowed and then bowed to Wei Lan. Wei Lan said, "To return from the darkness into the light is within the purview of Heaven. It's there you should direct your thanks. But this is a place for immortals, and your mortal kind would do well to hurry back down the mountain without delay."

Chi and Kong merely stood on that summit, gazing down from the void. They took in this human world of red dust and found it utterly drab and ordinary, with myriad paths and thousands of streams unfolding before their eyes. Again they wept, saying, "Until now our eyes have been closed, and we foolishly thought there were countless uses for them in the world. Now we've seen with open eyes and have awoken to the fact that all is flowers of ignorance and flames of illusion. There's nothing to hold on to. Now we can see we're suffering through seas of degradation and mountains of injustice, seeking calamity in the midst of calamity, where the prick of each new disaster troubles our eyes. It was better when our eyes were closed but we were living free and easy. Your disciples were happy to ascend this mountain with our eyes shut, but we don't dare go down again with them open."

The Immortal Wei Lan was unmoved by their entreaties and said to them, "There's a gulf between this place and the mortal world. Celestial officials frequently come here for audiences, and it wouldn't be right for you to remain. One day long ago I borrowed a cloth bag at the place of the Great Teacher Maitreya, a bag that was completely empty, but it could hold a great chiliocosmos.[13] The fortunes of those trained in loyalty, filial piety, chastity, and righteousness are fated to rise, and they can be counted on to build a better world. You commonplace strivers with no future have been singled out by Heaven for punishment. How could you live with the Upright and the True Gentlemen?[14] I have no choice but to make manifest another divine way for you."

He told the immortal boy to borrow a wine jug from Du Kang and instructed the two men to enter and find shelter inside.[15] At first the mouth of the jug looked very small to Chi Xian and Kong Ming, but upon lifting it to look inside, they saw that it was spacious, and so the two of them crawled into the jug together. They lifted their heads and looked all around and saw a level, open expanse with no outlines of city walls or tall buildings to be seen.

Taking advantage of the warm and sunny weather, they walked toward a market. They found the customs gracious, and interactions between people were courteous, harmonious, and happy, totally without expressions of pleasure, anger, love, or hate. The people were free and unfettered, following their hearts and wearing no hats to cover their heads. Some chanted poems or sang songs, some played guessing games, others partook in contests of strength, and still others shouted at one another, but never out of prejudice or hard feelings. They didn't need silk or cloth for their clothing or the five cereals for their food. They'd yammer on stupidly, not caring about the height of Heaven or the depth of the Earth. As for the seasons, they knew neither winter, nor summer, nor even night nor day. When they wanted to travel, they traveled but didn't need boat, cart, ass, or horse. If they wanted to sleep, they slept but required no bed pad, pillow, or quilt. They thought nothing of living with birds and beasts, fishes, and turtles and never suffered from maladies or fell ill. They plowed the land without any plan in mind, and taxes and levies were not forced upon them. Truly, "in the world of the jug, days and months were like this. This world stood apart from the world of men."

Chi and Kong were then told to sit on top of Mount Kunlun, where they opened their eyes wide and watched the Lightning Arhat let fly bursts of thunder, wind, hail, and rain, cleansing all the world of the fires of sin and the ashes of cataclysm. Afterward they emerged with the Free-and-Easy Arhat and wandered free and unfettered through the world, enjoying lives of ease, comfort, peace, and tranquility.

"This story was really just mysterious and lacking in substance,"[16] said the youth, "and quite unworthy of your honorable ears at that. Still, since it seems to have held my host's interest and received the patronage of all present, I submit these humble remarks in the hope they might inspire others to bring jade out of a brick and give us a better tale."

The group said, "As we listened to your lofty tale, it swept over us like a cooling breeze. What do you say to each of us riding it home to a happy evening of ease and comfort tonight in the world inside Du Kang's jar?"

GENERAL COMMENTS

This chapter pricks the heart and startles the eyes. In turn, Chi Xian, Kong Ming, and the Patriarch Chen Tuan, wittily "using Chan master blows and shouts," enlightened folk about their evil ways. Even all the Three Great Teachings with their clear language could do no better![17]

How ingenious to conclude matters with wine! When all things under Heaven get to the point that nothing can be done about them, only intoxication can melt them away. Thus Liu Ling carried his shovel along with his wine bottle, and Ruan Ji remained drunk for sixty days. Both were men of broad vision and high quality, and they did not merely sink into the constant drinking of wine.[18] I've heard that old man Aina also relied on wine and yet had astonishing skill in helping others recover from blindness. Surely there must be an allegory in that.

Translated by Alexander Wille

Liu the Brave Tests a Horse on the Yuyang Road

One evening of "metal" wind and the entire land is encircled in autumn.[1] When autumn arrives with the rustling of many branches, the thriving life within each species of plant fades. In the same way, all people under heaven must give way when their time for earning fame or making profit has passed.

There is only one species, a runner bean, whose flowers bloom all the more gloriously when fall arrives and the wind blows from the west, whose pods grow full and thick with beans like the rounded heads of nails.[2] How unlike the pods produced in the fourth and fifth months of midsummer that are shriveled, flat, and fleshless. According to the proverb, "When the northwest wind blows, the goat's-eye beans take husbands." Which is merely to say that when autumn comes, the pods grow abundant, gradually ripening into a crop of beans and leaving seeds for the following year.

When the autumn winds begin to blow, the pods produce their many beans, but the clothing people have to wear seems to grow thinner as the cold-soughing wind forces its way up their backs. Those from families of means have more clothing at hand and need only to reach into their boxes and baskets to dress warmly. But how could the idlers and itinerants—those who spend every copper as soon as they get it, who lack even enough rice in their jars for the next day—have enough clothing to ward off the cold?

Shameful ideas and harmful impulses arise in people who have no other means. Those who think small can manage, through their own ingenuity, to pilfer and, depending on their luck, glean either a little or a lot from their thieving. Some sweeten a few mouths in advance, hoping through bribery to avoid exposure and defeat. Those who think bigger band together with their wolf and dog companions and swear blood oaths and hunt up swords, spears, bows, and arrows before gathering in one place. They inquire in advance as to which households are rich, which are well off, which are defended, and which are not. Taking advantage of rainy, moonless nights or times when the owners are busy and exhausted, they carry flaming branches and scale the walls on rope ladders, chopping open doors or digging holes through the walls, shouting to make themselves sound brave. With daggers in their hands they capture the wealthy and threaten them with death unless they reveal their treasures. If a response is not forthcoming, they bind their victims, draw their bows taut, heat irons for torture, and by whatever means bundle gold, pearls, bolts of satin, utensils, and clothing into their bags before fleeing. If news of the robbery spreads, making their situation dangerous, they start a fire and take to the road. Then they choose a secluded place for portioning out the spoils before scattering like the stars.

Luck determines the outcome of these raids. Some men steal money and treasures, some steal tattered clothing, and there are those who, after all their efforts, seize nothing before being slain or captured. Without a single coin touching their hands or one bowl of noodles reaching their stomachs, they're interrogated and, following what the law states, "the offenders shall, without distinction between principals and accessories, be punished by decapitation."[3]

In this way a man from a decent, blameless, and ordinary family can bring his life to a contemptible ruin if in his youth he did not respect the instructions of his parents and uncles or the advice of his brothers and friends. Instead, such men pass their days cavorting with fancy women or idly gambling and are brought to this state by the good food, fine clothing, ready cash, and haughty behavior to which they have become accustomed.

It goes without saying that their grandfathers and fathers had not prevented them from following this path! We should all take care in choosing our sons' friends from childhood. When they meet indolent young fellows, we can't allow them to become close friends. Needless to say, children might go along with them. Children shouldn't be spoiled when their minds are immature and can be influenced by bad examples. This is what is meant by "nipping it in the bud."

Your humble servant lived in the capital for several years during a time when an imperial decree was in force to crack down on robbers and thieves. I observed the Imperial Bodyguards, the Secret Service, and the capital's army battalion that was responsible for arresting bandits both inside and outside the palace.[4] The men who belonged to the Imperial Bodyguards and the Secret Service were known as the company leaders and chiefs, and all came from the battalion commanders. The men who belonged to the imperial capital's five security force stations were called "rotating hands."[5] When deadline inspections took place on the third, sixth, and ninth days, the process was perfunctory unless the local authorities were being stringent.[6] If there had been any incidents, the higher authorities held strictly to the deadlines. Then bandits were rounded up one after another within a few days. Rounding up bandits seemed as effortless as catching turtles in a tub. Who knows what kind of magic they used?

By chance I met one of these rotating hands and happened to ask him how the arrests were managed. The deputy was forthright enough in his explanation. "Most of these men aren't real bandits. All of the ones brought in over the past few days came from groups of men we planted ahead of time. When the higher-ups get anxious for arrests, we lower-downs have some that are ready."

Hearing this filled me with panic. I said, "How can bandits be planted like melons or cabbages to be ready when needed?"

The deputy said, "Our organization in Beijing has no fewer than ten thousand men. The company leaders and chiefs usually pass out some money for expenses and send a group of two or three, or maybe five or six, runners four or five hundred *li* outside the capital, either to villages and markets or to larger gathering places, where they stay in one of the temples. When they come upon gambling dens or whorehouses, they work themselves in among the customers, helping arrange for prostitutes or egging them on in gambling, spending liberally, playing the part of lowlifes, and acting as if money means nothing to them. They treat the men there like brothers and the whores like sisters. Naturally they get to be on good terms with unworthy young men there, joining them for feasting every day and drunken singing at night. When they meet young men with money, they cheat them out of all they're worth—the poor ones they lavish money on and trick them into becoming Longyangs.[7]

"Once it's clear that a young man has no money left, they coax him into losing at gambling. When people come to settle accounts, one of the runners vouches for him. From the moment the runners promise to repay his debts, he might as well have sold himself to them. After a few days they stop pretending and demand that he return the money with interest, but now he has no one to back him. In the meantime they pull in a few real thieves who seduce the young man by telling him how easy it is to get rich, assuring him that money will fall right into his hands. Without his knowing what's happening, they lure him to some out-of-the-way place to pull off one or two jobs, which go smoothly. The young man's mind is at ease. He can eat enough to grow fat and pass as a highwayman.

"Supposing there's an incident in the city of Beijing. The deadline inspections will be strict, so he's taken into custody and handed the blame. Even though the recovered goods don't match what was stolen, and it goes without saying that the charges against him are unjust, these young men give up their lives without complaint. They sing even as they're bound and led to the execution site. Meanwhile, the bands of real thieves enjoy themselves at home in peace. All we have to do is collect a regular tribute from them every month and each quarter. What would the rotating hands and their bosses do for a living if all the real bandits were arrested?" These abuses had been going on in the capital for many years, but only the rotating hands knew about it, while outsiders remained in the dark.

Now I'll tell about a young man who carelessly listened to what someone told him to do and couldn't escape losing his life for nothing. His surname was Liu, with the given name Bao (Leopard), and he lived in Zunhua County of Shuntian Prefecture near Beijing. His father, who was called "Liu the Loyal Official," had succeeded in the provincial civil service examinations in 1600. His first appointment was to serve as magistrate in Shanyang County of Huai'an Prefecture. Through this office he amassed ten or twenty thousand ounces of silver for himself. As an official he was overbearing and biased by nature. His governance of the common people was harsh and pitiless, leading to the wrongful deaths of many. He was later promoted to secretary of a bureau in the Ministry of Works. When the Ministry of Personnel conducted its triennial inspection, Liu the Loyal Official was punished for his avarice and ruthlessness and reduced to passing idle days in retirement.

Between his wife and four concubines he had only one son, a boy who was badly spoiled, as is usually the case. When the son reached fifteen or sixteen *sui*, his father had a stroke and had to remain at home, unable get out of bed. The household's outlay and income were committed to the son's management. At first, still being young, he couldn't wreak too much havoc, even if he acted out at home, putting on airs like the son of a high official, beating and scolding both family members and servants, high and low alike.

Unexpectedly, when he was nineteen *sui*, his father's life was extinguished. The young man regularly bullied his mothers, the wife and the concubines, as if they were beneath him, and they dared not even take a breath. Many young low-lifes became his sworn brothers, enticing him into visiting prostitutes and luring him into gambling. In the company of ten or twenty household servants and freeloaders, Liu Bao would ride off with some thirty mules from their stable.[8] Whether they ended up in Beijing, Tongwan, or Tianjin, each place had its own class of spongers and sycophants who would become Liu Bao's friends, cajoling him into spending his money with a free hand.

There would have been a limit if he'd spent his money only at the whore-houses. Who knew that he'd go from whoring to gambling? There would still have been a limit if he'd been the only one losing money. Who knew that he'd lose and so would his companions? There might still have been a limit to how much Liu Bao paid on their behalf if his companions had really lost. Who knew that he'd really lose, while the others only pretended to lose, or that there would be no way of telling the true from the false, and no end to it? The several thousand ounces of silver Liu Bao had brought along in his leather cases and gift boxes lasted barely ten days before they were spilled out and spent. He wrote letters home asking his family to send money. At the same time, because he couldn't hold out until it reached him, he sold the mules at a heavy loss. What a pity! The family's immense fortune was squandered within two or three years. His moth-ers had no way of recovering the money, and within a few years they all died of anger. Three servants remained, but, suffering constant hunger and want, they fled elsewhere. Only Liu Bao was left to wander from place to place by himself. All of his family and friends had come to detest him.

One day he heard that the market town of Jizhou in the ancient Yuyang region was setting up a local militia headquarters for the governor-general. The fifty or sixty thousand troops and cavalry being raised would form a bustling community at the garrison, with goods in abundance. Zunhua Prefecture was only seventy or eighty *li* from Jizhou. Liu Bao thought, "Here, in the land of my ancestors, there isn't one person who will take pity on me. I'm like a visitor in a strange land. In my present state, I can search from morning to evening without even finding a place where I might get a bowl of thin gruel. It would be better for me to put up with my empty stomach and make my way to Jizhou. Maybe some-one will give me a full meal here or there based on our former friendship." His mind made up, Liu Bao set off at once, heading west out of the city gates along the main road, meandering along the way.

Liu Bao was fated to be both lucky and unlucky at the same time. He had walked no more than two *li* or so when he came upon a friend he'd met some three or five years earlier as a customer at the brothel of Madame Xue within the city walls of Tianjin. He was a large, brawny man whose stalwart appearance had drawn the notice of the governor-general, who felt that he was officer mate-rial. When the time came for recruitment, the governor-general promoted him to Red Banner Company commander. Traveling all over and enlisting men with-out a clear plan, he was riding along on his horse, not paying attention, when he ran straight into Liu Bao and only then looked at him carefully. Liu Bao realized that the man looked familiar and lowered his head to avoid being recognized.

The horse had already gone some distance when the man reined it in, turned back, and asked, "Could that be Brother Liu walking along the road?"

Liu Bao heard these words and knew he couldn't hide at this, his most desolate moment, when he was so eager for someone to take notice of him. He raised his head to answer, "I am your humble servant."

The man approached and jumped down from his horse to salute Liu Bao formally, asking, "Brother Liu, how did you come to be in this state?"

Liu Bao said, "In the past I made mistakes, and now I've come to this."

Then Liu Bao asked the man's name, and he said, "Back when you were spending so freely, like a man made out of money, you didn't even learn my name. I, your younger brother, am surnamed Li, with the given name Ying, and they call me "Dingshan" (Rock Solid). I come from Taiyuan Prefecture in Shanxi. More than five years have passed since we met at Madame Xue's brothel in Tianjin. I can see that you have no means of support. You should come live with me in Jizhou. If you can read, you can be a clerk in my camp. If you're strong, you can enlist in my division and draw a monthly grain ration. After you live in comfort for a while, I'll gradually help you make a way ahead for yourself, as long as you repent and correct the error of your ways. Besides, you're still young. Follow the regulations as closely as you'd follow the format of the examination essays and act in keeping with your lot in life. Like the light of the sun as it rises, your prospects will improve!"

Then he called an attendant to bring an extra horse up from behind for Liu Bao to ride, and they set off toward Jizhou. Liu Bao followed and so came to live in the army camp. Commander Li found him a few items of clothing to wear as well as food and drink. Before half a month had passed, Liu Bao's "surroundings transformed his bearing, just as the food he ate changed his body," and he regained the appearance of a healthy young man.[9]

Who could have known that a man like this one, destined to return to his vagabond ways, would start to cause trouble once he had eaten his fill? Liu Bao made a few friends who would drag him along to the shops for a grand, indulgent meal. At first the others pitied him and didn't expect him to return the treat, at least until the monthly rations were distributed, when Commander Li placed Liu Bao's name in an empty ration spot. Once Liu Bao had received his ration, he could hardly wait for daybreak so that he could invite his friends to a feast in return. So before the month was half over, he had used up his entire ration. Commander Li believed that since Liu Bao had been given a monthly ration, he wouldn't have to worry about other items such as clothing and food, yet Liu Bao was as impoverished and helpless as before.

One night as he lay on his cold straw mat, he sighed aloud, "And so I, Liu Bao, am stranded without a single coin to my name. I should find a rope and hang myself from the rafters like Su Qin or cut my own throat like the Hegemon King of Chu on the banks of the Wu River and just be done with it."[10]

He never expected one of the division's retainers who lived in the next room, a man named Huang Xiong, to respond, "Liu, old fellow! There's no reason to disturb my sleep with your moaning and griping. Come over to my room, and I'll show you a better way out." Believing Huang Xiong to have good intentions, Liu Bao leaped out of bed and went over to hear what he had to say.

Huang Xiong said, "I can see that you're not stunted, lame, deaf, or blind. You're registered for monthly rations from the camp, but how could that be enough for real men like us? Each month we only get as much as household servants. Our daily expenses are so much greater than the rations that we have to rely on other sources just to get by."

Liu Bao heard these words but was baffled by them. Again and again he asked what this meant, until Huang Xiong said, "You idiot, do I have to explain it to you? Do we have the fingers of Chunyang Lü?[11] As long as you have a bow hooked over your arm, a few arrows at your waist, and a horse to ride, more gold, pearls, and riches will find their way to you than you can spend. As long as you're with the army, you enjoy the protection of our commanders. No one will come to investigate. These days the officers who wear the finest uniforms and ride in carriages or on horseback—who among them didn't start out along this path?"

Liu Bao said, "I've had this same idea. But what could I do without any legs to ride?"

Huang Xiong said, "Aren't there legs everywhere you look? It's not hard, not at all. My horse needs training for the next few days, so it's not available. But there's a brother in the main camp whose horse hasn't had its turn for training yet, so it will be free. If I have a word with him, you will be able to borrow it."

After hearing all this, Liu Bao thought to himself, "I can see that these real men have as much money as they want in their pouches, and they wear new clothes. If that didn't come from doing this kind of work, where did they come from?" For the moment, though, he didn't want to admit that Huang Xiong was giving him good advice or agree to what he proposed too quickly. So he countered, "I'm indebted to you, Elder Brother, for instructing me, because I know these words are only meant to trick me. But what if someone heard these rash words and did what you suggest? From then on, he'd be under your control. If we didn't get along or I didn't do what you wanted, you might spread rumors about me. For the rest of my life I'd be paying you off, and even that wouldn't be enough. I won't do it, I won't!"

Although these fine-sounding words suggested a firm refusal, Liu Bao's ill-omened meteor shone for a moment in this clever answer. He was afraid that if he openly agreed to do this evil deed, people would find out, making it more difficult for him to succeed. He walked away as he was speaking and returned to his own room.

Closing the door with a bang, Liu sighed, "I know what your good advice amounts to—you're trying to get me into trouble." He continued to sigh instead of sleeping.

Huang Xiong spoke again, "You little fool, I've clearly shown you the way, but you won't believe me. Now I worry that when the rest of us are ready to pull off a job, you'll get greedy eyes and spread rumors about us. If that information is leaked, your life will be in danger."

Liu Bao answered, trying again to show off his cleverness. "Elder Brother! Why threaten me with violence? You don't really think I'll turn around and betray you. You only want to trick me into believing you and following this path. I have a plan of my own. Don't try to fool me."

The sky had grown light before he finished speaking, so Liu Bao rose and went into General Li's residence to await his orders.

Huang Xiong said to himself, "That young guy's planning to do the job himself, no matter what he says. He's just afraid I'll have control over him afterward, so he lies and says he won't do it. Troops and cavalry are needed at the frontier, so there are men everywhere along the road armed with swords at their waists and carrying bows and arrows. With a little bad luck he won't be able to pull it off. I was just about to set out on the road with this young guy as my accomplice, but he pretended to be all clean and innocent. Now I really will snare him and lead him onto this path after all."

Another half month passed, and the time for the monthly rations came again. Liu Bao was starry-eyed in anticipation of the lined archer's uniform that he was going to have made to give himself a little class. As he walked along the barrier of sharpened spikes in front of the headquarters, he collided unexpectedly with a drunk. This man's name was Zhu Long (Dragon), but he was nicknamed the Red-Faced Tiger. He was a bully who knew how to use his considerable muscle. It was costly for the unlucky man who ran into him, who might even have to pay for feasting and drinking until Zhu Long was willing to let him go. On this day the office Liu Bao was visiting had not opened yet, and he was unprepared when Zhu Long dealt him a sharp blow like a falcon strike on the upper arm.

Startled, he struck back, shouting, "You must be drunk. Why did you hit me so hard without any warning?"

Zhu Long glanced sidelong at him and said, "Why are you wearing my robe instead of giving it back, little fellow?"

Liu Bao said, "I've never even seen you before. What are you talking about?"

Some men nearby came over to intercede, saying to Zhu Long, "You've been drinking. You must have mistaken him for someone else."

Zhu Long insisted on what he'd said. The people in the crowd all knew his old ways. Once he'd seized hold of something, no one could talk him out of it.

Just then, who did Liu Bao see but Huang Xiong, who came over and said, "Brother Zhu, this man is my younger brother, so you can rest assured that I have a stake in this. Let him go." Liu Bao wanted to fight but couldn't after what Huang Xiong said.

Several of the men nearby peered down at him and said, "How can you not know Brother Zhu when you earn your wages in the camp? He might have offended you just now, but you shouldn't have lifted a hand against him. Even if you had not hit Brother Zhu, you've offended him." Liu Bao became even more enraged by their words, not knowing why the people in the crowd were shielding Zhu Long.

Huang Xiong said, "Brother Liu, don't lose your temper. Go apologize to him. He'll be sitting in the shop. Hurry home and pull together a little silver to bring back. If you don't have any, pawn some clothing at the loan shop."

Liu Bao listened, but it was clear even without his opening his mouth that he had no money at all and would need Huang Xiong's help. Huang Xiong said, "I see you've made no provisions. Take the month's ration instead and sign it over to someone else, and get whatever you can for it."

The people gathered around all said the same thing. Liu Bao was new to the army and unaware of its taboos, so everyone made allowances for him. There was no other way. He had to take the monthly ration and exchange it for six-tenths of an ounce of silver at a qian of interest per day.

In two days there was nothing left of his ration. Liu Bao made careful inquiries. As it turned out, Zhu Long was the brother-in-law of the official in charge and a member of the imperial family, so he could get away with anything. Instead of picking on the others, though, he deliberately sought out Liu Bao, and it was only by good fortune that Huang Xiong was there to intervene and make apologies. Huang Xiong was obviously acting with malicious intent, forcing Liu Bao to spend all his money without allowing him to save even a little for himself. Liu Bao later guessed what was happening and came up with a plan to deal with

Huang Xiong. Every evening he'd go to Huang Xiong's room to talk with him, and every morning he'd leave with him, showing eager affection.

One day Huang Xiong caught a chill from the wind and requested leave to stay home from the official in charge. His horse was set loose to graze outside the walls of the encampment. Liu Bao spied Huang Xiong's downfall in this, but he only said, "Tomorrow one of my brothers requested that I be part of the detachment for the military tactics headquarters, so I need to borrow Brother Huang's uniform and belt."

Huang Xiong was in a feverish state and agreed to this. Liu Bao took the bow and a quiver of arrows hanging on the wall. He also took the saddle and bridle and stealthily carried them outside the camp. Before dawn he was outside of town and had saddled the horse, which he rode seventy or eighty *li* to Bangjun Market in Three Rivers County, where he ducked into a dark forest.

Before long he caught sight of a scrawny old man riding a braying donkey with a covered bag sitting beneath him. Liu Bao judged the bag to be fairly heavy. He figured the old man was a wealthy villager carrying money. The horse leaped out, and Liu Bang, faking a Westerner's accent, shouted, "Dismount and pay your ol' man the highway toll!"[12]

The old man was unflustered. Raising his whip and pointing with the tip, he said, "There's plenty of this 'highway toll' here for you. But I'm more than seventy years old. There's no need to scare me or wait for me to get down slowly from this beast. You come over to take the bag. My arms are so feeble, I really can't lift it."

Liu Bao took this to be true. He brought the horse alongside the donkey and leaned over to take the bag. He never expected the old man to land a blow like a thousandweight of gold on him that knocked him over. The old man pulled Liu Bao to the ground, drew out a sharp dagger from the hollow whip handle, and pointed it at him, cursing, "Stupid child, still stinking of your mother's milk! I may be old but I've traveled back and forth on this Yuyang Road for more than fifty years, and I've taken care of I don't know how many bandits. Just because you see my wrinkled chicken-skin face you think you can meddle with me!" Even before he finished, he moved to gouge out both of Liu Bao's eyes with the knife.

Liu Bao cried out in a loud voice, "I have eyes but cannot see! I never dared do such things before. Now my eighty-year-old mother is sick and near to death, and I have no other way of saving her, so I was forced to do it. I didn't know I'd offend one as mighty as you. I beg you to pardon me!"

The old man said, "Stinking young man, you're not worth dirtying my blade! I'll only cut off two of your fingers as a warning for the future."

At this most critical moment, what did Liu Bao see but another horse leaping out of the woods? Astride the horse sat a large, gallant man with a dark face and a curly beard, who said, "Old man, your punishment for him isn't wrong, but you should take pity on him because of what he said about his mother's illness. If he loses two fingers, he'll never be able to get them back!"

From his sleeve he pulled out five ounces of silver for the old man, a gift to celebrate his longevity, then asked his name. The old man thanked him with a smile but wouldn't accept the money, nor would he give his name. All he did was cut off the army horse's branded tail with his knife. In great pain, the horse tore back along the way it had come. The old man got on his donkey and proudly rode away.

Liu Bao rose, expressing his gratitude to the large fellow. The man said, "I have an unused horse behind me. Hurry up and get on. If you delay, the local patrol will be here."

Liu Bao hurriedly mounted the horse and rode swiftly away after him. The man said, "My people have been riding along the Handan Road for more than twenty years.[13] Before any job we find out everything about our targets, starting when they set out on the road. We spy to see how many guards and companions they may have and follow to see who's bringing up the rear. We also have four or five men disguised as merchants along the way who trade off every thirty or fifty *li*. They lodge with those merchants overnight, so as not to arouse their suspicions. All we have to do is put arrow to bow in the middle of the road, and every one of them submits. If we blundered along like you, we would have been defeated every time! Now we've arrived in Baixiang County, a thousand *li* from Yuyang. We can trust that no one here will notice us."

Then he led Liu Bao to a deserted temple and, under the seated Buddha, took out four ingots of silver and ten ounces in small pieces for Liu to take back secretly to his hometown. He said, "Guard this money well. Now you'll be able to cure your mother's illness."

Liu Bao removed his inner garment and wrapped the silver inside. He was about to ask the man's name so that he could thank him properly when the man mounted his horse and, holding the reins of the riderless one, vanished like mist without even saying farewell.

Liu Bao had come into a great treasure. Trying not to attract notice, he became a laborer in the countryside and, not daring to return to Jizhou, went directly to Qian'an County in Yongping Prefecture. At first he plowed and planted for hire. Then, after a few years, he slowly accumulated his own farmland. He knew his body was still whole only through an accident of fortune and reformed his ways, becoming a common farmer. He took a wife from nearby and so lived out his life. But we'll say no more of this.

Instead I'll tell about how the army horse whose branded tail had been sliced off by the old man galloped back to the training camp. The local headman for Bangjun Market learned of this affair and prepared a report on it.[14] Soon each headquarters knew about the incident. The governor-general for the Jizhou garrison promptly reviewed the case and compiled a crime report, which was forwarded to the circuit for investigation. The old man also brought the horse's tail with its brand mark to the circuit to report what had happened. Examination soon determined it to be Huang Xiong's horse. Huang Xiong had been ill, and he claimed ignorance, saying he knew only that Liu Bao had borrowed the horse from him. When Liu Bao was nowhere to be found, Huang Xiong could not continue to declare his innocence and had to accept the guilt in Liu Bao's place. A full report was submitted to the governor-general, who sentenced Huang Xiong to be punished according to the law. He was immediately beheaded and his head displayed on a stake. This was the retribution for Huang Xiong's evil intentions, which had now turned back onto himself.

Let me tell again of Liu Bao. He took refuge in Qian'an and became a commoner content with his lot, a man who had reformed himself and begun a new life. Even Heaven ought to have pardoned him. Who could have predicted the great drought that year? The ground in the paddy fields cracked until it looked like a tortoise shell, leaving no hope for an autumn harvest. The only way out was to bring in laborers on yearlong contracts to reclaim more land. Unfortunately, these laborers were all in urgent demand, so there was no one to be found.

Suddenly ten or so men from Fengyang Prefecture arrived in the village. They were troops who had been serving rotational duty to work on the border wall and were heading back after finishing their work, so they were at leisure. Liu Bao asked if they'd take the opportunity to do a few days' work, to be paid as was customary. The soldiers immediately agreed. Within two days the land reclamation was complete, and the men went to his house to wait for their wages to be counted out.

At that time Liu Bao didn't have enough money on hand to pay them, so he stealthily unearthed the two remaining ingots of silver, which he'd buried under the stove. Taking advantage of the moonlit night, he heated some of the silver over a charcoal fire until it was red hot and then cut it apart with a chisel.[15] He was unaware that the troops had heard him hammering the silver, crept up to the eaves, and seen the shape of a large ingot. They formed a plan at once and swarmed in, swept up the silver, and disappeared in who knows what direction.

Liu Bao could do nothing but sigh. This is precisely what is meant by the expression "easy come, easy go." But let's say no more of this.

To continue the story of the soldiers, once they had taken possession of the two large ingots, they traveled gleefully through Zhen and Bao Prefectures and arrived at Bianliang, where they decided to divide the silver among themselves. Without planning things out beforehand, they boldly went to a metalsmith to have the ingots cut into pieces but were met there by a detachment of police looking for bandits. One of the officers stepped in and said, "You'll lose nearly half an ounce if you cut it into pieces. Why not come to my shop and exchange it for small pieces of silver? That would be advantageous for both parties."

So they took the ingots and followed the officers into a large house. After taking one look at the ingots, the police recognized the stamp and shouted, "Arrest these thieves, arrest them!" Some twenty or thirty men swiftly came out and shackled the soldiers.

As it turned out, the ingots had been stolen by a bandit chief three years earlier outside the town of Bianliang from an official transport from Jiangxi. The theft had been a lingering issue for the local officials and common people because the required compensation was still not completely paid off. Several bands of highwaymen were being held in jail, but they weren't the ones who had committed the crime. The police were taking more bandits into custody every few days but still had not recovered the stolen money. What doubt could there be in this case when they saw the stamp marked clearly on the ingots?

The rotational troops were sent to the central military defense headquarters. The men cried out that they were being unjustly treated, saying, "We were serving in rotation together to work on the border wall and received the silver to pay for vegetables and salt."

The official said, "Even though, as rotational troops, you receive money to buy your vegetables and salt, those wages are paid in small pieces. So where did you get these large ingots? Besides, those rations have not been distributed yet. How could the ingots have been given to you?"

The officials began to use torture, which brought out, little by little, the details of the men's confession that they had stolen the ingots from the home of Liu Bao of Qian'an. The circuit intendent then sent the case to the provincial grand coordinator, who at once transferred the documents to the supervisory court at Jizhou. Then runners escorted the accused to Henan for a confrontation by his accusers. Liu Bao testified to his earlier attempt to use a horse for banditry and told of how the big fellow had presented him with the money. He recounted his story from the beginning, and it was entered item by item into the case documents. Soldiers and guards were assigned to escort him to the capital.

As they came to Shunde Prefecture in Hebei, they suddenly crossed paths with a large man riding along the road half drunk. Liu Bao went forward and poured out his entire tale of woe to him. Hearing this, the men guarding Liu Bao realized that he was speaking to the powerful bandit who had stolen the ingots, a man who had been hunted everywhere without a trace of him being found.

One member of the escort was feeling clever and praised him profusely, "What a gallant warrior! Drifting along, he meets someone, saves his life, and even presents him with money. Today that man's fate is misfortune, and here everything is exposed. This lofty justice of yours deserves our great admiration!"

They tried asking the bandit to come to the inn so they could get the whole story from him, but he declined. Someone took advantage of the moment and hacked at his horse's leg, knocking it to the ground. As one, they pushed forward and bound him. The local people said, "You may have captured him, but you must be cautious. If news of this leaks out, you won't get thirty *li* before horsemen will be pursuing you to snatch him away, and your lives could well be lost."

One man said, "We have a way of handling this. This bandit has killed many people. It will be difficult to escort him any distance. He'll throw off the ropes if they loosen. Tie him backward on the horse and cut his belly open with a dagger. Pull out his guts and tie them to a tree with a rope, whip the horse, and as the horse gallops away, his intestines will all come out. Wouldn't that put us at ease and provide some entertainment?"

The crowd said, "Yes, let's do that!"

So it was done. Then his head was chopped off and discarded five or six *li* away so no one would ever know.

Afterward, Liu Bao was escorted to Bianliang, where he confessed item by item. He was charged with a capital offense having no statute of limitations for the armed robbery case that had been pending further investigation these five or six years. Of the men who had been wrongly imprisoned, half had already died, but the others were set free because they didn't have the stolen goods.

Thus it can be seen that no crime takes place between heaven and earth that is not subject to the principle of retribution. At the most critical moment of his life, the rash young Liu Bao suddenly met the bandit Li, who was moved to pity by Liu Bao's account of his mother's illness, gave him money, and commanded him to flee.[16] The silver lay for five or six years hidden under the stove, where, unknown to ghost and god alike, it could have remained a secret. Instead, when the rotational troops from Fengyang arrived, it was revealed in the middle of the night by the sound of Liu Bao's chisel. The great bandit Li committed evil acts along the Handan Road for twenty years, but he was moved to rescue a man and show him kindness. Then he chanced to meet the same man on the road under guard, and the bandit's life ended at the hands of Liu Bao's escort. Huang Xiong, from earlier in our tale, had evil intentions and was executed before his time for the wrong crime.

The artfulness of the Way of Heaven in levying retribution is truly as marvelous as a mustard seed falling through the eye of a needle—but it never misses.[17] Thus it can be seen that those who are in dire straits shouldn't listen to the words of wicked men. A single wrong decision and your entire life hangs on the brink. For all your cleverness and ingenuity, you cannot evade retribution. The only question is whether it will arrive early or late. Heaven regards humankind as a set of puppets to be manipulated.

The listeners responded, "We sit under the bean arbor, yet it's as though we're standing at the outside of a circle, watching the affairs of the world with detachment. This experience is no less enlightening than a Peach Blossom Spring utopia or the cave heaven of the Daoists!"

General Comments

From ancient times, the greater part of all disorders under heaven has been banditry arising from hunger and cold. The rulers responsible for shepherding the people all concern themselves with suppressing bandits. Those who keep the records reflect on what takes place beneath their windows, and who among them does not consider policies for wiping out banditry? As some have correctly said, there are those who copy their predecessors, while others regularly produce new theories. Every one of the theories may be reliable and worthy of notice, yet answering a strategy with another strategy seems to be just another exercise from the civil service examinations used for government promotion. Who is willing to implement these policies?

Eventually thieves who "draw lots" fill the city and robbers who "hide in marshes" terrify the populace, but the government's hands remain tied.[18] Without a strategy, officials sit by and watch the situation fester. No one does anything. At worst, administrators open the gates and welcome the bandits. With death raining down, they regret that the study of bandit suppression seemed to have had little relevance before.

Alas! This calamity is caused by the inattention of pedantic Confucians. Would it not be better to take this speaker's entire tale as a warning intended to awaken the foolish and enlighten the despotic? Without exception, great bandits would meet the executioner's blade,[19] while imperial institutions would continue to be as bright as the heavenly bodies. Truly, this is a venerable theory on the suppression of banditry.

Translated by Annelise Finegan Wasmoen

Freeloader Jia Forms
a League on Tiger Hill

The Register of Edibles says:

> The scarlet runner bean should be planted in the second month. Its
> tendrils extend and bind, its leaves are the size of a cup, round with a point.
> Its flowers are shaped like small moths and appear to have wings and tails.
> Its pods come in more than ten varieties: long, round, like a pig's ear, like
> a sickle, like a dragon's claw, like a tiger's claw, among others. They bind
> together to form branches and are most prolific after White Dew.[1] When
> the pods are tender, they can be used in vegetarian dishes or for making a
> tea—when the beans are mature, they may be shelled and boiled for eat-
> ing. The beans come in four colors: black, white, red, and multicolored. Only
> the white beans may be used in medicines—their flavor is sweet and warm,
> and they have no toxins. Their primary use is for controlling and harmoniz-
> ing the central and lower *qi*, to bolster the five viscera, to inhibit vomiting, to
> dispel summer *qi*, to warm the stomach, to purge wet heat, to treat cholera,
> and to control diarrhea, as well as to relieve the effects of globefish poison,
> alcohol, and all types of plant poisons.[2]

Since this particular variety has so many benefits, why shouldn't people grow
it? It has yet another marvelous quality. All cucurbits, eggplants, and other small
vegetables are divided between those suitable for growing in the south and
varieties that grow better in the north or those suitable for the east and varieties that grow better in the west. Only the scarlet runner bean can be cultivated
everywhere. Only the pig's ear, sickle, and tiger claw—these three varieties—
mature late with large, broad pods that are especially tasty when boiled. Only
the dragon's claw variety appears to have large beans, but inside they are hollow.

Just look, and you'll see through them. When you eat them, they're bland and without flavor. They grow only in the Suzhou region—no other area has them. If you happen to mention them, people won't believe you. If someone here today can explain the reason for this hollowness while we're idly talking, he might be able to add to the *Materia Medica* for edibles so that others may know about it, too.[3]

One among the crowd said, "This is the effect of the local soil and weather. All the rest of the world's people are trustworthy, and so the beans they raise have thick and tasty seeds. Only in Suzhou are values so distorted and the locals so prone to exaggeration that you can't believe a word they say. So it's appropriate that the pods of the beans they grow there are hollow as well."

"Suzhou is one of the most famous places under Heaven. Ever since antiquity there have been stalwart fellows and auspicious omens galore there," the crowd said. "Even famous scholars of the Neo-Confucian school have hardly been scarce—each has appeared on the heels of another.[4] How could you see those people as faithless and superficial? Surely there have been some extraordinary events there. Tell us some of those exceptional tales! If we meet a Suzhou man with a glib tongue in the future, we'll have some acid remarks ready to answer him with."

The man spoke.

ON SUZHOU CUSTOMS

Suzhou customs are all show and no substance. One could not explain them all in one sitting. Even Mount Tiger Hill—no bigger than a fist—is filled with strange things. From the Shantang River Bridge outside the Chang Gate it is only seven *li* to Tiger Hill, but in addition to several traders large and small on one side of it, all the people living in the houses that line the riverbank and hang over the water on the other side of the Halfway Bridge depend on Tiger Hill for their income. Who knows just how many of them make fake goods for a living? Even if they open stalls only a couple of board doors wide and sell just a few miscellaneous goods or some food items, from far away you can see them one after another putting out their goods, and surprisingly it is both busy and orderly. If you look closely at their goods, it's just as the local expression says—essays from the Hanlin Academy, swords and spears from the Imperial Armory, medicines from the Royal Academy of Physicians—everything has a great name but nothing is genuine. Half are made to cheat travelers from distant parts, and the other half are things made to fool children.

It's not just people from other places who call them fakes—even several scholars and learned men of the area have written "bamboo branch songs" or doggerel verses about them. The way they enumerate their faults is particularly interesting. I still recall some that describe the tiny shops on the bank by the Halfway Bridge and then gradually extend to the shops at the head of Full Cup Bridge:

> The view becomes lovelier as you follow the Shantang Road,
> With calls of hidden crows among willows along the shore.
> How much of springtime's beauties remain here to be seen?
> Just view the jasmine flowers there before their very doors!

Curio stands—

> Winding walks quiet, secluded: elegance abounds.
> Objects of many sorts lie arranged on trays.
> Inside the shop a small room, a tiny tea alcove,
> But plum blooms and bamboo mats impede the visitor's gaze.

A "pure visitor" house—with nothing besides tea utensils, a stove, and a vase, a room no larger than the palm of a hand—will be divided into two sections, awaiting customers here to pass the time and arrange for whores and gambling—

> Outside they run a little shop, a study lies within,
> With tea utensils, a flower bowl, little wicker chairs,
> An incense pot, a stove and vase, tiny bamboo tables,
> And on the wall, a half-fake "Dong Qichang" hanging there.[5]

The tea huts, which also sell wheat flour breads—

> Flat breads in the teashops as hard as bricks,
> Salty—no, not salty—sweet—no, not sweet;
> Only elders returning home from provinces to the north
> Finish up one plate, then want another one to eat!

The wine shops, where "red skirts" manage the stove—

> Wine shop newly opened at Halfway Bridge,
> At the stove a charming maiden attracts better than a sign.
> The wandering guest may ply her with loads of saucy talk,
> But even though half drunk he still would taste her wine.

Snack stands, where every kind of snack has either plum sauce and sour vinegar or is mixed with rock sugar—

> Tiger Hill snack baskets are certainly the worst,
> But ardent fans all claim that these are truly great.
> Chopped and pickled ingredients, beyond all recognition,
> If they do not dump in vinegar, these surely will be sweet!

Trotters and stomach with sesame sugar—

> They used to praise that sesame sugar sold at Tiger Hill;
> I've also heard that the local pork is what they like to boast.[6]
> Just recently I chanced to sample both these kinds of snacks,
> Their tough stomach and coarse sugar would fill only a hungry ghost!

Seafood shops—

> Shrimp eggs on salted fish were famous on Tiger Hill,
> But nowadays dried fish are served up here as well.
> Gold carp with soy sauce may come in many flavors,
> Though anchovies and bitterlings are all just boiled in oil.

Leaf tea—

> Tiger Hill tea prices double when it's fresh,
> But one can't tell the true leaf from the fake.
> All say those grown here on the Hill are exceptionally fine,
> But surely they were really grown out near Heaven's Lake![7]

Woven-mat shops—

> Along the bench, all five feet long, he works upon his loom,
> For Honest Zhang's his name as is his trade;
> You may have found a fine one, but he'll stealthily switch,
> And you'll find he adds a bit more with his pitch!

Flowering plants—

> "Once crabs are done flowering, tree peonies make their show;
> Our bush peonies and azaleas each blossom in profusion."
> For twiggy stems and grassy roots that people do not recognize,
> They'll make up fancy plant names to leave their buyers in confusion.

Miniature landscapes—

> Rounded, rounded banister to tiny, tiny window,
> Bent branches in this *penjing*,[8] a winding corridor appears,
> Cleverly created with a choice of Xuanzhou rocks,
> Makes this all so natural, to win admiring cheers.

Huangshu incense—

> Here a box of *huangshu* incense: nothing real is meant.
> All of it so nicely wrapped, wound with decorative bands.
> They will say it's really what is known as *ompa* scent,
> Yet before you even light it, it will irritate your hands.[9]

The gentleman—

> In manner oh so dignified, his air is all so grand;
> Clothed all in finest silks, he feigns such nonchalance.
> In days to come he'll surely risk becoming simply bored,
> But for now he hopes you'll treat him as a stylish "gentleman."

The "fashionable" tarts—

> Prostitutes so fashionable, thin makeup makes them chic,
> Loosely done-up hair, oiled shiny and so sleek;

"Flying" temple locks on kingfisher feathers borne,
Revealing pairs of two-inch clips made of rhino horn.

The old tarts

Daubed-on rouge, smeared-on powder, mottled by flowing sweat,
Dressed up in the queerest way, their words meander still;
Their johns are no encouragement, their pimps of little help,
They must bring in their own guests from up on Tiger Hill.

Love nests—

"Silk workshops" for the village whores dolled up not quite in style,
Removing layers of black turbans, shiny foreheads do prevail;
Old material seems like gold; pearls may look like grain.
These sparrows, aping pheasants, sport long and colorful tails.

The monks—

Three things about Buddhist monks are all too common now:
Gambling and drinking wine and keeping women on the side.
Nowadays they keep close ties with friends at the local court,
Familiar with all the services the fixers can provide.

The beggars—

Disheveled hair, dirty faces, and all with empty hands,
Worn and tattered clothing, shoulders both worn through,
Short, despised—morn and evening standing by the shrine.
Every word they utter is "Give us your coppers, do!"

The old catamites—

Nowadays the "masculine style" has become the latest fashion.
Odd and homely country boys compete for older guys;
Grease may cover their lips, all three inches thick,
As in the gambling parlors they play "backdoor-wise."

The young scholars—

> So frivolously showing their finery, these elegant young men,
> Accoutred all in fine silk gauze, wearing embroidered slippers,
> Felt hats so shiny, dimples pressed into their cheeks,
> Sweat bands they mop, their fans painted by famous hands.

The big-footed women—

> Aunties from the countryside are all so very strange;
> The scarves with which they mop their chests are tattered it would
>   seem.
> White shirts with open sleeves, they wear them inside out;
> Their feet so big that when they walk they slap like a brace of bream.

The "mourning sons" coffin bearers stay mostly along the Shantang River, but of these "mourning sons," none will go home sober—

> People sigh to see "bereaved sons" drink the "yellow soup,"
> Their faces just as red as Lord Guan in the Pudong temple.[10]
> If they don't use the mourner's staff to keep them on their feet,
> They're all too likely to stumble and fall down right there in the street.

These poems are all about those who depend on Tiger Hill for their livelihood. Most may be cheating a bit, but they're only leaning on its shadow. Because they're just feeding their families, we should overlook their transgressions.

But there's another bunch that are like floating duckweed on the waves, like the maggots who live in the stink of shit—they stand as a group and sit as a bunch. They come without being called. You can shoo them away, but you can't get rid of them. They are called "old freeloaders."[11] I don't know why they originally took this name. Some suppose that it's because they're all single and can go wherever their feet take them, and no matter whether it's houses or paintings or gardens, antiques or women, they don't pay a cent for them. They get to appreciate them all for free. One name for them is "bamboo strips" (meaning "fixers"), and another is "nap boards" (meaning "spongers"). These are expressions used in the brothels.

For example, if one of the brothel's clients lacks connections and stands outside the door and starts to cry because he's unable to enjoy himself there, he needs one of these "bamboo strips" to get him in, and that's why they're called "bamboo strips." If some big shot goes whoring, one of these flatterers will keep him company while he drinks until it's so late that the alley gates have all been closed for the night. Since he can't leave, he borrows a plank bench to catch a nap until daylight. That's why they're called "nap boards."[12]

This is all common knowledge nowadays, so it goes without saying. But I was thinking about the type of fellow who has nothing worth pawning when he needs to buy his seven daily necessities.[13] He gets up in the morning and goes down to the mouth of a stream where he washes his face, and with the few coppers he has left over from the previous night he buys himself a few jasmine flowers that he puts on his head and then puts his hat on over them. Then he goes out wearing his thousand-stitched, hundreds-of-patches worn-out Daoist robe, and with no particular purpose he trusts his fate to wherever his ten toes may take him.[14] If there's someone who's on his way whoring, then he'll go along—either going up to a widow's door, seeking out a whore in a "private nest," or finding a boy to trick. If there's one who wants to gamble, he'll go to the gambling den with him. It doesn't matter what he plays. He knows all the games—cards, throwing dice, struggles and jabs.[15] And if he's really hard up financially, he'll pinch tips from behind the back of some wealthy big shot and put aside a little something for the future. But now I'll tell you my main story.

It was summer, just after the Dragon Boat festival in the fifth month, and the wealthy big shots had already watched the dragon boat races. Not many people were coming and going. A group of these freeloaders had no "business" and so were truly bored to death. They gathered at places along the Shantang or in the teashops and antique shops below the second mountain gate on Tiger Hill, looking for all the world like herons, each with a leg bent standing on a sandbar, their eyes longing for someone of the sort they recognized to appear.

Several people suddenly walked in through the great mountain gate. In front was a "gentleman" wearing a very stylish square administrator's hat on his head with an official green, stiff gauze Daoist robe and on his feet soy-sauce-colored thick-soled satin shoes. In his hand he carried a conch-shell-edged sandalwood-staved gold-covered paper folding fan. He was thirty years old, more or less, and he had a square face and large ears, with extended sideburns and a short beard.

Behind him followed four bondservants wearing eight-trigrams felt hats and tight-sleeved archery jackets. All carried felt bags, calling-card boxes, canes, umbrellas, and the like as they plodded along up the hill. All the free-loaders thought he must be from the northwest and didn't pay him much attention. They watched as he climbed to Thousand Man Rock, where he stood to look all around. Then he went straight up to the Hall of the King of Heaven, where he bowed four times to the Buddha Maitreya. Several of the monks fund-raising for "oil and flowers" came out with their pledge books to engage him in conversation and beg him for a donation. Thereupon he wrote out a donation pledge:[16] "Ma Cai, faithful follower and official from Pingyang in Shanxi, donates ten ounces of silver." The group of monks immediately became polite and formal and invited Master Ma into the abbot's quarters for tea.

"I wouldn't trouble you to provide me with tea," this Ma Cai said. "But I do have a concern I wish to raise. Might there be a professional chanteuse in the vicinity?"

Not understanding his manner of speaking, they answered, saying, "We have no butterfish sauce here.[17] But if you wish to buy rose sauce or plum-blossom sauce, shrimp-egg-covered fish, or preserved olives, you can get them all at Mr. Ge's shop in Pure Street Market in the city."

"Not that," said Ma Cai. "Presently I'll secure a vessel on the river, and I wish to engage a lutenist to play the *pipa* and vocalize some songs."

By now the monks could understand him, and they answered in official speech,[18] saying, "We don't call our singers 'professional chanteuses' here in Suzhou. Any one who has become famous and made a name for herself is called a 'songstress,' and the ones who are not well known and just drift back and forth are called 'pure visitors.'"

"I'm acquainted with the concept of songstress, but I don't wish to have one," Ma Cai said. "I'd prefer one who has not yet turned professional and 'just drifts back and forth.' That would suit me. But I'm curious—what does this term 'pure visitor' imply?"

"Tiger Hill is a world-famous mountain," the monks said, "a place where traveling merchants and men in office gather, and people come here in great numbers to be entertained. On holidays, when they're here to drink and wander around the mountain, it's just not as interesting if they don't have friends who have the leisure time to have fun with them."

"Being a drinking companion can't be called a 'pure' occupation, nor can someone you're having fun with be called a 'visitor,'" Ma Cai said.

"But such people are on their own and eat at other people's houses," the monks said, "so why wouldn't you call them 'visitors'? Most of them have no families and no homes and not enough clothing and food to get by on, so why wouldn't you call them 'pure'?"

"Would it be possible for me to engage several to accompany me in my recreations?" Ma Cai said.

"Yes, yes," the monks said, and they quickly went out to the threshold of the front gate of the temple hall and beckoned.

Two or three ran up the fifty-three stone steps, saying, "Is that gentleman looking for some freeloader friends to keep him company? I'll go, I'll go!"[19]

"Don't raise such a ruckus," the monk said. "A bunch of you should go together, and he'll select the ones he wants."

Everyone in this group had a nickname.

One was called "Monkey Fried in Oil" Qiang She (Strong Tongue). He was the son of Qiang Mengqiao and was given this nickname because he was small and short, was constantly getting into trouble, and just could not relax.

Another was nicknamed "Leather Painted Face" Xu Fobao (Salvageable) because he was rather dull-witted.[20] When a wealthy patron asked him something, he'd answer with only a word or two. When no one was paying any attention to him, he'd drink all by himself until he was red in the face and then fall asleep on a table and snore.

The third, an older man, was called Zhu Sanxing (Three Stars). Close to seventy years of age, his face was all wrinkles, his eyesight was dim, his whiskers and the hair on his temples were dyed dark green, and his back was bent like a drawn bow. He depended on being treated like an "uncle" from the older generation and so took the lead over the others. This irritated people to the extent that they changed his nickname from Sanxing to Sanjie (Three Invitations/Three Festivals).[21] Because he had been somewhat good-looking in his youth, had a clear singing voice, and performed opera rather well, people would request his presence. He put on airs and made people come to get him three times before he accepted "invitations." In middle age his throat gave out on him, and everyone rejected him. On the Qingming Festival he would walk into someone's house, and the occupants could not get him to leave. Only after the Dragon Boat and Mid-Autumn festivals was he willing to move on—these were "his festivals." And so now his lot in old age was ruination, and people had made up a joke about him. It said that in his youth he was cold and poor, another Lü Mengzheng, in middle age he fell on hard times that he couldn't bear, just like Zheng Yuanhe in his middle years, and in his present "stage" he was old and decrepit, becoming senile, fit only to be put out in the gutter, like old Governor Cai in his later years. He even had stiff joints like the "joints" of bamboo.[22]

A monk escorted the three of them in, and Ma Cai was overjoyed. "This honorable place has so many men of talent!" he said. "How did you manage to get several of them with just a single wave of your hand?"

"We younger ones have only modest talent," the freeloaders said, "but we depend on such as you, sir, to enrich and nurture our modest talent."[23] Ma Cai took Qiang She by the hand and was about to take leave of the monk.

Qiang She stopped the monk with his hand, saying, "If Master Ma wishes to enjoy the waters and climb the hill, to 'seek the flowers and inquire about willows,' he surely can't do without an abbot along if he wants to have a fine time. That we should be together today was indeed rare good fortune. Surely you can't part with Master Ma either? Moreover, since Master Ma has pledged a contribution, you should cash it and put it in the collection box so that the god Weiduo won't be angry at you."[24]

"Just so, just so," said Ma Cai. "We'll go together, go together. But I still need to engage a prostitute, and I fear that this would be a little awkward for the abbot."

"The abbot has no prohibitions about such humble places," said Old Zhu. "He's an old customer himself. It's what they mean by 'Form is emptiness, and emptiness is form.'"[25]

They spoke more nonsense of this sort as they made their way to the Gu Family Garden. Xu Fobao said, "This is Yan Saiguan, who recently moved here from Yangzhou. Wait while I knock on the door so we can go in."

"Yesterday several customers from Xuye Gate came to invite her out," was the answer from within.

Then they went to look for Old Fourth Wu at the Han Family Garden near the Shantang Bridge. There they were told, "Squire Xu from Taicang is giving a banquet, and she won't be available." Altogether they visited three or four houses without seeing so much as a shadow.

By then Ma Cai was becoming impatient. "These bawdy wenches seem to have hidden themselves away on purpose. I'm certainly not going to eat anyone up!"

Together the freeloaders assured him, "Don't be impatient, Master Ma. Our humble location is a way station for traveling merchants, and a lot of people come through here. And recently they've added more officers to the brigade.[26] That led to more brawls getting out of control, so that even the whores can't be stationed here for long. We have only these few whores, and it appears in truth that none of them is free."

Qiang She said, "Now there's Old First Xu. She's a skinny little thing, but she has such a pretty face. She and Master Ma have a lot in common—they'd hit it off right from the start. You two take Master Ma up on the bridge to sit for a while and wait for me to go ahead and see. I'm just afraid she might still be asleep at this time."

He couldn't have known that Old First had long since finished washing and combing for her morning toilette and was just in the middle of washing her feet in a wooden basin in the kitchen. "Don't come in," she called out to him, but Qiang She was already standing in front of her.

Startled, he said, "Old First, when I came around here in the past, I never knew you ever left 'a pair of dry feet.'"[27]

"You came to tease me again, you little tortoise bastard!" she said. "How could I have a pair of dry feet?"

Qiang She said, "Well, if they weren't dry, why would you be soaking your feet until they swell up?"

Old First raised her feet and splashed water right on Qiang She's face.

"Stinky old whore," he said, laughing. "I had intended to send along a temporary husband for you, and yet you treat me to some dirty water!"

"Oh, really?" Old First said. Hastily she wiped her feet and put on shoes and clothing to go out and meet Ma Cai, happy as could be. She dusted off a seat for him and called for tea, all very busily.

Without even stating his name, Ma Cai opened his mouth and said, "I won't take tea in such backward surroundings. Let's go down to my water-craft and have some wine."

The freeloaders led the way, and so they all went down to the wine boat together. Aside, Ma Cai pulled out the money pouch hanging from his belt, took out a piece of silver and gave it to his servant, and sent him off to buy food and wine.

Unable to wait, Ma Cai at once asked Old First to sing a song. Old First said, "We only learned how to 'sleep.' How would we know how to sing some sort of song?"

Zhu Sanxing said, "Her renditions of 'Weeping to High Heaven,' 'Goat on the Mountain Slope,' 'Twisted Silver Bracelet,' and 'Lad from Jade River' are absolutely the best around here."

"If you know how to sing," said Ma Cai, "why do you say that you don't? Is it because we've just met and my face is strange to you? Since we're getting well acquainted today, you should sing from morning to evening, and then from evening you ought to go on singing through to daylight."

The freeloaders all said, "No one else could boast of this, but Old First's strength is second to none. With Old First as number one, Suzhou doesn't have a number two."

After being flattered so nicely, Old First could only stretch her neck and yell nonstop in response.

Soon they seated themselves at a table set with dishes including stewed pig's head, seared ox stomach and smoked pork trotters, chicken boiled in broth—about seven or eight dishes altogether, with big plates and big pieces all piled on one another. The servants brought out several jugs of warmed wine and had poured several rounds when Ma Cai said, "Cheers!" and Old First downed several cups at a single breath. Fobao matched her cup for cup.

Seeing that Old First was relaxed and happy, Qiang She made a couple of demon faces to tease her and began to chat with her in Suzhou local slang, *gee-lee, goo-lu*, just as friends arriving at the army camp might strike up a conversation in their hometown tongue. It made Ma Cai raise his eyes to the sky, not understanding what it was all about.

One of his bondservants made up some additional expenses to explain what he spent on all of this, fearing that the host was keeping his own account. In order to cover up what he was doing, he brushed the host's ear and said, "These southern barbarians are swearing at you, Master." Being quick-tempered, Ma Cai took a bowl of fatty pork stewed in soy sauce, splashed it on the faces of the freeloaders, and began to hit them with his fists, *bim-bam*.

Xu Fobao escaped off the boat, and Old Zhu stood stock-still against the wall. Grease stained all of Old First Xu's clothing, and she began bawling, *wa-wa*, nonstop. Qiang She sat at her left and so could not easily get away. With one hand pressing down on the corner of the table, he cried, "Now the whole damned thing is ruined!"

The servant again turned to the host and said, "Now he'll beat you to death, m'lord!"[28]

This made Ma Cai even angrier, and he picked up a footstool and went after Qiang She. Fearing for his life, Qiang ran out onto the stern of the boat, leaped into the water, and disappeared. "Now you've caused a homicide, Your Honor," the servant remarked.

Anxious, Ma Cai went out to the stern and asked the boatman. The boatman said, "No matter. He's just been blown by the wind over to the other bank."

"Why didn't he sink?" asked the servant.

"Some people are like cuttlebone," the boatman said. "How could they sink?"

This is how a group of freeloaders happened to provoke some ugly gossip. But we'll speak no more of this.

Instead I'll tell of an old freeloader named Jia Jingshan. From the time he was young he had served as his young master's study mate. Although he never really understood literary composition, he'd mastered the manners of the group of those who are obsessed with writing.

One day he heard that Qiang She, Xu Fobao, and Zhu Sanxing had gotten themselves into trouble, and the more it was described, the worse they seemed to have behaved. So he gathered together ten or so of the older freeloaders, and in good order they went off to the Thousand-Acre Cloud Pavilion on Tiger Hill, where he sat them down in order of rank and presented this statement. He said, "Our profession cannot be said to be either lofty or lowbrow. Yesterday I received word that several of our number endured a very awkward situation. Situations like this happen often because there has never been a discussion of our arts, some of us aren't very smart, and we've presented ourselves in a fashion that is too low-class. This is why others see us as frivolous lowlifes. We must begin to show respect for ourselves, like the learned scholars do. We should form a great society and burn an oath to show our allegiance."[29]

"Which deity should be the patron for our society?" the freeloaders asked.

"We play flutes and sing songs," Jingshan said. "We help fill in for professional musicians, so all the other gods are irrelevant. As I recall, when he was just starting out, Wu Zixu played the flute for a living here in the market at Wu (Suzhou), and he passed down his scores. Lord Bopi praised butts and patted bottoms here,[30] and so he passed down those manners. These were our founders. When we drink water, we shouldn't forget the source."

"No, no, we shouldn't," the freeloaders all said. "Wu Zixu was a stalwart and a hero, but Bopi was a petty man of foul reputation. They shouldn't sit together."

"In our business," said Jingshan, "whether high or low, we're all the same. When opportunity presents itself, we fulfill the role of a stalwart, but when the time isn't right, even though whatever we do might be smelly, the gods won't blame us for it."

"We don't dare bother Wu Zixu," the freeloaders said, "so if we exchanged him for Zheng Yuanhe instead, he'd be closer to us. By the way, how should we dress?"

"We should wear top *guowen* on our heads."

"What's a *guowen*?" said the crowd.

"In the past we wore topknot hats when we were just sitting around and not going out," Jingshan said. "If we were to change into tall hats and broad robes, people would all make ghost faces to ridicule us. Only when we wear the *guowen*, which is neither tall nor flat, will people not notice the change. If we wear quilted straight-seam robes that are halfway new and not worn out, dark green or deep black, then when people see us, all our clothes won't be brand-new, so we can claim that we're not spendthrifts. On our feet we'll wear those travelers' broad, brown straw shoes—they'd look rather elegant and wouldn't be seen as too extravagant.

"When we hail each other along the road, we'll all call each other 'Elder League Brothers.' The younger ones should call us 'League Uncles.' When we see a big shot, we should call him 'Your Honor,' or if he's lacking a little, we'll call him 'Old Master.' And if you're teaching tunes in someone's home, we'll all say 'your humble servant's host' and 'your honorable household.' As to young men who study the opera with us, we should call them our 'humble students and disciples.' We won't rank people according to their character or material things. We'll refer to them all as 'immortals,' and when we encounter their bondservants, we'll refer to them all as 'sir.'"

As he was giving his lecture, Qiang She, the fellow who had been beaten the day before, said, "Two medium-size painted passenger boats have entered the mouth of the river. Both display broad yellow umbrellas. I think it must be a traveling official mooring here. Old Uncle, you should bestir yourself. Find a way to make yourself useful to him."

Hearing this, Jingshan hurried down Tiger Hill. There he saw, leaning on the handrail of the boat, their new patron with an upright cloud hat on his head and wearing a mountain silk Daoist robe and tall red cloud shoes. Together with two countrymen from the Wonton Bookshop in Xiang Alley inside the Chang Gate, he chatted in their local speech as they walked up the hill.

Jingshan quietly sidled up to one of the bondservants and made some discreet inquiries. He learned that this was a palace graduate of the class of 1613, a man from Jishui in Ji'an Prefecture named Liu Qian (Modest Liu). He had served in the Office of Government Communications and was on his way home after retiring. He wanted to buy a few elegant knickknacks and curios in Suzhou, procure some exquisite *objets de vertu*, and locate several handsome youths and good-looking girls whom he could train for two acting troupes.

Hearing this, Jingshan unconsciously began nodding smugly, to say nothing of the seventeen or eighteen dimples added to his smiling face. Even the joints of his bones began to twist. In a single breath it was "This would be right for Great Uncle," and "That, sir, would not be so fitting." Taking advantage of a lull in the conversation, Jingshan dragged the servant into a shop to have some tea and to inquire about his master's fellow graduates, his fellow countrymen, his relatives. Committing each and every one to memory, he then turned and went off to the Wonton Bookshop to ask Liu's two relatives there to put in a good word for him. And they did indeed mention him to Lord Liu.

"Since you all do business hereabouts," Lord Liu said, "for a sojourner such as myself to patronize the establishments here, I simply must have the recommendations of some local person of stature."

Jingshan saw an opening for himself, but he felt that Lord Liu posed a difficult challenge, and so he waited two whole days just like an ant in a hot wok that could not climb out or a grub trying to drill through a hard bone. But fortunately the servant was an old acquaintance of one Wu Songquan, who ran the Virtue Abounds satin shop over by the Chang Gate. It happened that the servant had invited Wu to come over to sell goods and set up an account. By coincidence Lord Liu had not yet returned from visiting, so Jingshan took advantage of his passing acquaintance and hastened to fawn on Wu Songquan, begging Wu to employ his weighty words and recommend him.

Now this Anhui man liked to flaunt his authority and in the end agreed to do so. Before long they both went down to Lord Liu's boat. There Jingshan looked around and held forth in fulsome praise, saying that Lord Liu's artworks were all exquisite and that he had an exceptionally refined eye. No matter whether paintings or calligraphy, bronzes or pottery, objects or utensils, Jingshan understood them all "right down to the bone." In fact, he was himself an old curio personified.[31] Lord Liu laughed and asked his book page to take a decorated bronze goblet out of its case and let Jingshan appreciate it. Jingshan began to praise the piece in a loud voice even before the page had unwrapped it.

"Might this be in the manner of the Three Dynasties of antiquity?" Lord Liu asked.

"This treasure has all the right patina. This must have been kept in Your Honor's family for seventeen or eighteen generations," said Jingshan.

Lord Liu laughed and said, "That's not the period of time I was referring to."[32]

"But in truth I've never seen utensils from the Three Dynasties," Jingshan said in the next breath. "My ignorant eyes are good enough only for two and a half dynasties, and not a bit more."

Lord Liu then took out a famous old painting of early plum blossoms in the snow for him to see, but it had no artist's signature or seal in any of its four corners.

Jingshan opened his mouth and said, "Does Your Honor recognize whose painting this is?"

"A man of the Song or Yuan dynasty," Lord Liu said. "He didn't put his seal on it, so unfortunately I don't know."

"No, not Song or Yuan. It must have been painted by Zhang Chang of the Jin dynasty," Jingshan said.[33]

Lord Liu laughed again and said, "It seems that you, sir, have not been much concerned with paintings, calligraphy, and curios. You must be more concerned with notes and scales. I wish to find several elegant young women who might be taught to sing opera. Are there any available?"

"Yes, yes indeed," Jingshan said. "It's just that it would take some time to find some in the area who are mature. But if you have the time, and don't go about it carelessly, you can find the right faces, eyes, feet, and hands, without question. But you also have to ask their parents about whether they have had any smallpox pustules, whether they have any hidden infections on their bodies, whether they have any kind of bad temper in their bellies, whether or not they have to get up at night to pee, and how good their throats are for singing. The parents may not be willing to let them go so far away. But it happens that I, your student, have carefully selected girls for several old gentlemen. These girls have become ever more attractive with age. Those gentlemen took them as concubines, and they all gave birth to sons. Their relatives still go to visit them regularly. So everyone says that I, your student, am reliable in such matters, and those who have girls for sale trust me in this business. If Your Honor had not asked, your student wouldn't have dared mention them. Since Your Honor is looking for some, you'll see that your student has not been exaggerating. No one else would dare make such promises."

"Then I'll rely on you," Lord Liu said.

Jingshan also asked, "How long will you be anchored here, Your Honor?"

"Let's not be concerned with dates. I'll leave only when this matter is settled," said Lord Liu. He made up a list of bolts of satin with Songquan, and together they took their leave.

Jingshan then went to meet his various friends. They looked high and low, but they could find no leads on any available girls. With no other alternative, all he could do was go to his niece and talk her and another girl from that neighborhood into going with him to Tiger Hill to have some fun.

He took them directly to the boat. Lord Liu took a look at them and said, "Male leads, female leads, villains, and clowns—I have need of them all, so I don't need to examine them too carefully. But I must ask what their prices are."

"If they were older, their families would not allow them to leave home," Jingshan said. "But hearing that Your Honor would give them special treatment, and that I, your student, would be serving as the go-between, only then were they willing to let these two girls go. In the past, girls cost only twenty ounces of silver, but now they're only willing to part with them for forty ounces each."

"Ten ounces more than the old price, and that settles it," Lord Liu said.

Jingshan's first impulse was to counter the offer in order to increase his own percentage. How could he have known that Lord Liu would produce the silver on the spot and have his servant go with him to Wu Songquan's shop to sign the contract and pay him off? But Jingshan again came up with another thought. "If he's going to make up a contract, he'll still need to hire me to tutor them. Why not match him scheme for scheme and get a little cash in hand to play with?" He wrote out the contract at once, received the payment, including his "wine-and-water" fee for serving as middleman. Then he asked Songquan to cosign as guarantor.

Jingshan picked up the silver and walked back onto the boat, where he reported, "Your Honor, even though you've purchased these girls, their parents want to make them several pieces of clothing and some shoes. This will be my responsibility. It will probably take five or six days. If Your Honor wants to have them learn opera, there is no place better than in my home. Although I'll be at your beck and call, my wife can also teach them opera. If by chance Your Honor is anxious about this matter, I'll just leave this silver here with you."

"Wu Songquan's recommendation was not far from the truth," said Lord Liu. "I'll trouble your honorable spouse to devote herself to this, and when the time comes, all these efforts will be recompensed."

Jingshan happily took the silver and went home and had a splendid time, but that's not in our story.

He had not expected this group of spongers to become so tight-knit that when they realized that Jia Jingshan had worked out a little advantage for himself, they wanted to get in on the action, too. One among them, Gu Qingzhi, also went to the boat to check the prospects. There he overheard that Lord Liu had sent someone to fetch a Doctor Yang Chong'an to compound some medicines for him.

Now Qingzhi and Chong'an had a nodding acquaintance, so in a single breath he hustled over to the Yang house to beg for an introduction. Together he and Chong'an went to the boat. Lord Liu met them and engaged them in small talk, and when it became convenient, Chong'an started praising Qingzhi highly. Lord Liu was extremely affable and kept them there for lunch.

"Yesterday Jia Jingshan came to see me, and I entrusted him with finding me two young girls," he said, "and he'll keep them at his house to be trained in opera. I've also bought several boys who are no more than fifteen or sixteen, and I also want them to learn to sing. But I wonder, is he able to teach them?"

"Fifteen or sixteen is just the age when children's singing voices are developing," said Qingzhi. "Not hard to teach at all. May I be so bold as to offer my services?"

"Do you know this Jia Jingshan?" asked Lord Liu.

Qingzhi looked first at Chong'an, who was busily writing prescriptions, then quietly said, "Although I'm acquainted with Jingshan, we young ones don't sit with him."

"Is he deficient in character?" Lord Liu asked. "What does he do that's improper?"

Qingzhi lifted his hand and lightly touched his nose with his fingers, then made a sign with his hands and said, "You should very carefully inspect the girls you entrusted him to buy for you."

Lord Liu then nodded his head, and Chong'an came forward with the prescriptions and explained them.

Now Lord Liu generally preferred the masculine style, and the boys he wanted to train to sing were all Lord Liu's young Lord Longyangs.[34] Qingzhi observed that Lord Liu expressed special concern for them and began to develop a plan for his own benefit. Pretending to speak to Chong'an, he said, "I'm not very old, yet recently I've become impotent. I can no longer have normal relations." Believing this to be true, Lord Liu then entrusted him with teaching these youths. Within a few days, Gu Qingzhi had established himself as their teacher.

While on the one hand Qingzhi went to see Jingshan and have a look at the girls, on the other hand he also wanted his cut of the matchmaker's fee Jingshan received. Jingshan said, "*I'm* the one who recommended *you* to Lord Liu as a singing teacher," and so he expected a portion of Qingzhi's "tutor's meat" for his efforts.[35]

The two quarreled for a while, but the next day they went together to Lord Liu's boat. Breakfast was over, so they all went out the Chang Gate to buy some goods. Along the way they bought a few jade objects in Zhuan Zhu Alley. The two merely glanced at each other, but they continued to barter behind their backs by sticking out several fingers, reaching tacit agreements on their go-between fees from the shops as they went along.

At sunset, Lord Liu was returning from a banquet on a small boat. Jingshan surreptitiously took a ferry and caught up with him. When he saw Lord Liu, he started a conversation, saying pointedly, "Why didn't you bring your attendants along with you today? If you leave only Qingzhi on the boat, you should be cautious and personally look out for them. If they're seduced into ruining their bodies, then their singing voices won't be clear."

Now Lord Liu was single-mindedly committed to this path, and it was also extremely easy for him to be jealous. This comment from Jingshan moved him to check up on them. It was only because Qingzhi had said that he was physically incapable of intercourse that Lord Liu had taken no precautions. The day had come when Qingzhi was fated to be exposed.

During his noon rest the following day, Lord Liu did not hear the boys singing, so he quietly spied on them. What he saw was Qingzhi fully aroused, thrusting with that thing like the testicles of a seal, all virile and fierce as he carried out that business with one of the boys.

Seeing this, Lord Liu summoned them out, beat the boy thirty strokes, stripped off Qingzhi's clothes and hat, and, leading him by a straw rope around his neck and saying only that he had stolen some silver cups, sent him off to the county magistrate with Liu's own signature card. Blood follows prison and pursuit. They beat him *ling-ling ding-ding*. It was not until he sent his own handsome fifteen- or sixteen-year-old son to Liu's residence that the trial could be concluded. He was tattooed and sentenced to exile, dispatched to be a courier at Jingkou Station.[36]

Once this irritating nail had been plucked out of Jingshan's eye, he was able to realize his plan to the full. Everyone who had sold Liu calligraphy and paintings or curios had to pay him a cut. First they had to reach an under-standing with him, and only then could they complete the sale. Even those who were asking for the price they had been promised had to go through him—even the tips to the servants passed through his hands first. When-ever several of his disciples or old acquaintances came by, Jingshan joined them in composing pretentious verses and warped essays, reading sen-tences with the pauses in the wrong places.[37] They'd laugh until their noses collapsed and their mouths cracked out of shape.

But who would have thought that his good fortune should pass and disas-ter would come in its place? That gray one, Heaven, perversely plotted to cre-ate a disastrous coincidence for this fellow. Quite unexpectedly, through his nefarious arrangements, Jingshan had swindled a great amount of money in a very short time. Not wanting to reveal his hand to his wife, he stored it all in a wine pot under the bed. Day after day, in his satisfaction, he, his wife, and their daughter all drank a bit extra and then fell fast asleep. But then one night a thief pried the door out of its socket, entered, and found the stove and then the bedroom. He felt all around and discovered two wine pots under the bed. One was chock full of rice. But the other was only half full, and it had a big brick on top of it. Not knowing what was inside, the thief felt around, and there he found it. As he was about to go out the door, he knocked over an incense burner from the family shrine, which fell onto a chamber pot, making a loud crash. In their bed, husband and wife were startled awake. They felt around for the earthenware pot and cried out. But by then the thief was already far away. As they were crying for help, Lord Liu's men came to urge him to send the two girls to wait on the master. Jing-shan was beside himself—neither a road to heaven nor a door into the earth presented itself.

Jingshan's neighbors and people in the shops along the street spread the rumor that the girls he had sold were fabricated out of thin air, and only the silver he had lost was real. The official's servants cut him no slack. They imme-diately dragged him off to the boat to explain the situation. Lord Liu was very angry and sent him off right away with a note to the prefect demanding the girls. Jingshan's two hands were empty—he couldn't even form a ball out of mud. How could he remedy the situation? The original contract was sought out, and the guarantor was held responsible for the full sum. In addition, the prefect determined that Jingshan had abducted the girls.

Stuck in jail and with no deals to make, he could only send his own twelve- or thirteen-year-old daughter to the boat to work as Lord Liu's servant. And as with Gu Qingzhi's case, he, too, was punished with penal servitude and sent off to Jingkou Station. As before, the two men were forced to team up to meet and see off officials from the northern and southern docks. It was only right that freeloaders who depend on Tiger Hill should wind up like this. Even today when people talk about it, they still get a good laugh.

GENERAL COMMENTS

Suzhou freeloaders are frivolous and mean. Even though they belong to an interesting profession, they can be as harmful as a lizard. People know them for what they are and still allow themselves to be misled. Because of them, Tiger Hill is a tiger's lair.[38] How could it be worth the title of "famous mountain"? Aina has traveled to all the famous mountains and great rivers within the four seas, leaving a poem or writing a note about each one that sighs over their exceptional qualities. Why only at such an outstanding spot as Gusu [Suzhou] should he select this group of people so unworthy of consideration, try his hardest to find out about them, and be unrestrained in his efforts to joke about them? In addition to these freeloaders, all other forms of bad habits or scandalous actions, whether laughable or startling, pitiable or despicable—there is no end of detailed descriptions of them here.

If this gang of freeloaders were to read this story about themselves, they would grind their teeth in anger. Even so, there are deep meanings to be found hidden within Aina's words. Those who draw ghosts can provoke fear—those who set up pitfalls cause people to think of ways of avoiding them. One who knows about potential dangers will not be misled by them. If this group of people had no place where they could function, then they'd have no choice but to go straight and turn their deceptions into honesty. Then later visitors to Tiger Hill would instead have eminent knights and hermits to converse with and would be able to enjoy the snow and moon, the breeze and the blooms.[39] Then what would it matter if you were to wander Tiger Hill day after day!

Translated by Robert E. Hegel and Xu Yunjing

In Death, Commander Dang Beheads His Enemy

When the farmers celebrate the year, they always say, "Let there be autumn."[1] Why focus on this one word, "autumn"? During the spring when they plow and plant vegetables and wheat, what benefit can they get? By the fourth or fifth month, when it's time for summer weeding, if there are daily rains there will be rot in the fields and the major rivers will inundate the land, or if the heavens are clear and there is a severe drought and the sprouts and seeds dry up, then you may only get half a crop. But if you take advantage of the late summer to plant another crop of sprouts or rice seedlings, you can still hope that when autumn arrives, you'll have a crop. If by autumn the waters are still high and do not recede, or if the drought lingers and there is no rain, then the crops will break off at the roots and die, and there is no hope. Therefore, for prosperous years they emphasize only this word, "autumn."

Zhang Heyang's poem "Living among the Fields" says:

> The moving sun makes the noon pavilion hot;
> The dripping rain makes the bean blossoms cool.

Master Han Shan's poem "Farmer" says:

> As the purple clouds pile up, the rice grains fill;
> The white beans blossom as the geese and ducks hurry.[2]

Why is it that when talking about farming poetry, we regularly mention this kind of white bean? Because the white bean blossoms and produces beans at the same time. Now at this time, with the weather of early autumn, the rains have evened out, and you only have to look at the flourishing flowers on the bean arbor to know that this will be a year of rich harvests. Thus we can see that the appearance of this bean arbor is directly relevant to the harvest season.

At this time of the year, most of the farmers' work is already done. They only have to view their fields like clouds or brocade, and in a few days the phrases "may lowland crops fill the carts" and "abundantly they fill the households" will become reality.[3] Now everyone is sitting at leisure under the bean arbor, and your minds are all at ease. If the world were in turmoil and if the fields were nothing but random weeds and wild grasses, how could there possibly be a bean arbor? For the last several days, all of the stories told under this bean arbor have been idle talk of peace and contentment, so we can see that the world has enjoyed peace for a while now. These naive youths know nothing of the pain of home-lessness and the flames of war. So today let's invite back the old gent who told stories on other days and have him recount from the beginning his experience of those days of displacement and distress so that the youth may practice some skills at hand and cultivate some wisdom in their minds. That way, should a bad year turn into a time of chaos, they will still have something to rely on, something to support them.

Everyone said, "Right, right—let's go invite the old gent."

Now it so happened that the old gent was an elementary-school teacher and had been at the school for a long time without returning to the bean arbor. On this day he was taking advantage of the cool breeze to visit home.

Everyone asked him to come take a seat under the bean arbor, saying, "Our dear uncle has been away a long time, and we feel that the bean arbor has become a lonely place. Even though we've all told a few stories, they're nothing more than ordinary tales about things past and present. You, dear uncle, are much older, and we've heard that you've experienced much of the pain of the fighting and separations of war. We beg you to recount those previous events, and make us youngsters listen up, so that during this time of prosperity we won't dare trample our food grains or squander our health." The old gent began.

THE OLD GENTLEMAN'S TALE

If I speak of the situation of that time, it would scare you to death! I remember that in the forty-eighth year of the Wanli reign, Liaodong changed command.[4] The Taichang emperor died within a month, and the empire turned to the Tianqi emperor to take the throne, but he was still young and fool-ish and really knew nothing about the affairs of the world. He relied on the eunuch Wei Zhongxian to handle matters of recruiting soldiers and securing provisions for them, but Wei whittled the state treasury down to nothing.[5]

At that time the disruptions were still beyond the Shanhai Pass, and the lands within were still tranquil. Unexpectedly, the throne passed to the Chongzhen emperor, but his fate was worse than Tianqi's. As time passed, if it was not a multiyear drought, then it was floods—if it was not epidemics, then it was locusts covering the ground. He was also stingy by nature, and the inexperienced officials in charge of the Six Ministries branches at the provincial level didn't care at all about governing but only wanted to ingratiate themselves with their superiors. They presented an edict cutting funds for all the courier stations in the country.[6] This cut off the source of clothing for loafers and hoodlums, and so they then formed gangs and turned to banditry.

At first their numbers were small, and they just became mounted highwaymen who intercepted and cut off merchants, attacked villages, and plundered residences. Later, when higher officials found out and sent out cavalry and infantry to protect the land, these bandit gangs either gathered in the mountain forests or formed up in the marshes. At that time, if there had been a commander daring and clever enough to offer them amnesty, and if there had not been officials in court demanding that bribes be passed up through the chain of command and hamstringing his leadership, it would have been easy to eliminate them. Who would have expected the court to appoint Yuan Chonghuan as military commissioner of Liaodong at such a critical time for the empire?[7] Yuan had bragged to the court before this, saying that within five years he would achieve success and would live in the mansion of an esteemed official. Later, when the outcome was not as he'd hoped, he decided to make the first move and kill Commander Mao of Dongjiang.[8] When they heard the news that their commander in chief had been killed and that they had no one to rely on, his remaining thousand-plus troops who had gone to Shaanxi to buy horses rose up and rebelled when they were halfway there.

Hungry people gathered from all directions like clouds or fog and formed a powerful force. Whether to east or west, they didn't stop and so were called "roving bandits." At their head were several rebel leaders who were intelligent and pretended to be loyal and just who tricked ignorant people into joining them. Later, their strength was irresistible wherever they went.

The area of Shanxi is vast and extensive. Not only did every department, county, and prefecture lack troops and soldiers for defending themselves, but they also lacked precipitous mountains to serve as barriers, and so they lost cities and towns and had their cattle and horses stolen. No matter whether the offense was light or serious, the court sent secret police to capture the perpetrators and sentence and execute them without delay in accordance with the law. The officials in charge of protecting their area carefully weighed their alternatives—they had no choice but to submit to the roving bandits and become ringleaders in order to survive a little longer. Yet when the official troops arrived, what could they do?

At that time I happened to be walking down the road when I heard someone singing a borderland tune.[9] Then it was clear that all the people under heaven were crying out in anguish, as if they were being burned by fire. I hated that the heavens and the earth could not be overturned at once to fulfill their heartfelt hopes. His song went:

> Old man Heaven,
> You are getting old.
> Your ears are deaf and your eyes are blurry;
> You can't see people
> Nor hear their worries.
> Those who kill and burn enjoy splendor and glory,
> While those who read sutras just starve to death.
> Old man Heaven,
> If you can't be Heaven, then just cave in!
> If you can't be Heaven, then just cave in![10]

Strongmen arose everywhere, and although I can't recall all the factions, I can still remember their names and nicknames—the Big Fool (Liu Tong), Tiger Wang (Wang Guoquan), the Old Muslim (Ma Jinxiao), the Comet (Xu Shifu), the Dashing King (Gao Ruyue), the Dashing General (Li Zicheng), the Invincible (Yan Hong), the King Who Sweeps the Earth (Hui Dengxiang), the King Who Pacifies the World (He Jing), the Dashing Heaven Smasher (Han Guoji), the King Who Overturns Heaven (He Yilong), Muddling the Hundred Thousands (Liu Guolong), the Living King of Hell (Ma Shouying), the Golden Balance (Niu Chenghu), Tiger Who Pulls in the Oceans (Fan Shishou), Diamond's Rival (Xue Yougong), the Red Wolf (Liu Xiyao), the Tiger of Mount Ba (Li Yuan), Flying across the Plain (Xu Shibao), the Palace Rafters (Feng Jinxiao), Mother of Devils (Dong Guoxian), Eye in the Grass

(Sun Ren), Golden-Winged Bird (Wang Guoyao), Cao Cao (Luo Rucai), Nine Dragons (Guo Dacheng), a Peck of Grain (Sun Cheng'en), One-Footed Tiger (Liu Xingzi), Gold Money Leopard (Liu Fucheng), the Rough Zhang Fei (Yang Shiwei), a Chunk of Scorpions (Bai Guang'en), the Eighth Great King (Zhang Xianzhong), Prince Li (Li Yan), Heavenly King Deng (Deng Tingchen), the King of Hell's Nose (Liu Yue), Tiger in the Clouds (Zhang Degong), Third Monkey (Li Shao), Old Man in Charge (Kun Yikui).

Most of those strongmen had no cities, no local troops, and no military strongholds, so wherever the cavalry and infantry went, their families, old and young alike, simply followed them. Relying on armed force, the strongmen who stole the most donkeys and horses and rounded up the most youngsters became the leaders. Everyone over forty, both men and women, was killed. They spared only those between twelve and thirteen and between twenty-four and twenty-five or so, seeing them as valuable treasures. They swore brotherhood with them or declared them to be their sons. Why, you ask, didn't they want the older people? Because they had more years on them, and most had strong attachments to their families or their property, and the rebels worried that they would be disloyal.

They wanted only young men filled with the hot blood of youth and lacking all concern for themselves or their parents, and who knew nothing of right or wrong. In battle, the young men did not avoid the violence—even if cannon fire destroyed the entire front line, they'd swarm in from behind. When striking a well-fortified city, the young men would take scaling ladders, shields, long-handled hooks, and rope and climb up one by one. If the city didn't fall in one day, they'd attack the next day—if it didn't fall in ten days, they attacked ten more. During the day they'd take turns attacking, squad by squad. At night a group specialized in digging tunnels used burrowing equipment to tunnel from a *li* or two outside the city wall under the metal defenses and up into the city from all sides. Or they'd excavate one or two gaps, fill them with gunpowder, and then blow them up so that the city wall would collapse, and they'd all swarm into the city. Aside from the people they slaughtered inside the city, they'd spare the young men and lead them out of town.

At first, when they destroyed a city, they seized only money and women, but later the rebel leaders issued an order—if anyone took fifty ounces of silver or two women in addition to livestock, he'd be beheaded and his head would be impaled on a stake. The amount of treasure abandoned in these sacked cities was beyond counting. Some were greedy and couldn't help but secretly bury it, marking it clearly in hopes that later, in more peaceful days, they could dig it out and use it. Little did they know that they were going to die and have no chance to do so. And so it remained buried for a long time, its discovery left to individual luck.

As a result, the young men began to see money as being about as worthless as shit. All they wanted was to steal some food to eat, get some women, and create havoc. There were also the heartless ones, who amused themselves by taking a pregnant woman, gambling on whether there was a boy or a girl in her belly, and then cutting her open to see who was right. Some cut out people's hearts and lungs, strung them together, and smoke-dried them to eat as snacks with wine. There were also cruel forms of execution, like skinning people alive, gouging out their eyeballs, cutting off their noses, chopping off hands, and cutting off feet, even melting people. Who knows how many ways they had! One need only mention such scenes, and it causes people in times of great peace to remember the separation and the misery and to recall and regret all those events.

One day a traveling merchant was returning to the Huguang area along the road from Shaanxi and Henan. The travelers that he passed often had chopped-off noses or ears, or had both hands cut off, and seeing them made his blood run cold. Later he saw even more—they weren't rare. If there was someone who was even more badly injured, nobody would even believe it. For most people, if they were missing their ears, eyes, mouths, noses, hands, feet, or all four limbs, their wounds weren't fatal. It was only if the head had been chopped off that death would be instant, leaving no way of recovering.

In a small deserted village in the area of Luoyang County in Henan, a man happened to be riding into town when he encountered a violent storm. There was no place to take shelter, so he had to borrow the space under the eaves of a house to escape the rain for a while. But unexpectedly, the heavy rain came down in torrents and still had not stopped when evening came, so he was forced to beg boarding for the night in the person's home.

An old man came out and said, "My house is no bigger than a snail's shell—I dare not let you stay. You'll have to go on to the next village, about twenty or thirty *li* ahead. There's an inn there."

But with the sky getting darker, the man could not simply hurry along, and seeing that the old man's home had an empty side room that was closed off, he pleaded with him again. The old man said, "If the room were empty, there would be no problem with you staying there. But my younger brother is in there, and it wouldn't be convenient for you to stay with him."

The traveler said, "If it's only your honored brother, what would be inconvenient?"

The old man said, "It's a strange fate that you two should meet when you're in dire straits, but when you see him, don't be frightened."

The traveler said, "I've been traveling along the rivers and lakes for nearly twenty years. Whether you have an esteemed official or an honored guest, or an extremely fierce and evil person, I've certainly encountered their like before. What could I possibly be frightened of here in your home?" And he started to walk inside even before he'd finished speaking.

As they reached the side door, the old man gave it a light knock, and there was the sound of movement inside. He lifted the latch and pushed the door open with his other hand. The traveler followed the old man into the room, but when he raised his head to look, what should he see but a headless man standing at the left side of the door? When he saw this, he gave a loud shout, saying, "Oh no! Oh no! A ghost!" With his mouth still open, his two legs gave out, and he collapsed to the ground.

The old man immediately helped him up, saying, "I warned you in advance not to be afraid, and you insisted that you wouldn't be. Why are you suddenly so afraid now?"

The man just stood there blankly for a while and then asked, "What happened?"

The old man said, "Just sit and listen and I'll tell you." With one hand he pointed to the headless man and began.

My younger brother used to sell fabric for a living at Tongguan. The year before last he was being chased down the road home by some roving bandits, but when he was only thirty *li* from home, he was attacked by some local bandits who cut off his head with a knife, and he fell down on the ground. That night a bunch of wild dogs and wolves ate half of a corpse. They were going to eat my brother's corpse next, when his soul heard a voice at his ear, yelling, "Get out of here, beasts! The supervisor of the Meritorious Service Section hasn't inspected them yet. Why are you eating them already?"

After a short time, he saw several men and horses gathering around and checking off the names of the dead and wounded on the battleground. When the supervisor got to my brother, his name was not in the roster, so he checked another roster, and it turned out that my brother was listed as wounded but not dead and still had four years allotted to live.

The next day my brother came to his senses, and when he used his hand to feel his head, there was only a neck bone sticking out. That night I was still hiding out in the village, and I heard someone knocking on the door, and it was my brother's voice. Since there were also no lights in our deserted village, I could only help him into the room by his dark shadow. He then told me the whole story about how he had been injured in the other village. It was only in the daylight that I saw that he had no head. I had spent half the night talking with a headless man! At first I was also shocked, but I saw that his body was still warm, his arms and legs weren't stiff, and his throat made gurgling noises. I took some wheat porridge or rice gruel and spooned it in, and when he was almost full, the sound stopped. It's been like this for more than a year. Recently he learned how to weave mats. By doing this every day he can sell them for some money and support himself.

Once the traveler heard the man's clear explanation, he calmed down. And in the end, the one reason he wasn't drowsy after not sleeping all night was nothing other than the one word "fear." This was a marvel of a world in chaos—you couldn't say he was alive, nor could you say he was dead.[11]

Now I'll tell you another story of a person who was clearly dead but did the deeds of someone who was living. This story is set in the area of Ansai County in Yan'an Prefecture in Shaanxi, and the man's name was Dang Yiyuan. He had been upright and outspoken all his life, and in physical strength he surpassed other people. His family was also especially wealthy. Whenever ruffians or bullies did unjust or unlawful things in the area, he immediately eliminated them. If people were poor or going through difficult times, he'd provide resources to help them. Villagers near and far were all grateful for his generosity. Within a year or two, everyone everywhere admired his reputation, claiming it to be no less than that of Great Lord Chai Jin of Taiping Manor or Headquarters Clerk Song Jiang of Yuncheng County.[12]

At this time the roving bandits were not yet so widespread, and when the headmen of departments and counties heard warnings about bandits, the local gentry all recruited their farmhands, arranged monthly provisions of grain and weapons, and came up with a plan to defend themselves. The authorities also feared that there would be some unruly men among the people who would take advantage of the opportunity to stir up trouble, so they sent out an order that all areas where rebels were becoming active would have to pick people with both strength and wisdom to be installed as commander at the level of the cities and commanderies, as military training commissioner at the level of counties and departments, and as post commandant at the level of town forts and market strongholds, each to be elected publicly. If their talent and ability weren't sufficient, then they should not dare to accept the commission.

Although the orders of the imperial court were strict at that time, public morals were corrupted and weak. Some career-oriented officials wanted to squander resources that average people, who had no career prospects, could not even dream of. Yet when the time came to elect militia leaders, those same people became just like genuine officials. At that time justice was with the people—with one voice, gentry and the local headmen recommended Dang Yiyuan for the post. The official document was submitted to the superiors, and the authorities immediately sent down his commission. Dang Yiyuan then took up his post, and the matters of city defense and preparing equipment were all done appropriately. But that's not part of my story.

Instead I'll tell about a military training commissioner in Qingjian County of Yan'an Prefecture whose name was Nan Zhengzhong, the son of a very wealthy local gentry family. Throughout the county his family was considered an influential one. On ordinary days he especially liked to practice with his staff and spear and pretend to act with benevolence and justice. But by nature he was lustful, and when he saw that a family had a beautiful daughter, he was beside himself and simply had to get her in his clutches, regardless of the cost.

So how was a man of this character elected as militia commander? This happened because in peaceful times he had enjoyed becoming acquainted with the layabouts at the marketplace. If there was the slightest injustice in one of the local towns, they'd band together in a large group and stir up heaven and earth, stopping only when it suited them. For this reason everyone in the area, whether big or small, feared him, and behind his back they gave him the nickname "Playboy Jupiter."[13] Aside from Nan, no one else dared aspire to the post of militia commander.

One day he commanded people to sweep the martial arts hall outside the town and picked a day for training the manor's farmhands. Very early they prepared bright flags, sharp swords, and spears, and with horns blaring and drums beating, they lined up in neat formations to welcome him to the training grounds. The villagers had never seen anything like this before, and some who lived in the market had invited relatives over to stay with them and hung curtains in the doorways so they could enjoy watching the soldiers training.

From horseback, Commander Nan looked up suddenly and saw through a curtain a woman as delicate as a flower and as refined as precious jade.

He immediately reined in his horse and said deliberately, "Why are the troops in the front rank so sparse?" and hurriedly called for a clerk from the barracks to bring him the roster to examine. He ordered local headmen to quickly prepare a folding screen and a table and chair and set them up neatly facing the curtain. When all this had been arranged, he dismounted, sat down, and ordered the clerk to call the roll. That commander had one eye trained like an arrow on the inside of the curtain and went through a variety of flirtatious mannerisms and poses. Ultimately he wasted most of the day before he finally entered the training grounds, and even then, he only went through the motions before returning to the yamen.

Commander Nan dreamed about the girl all night long, but he could not think of a way forward. He had an orderly in his service named Li the Third, whose nickname was "Iron-Eating Worm." Knowing what was on his commander's mind, Li the Third picked two roses and purposefully walked up to him, saying, "I happened to pick these at the home of retired official Zhang on the street just ahead—one flower to present to you, sir, and one to present to the mistress."

The commander asked, "How is one rose enough for three or four mistresses?"

Li the Third said, "You can't get many flowers of this kind. You'll just have to give it to the one mistress who pleases you best, sir!"

The commander said, "Who do I have that pleases me? Yesterday I saw a woman who pleases me perfectly, but it would be hard to obtain her."

Li the Third pretended not to know what he meant and asked, "Where does she live?"

The commander told him the location of the woman behind the curtain. Li the Third said, "I know who she is. She is Ms. Dang, the wife of the county schoolteacher, Master Zhu Bofu, and she is Commander Dang's younger sister. How could you possibly get your hands on her?"

The commander said, "Come up with a plan for me, and you'll be handsomely rewarded!"

Li the Third, greedy for such a reward, schemed and planned, and after thinking for a moment, he said, "Let me have three days, and I'll get back to you."

The commander laughed happily, saying, "My heart is like an ant on a hot stove—you must get back to me later today!"

Li the Third agreed and promptly walked out of the residence.

He asked around and found out that Zhu Bofu was by nature fond of drinking and gambling, so he brought several strings of cash and, upon finding the place, gambled with him. He squandered the cash freely on purpose, so that he could entice Zhu into going with him to see the commander. This kind of back and forth went on for three days.

Then, just as the commander could no longer bear his desire for the girl, Li the Third came in and whispered in his ear about this and that. As soon as Commander Nan saw that Zhu Bofu was nothing more than a drinker with no sense of caution, he kept him for tea and flattered him repeatedly, saying, "My home has been lacking an 'honored guest.'" He immediately prepared a proper invitation for that very day. That afternoon he arranged for a luxurious wine feast, and they drank their fill all the way to the fifth watch at dawn the next day. Zhu Bofu was totally delighted, and the next day he sent an invitation to a return banquet via Li the Third.

After having stayed for three or four days, Zhu Bofu wanted to return home to let his family know and arrange for basic foodstuffs for the home. The commander said, "I know that you, Elder Brother, have a family to worry about, so I've already dispatched someone to send food to your home. If you won't hold my military background against me, then today, you, dear Elder Brother, and I can swear brotherhood, and upon paying respects as elder and younger brother, your wife could be invited to stay here with us. Wouldn't that be most convenient for both of us?"

Now being a muddle-headed drunk, Zhu Bofu immediately agreed and asked Li the Third to go to his home to inform his wife.

The woman replied, "The other day from the doorway I saw the commander moving about frivolously, and I'm afraid that going to stay at his residence would be inappropriate. It would be better for me to stay in the spare room of some relatives in the city, to be near his residence."

Li the Third saw that she spoke as if she knew much of what was going on, and he realized that if he pressed too hard she would not even consent to enter the city, which would ruin the whole affair. He could only mumble his agreement. So he prepared a cart with the basic necessities and sent her off to the city to stay with her relatives.

Seeing that things were working out, the commander was greatly relieved and immediately went with Zhu Bofu to visit Ms. Dang and invite her. He said that because they were family now, sworn brother and sister-in-law, they must come and see him. Zhu Bofu also urged his wife to come out and meet him. The commander pretended to be completely sincere and respectful, and Ms. Dang unknowingly fell into his trap and agreed to move into his residence. It goes without saying that everything they needed was supplied and provided. When flirtatious glances quickly came her way, Ms. Dang paid them no mind.

After several days, Li the Third sent for his wife to bring over some wine and snacks. She pretended she just was coming for a visit, but during the eating and drinking, she let slip mention of Commander Nan's romantic feelings. Ms. Dang listened quite impatiently but didn't say a word. Li the Third's wife just thought that the woman was tacitly in agreement, and, taking advantage of her own intoxication, she told the woman all about the commander's intention to set a trap by having her move in. She pulled out a gold-inlaid jasper hairpin and a white jade joined-hearts knot from the inside of her sleeve and handed them to Ms. Dang.

Ms. Dang knew in her heart that this was a plot, but she didn't refuse them and instead kept them at hand to serve as evidence. She called her husband over to discuss leaving at once, but unfortunately Zhu Bofu's mouth had been filled with sweets, and he believed wholeheartedly that the commander was a good man. So he scolded his wife instead, saying she was being unfair and stupid and was only causing problems. Ms. Dang had nowhere to turn and all she could do was write a letter to her elder brother, Commander Dang, letting him know everything that had happened.

When Commander Dang read the letter he was so furious that his hair stood on end, and he thought to himself, "In three days the new governor-general takes his post. Commander Nan and I will have to meet there in person to welcome him." Taking advantage of this opportunity, he gave secret orders to ten companions, who headed out on mules and horses.

The distance was less than two hundred or so *li*. They arrived in great haste and entered the gate of the Nan household. The gate guard could not stop them, and so they went straight into the flower garden where they helped Ms. Dang onto a horse. The tippler Zhu Bofu was still in a drunken stupor, so they paid him no mind and walked right out the door. The house staff immediately sent someone to report this to Commander Nan, who was at the pavilion designated for greeting officials. At once he began to shout at Commander Dang.

While their fellow officials were trying to calm them down, Li the Third took a horse and rushed to the Dang residence to inquire about Ms. Dang's whereabouts. Commander Nan didn't return home but instead gathered two or three hundred strong men and unexpectedly went to Commander Dang's residence, snatched the woman, and left.

Commander Dang heard about this on the road, and even though he had not brought many troops with him, he immediately set out in pursuit. After traveling a hundred *li*, he caught up with Commander Nan on a narrow road, and fighting erupted. Now Commander Dang's courage surpassed that of other men, and he managed to wound many of Nan's troops. Commander Nan had no mind to challenge him to a battle, so he simply fled first, taking the woman with him. The woman saw that she had fallen back into the hands of a bandit, so she let her hair down and acted crazy, cursing and scolding without end. As they turned toward a dangerous and precipitous mountain slope, she jerked her body violently this way and that, and the horse suddenly reared. Commander Nan loosened his grip a bit, and the woman fell over the cliff. How lamentable to see a woman as delicate as a flower and as refined as precious jade all smashed and broken! Commander Nan regretted it deeply.

Commander Dang knew that his sister had died protecting her chastity, and on the day appointed for the governor-general's office to review lawsuits, he wrote up a complaint and filed it jointly with Zhu Bofu. The governor saw the details of the case and slapped the table in fury. He immediately sent eight imperial agents with a warrant to find and arrest Commander Nan.

Now Commander Nan surmised that his sins were heavy, that his opponent was also very fierce, and that he would not be able to straighten this out later. Since he was used to acting like a bully and a strongman and had always had a rebellious heart, these various pressures left him with no other alternative. Beside him, that Iron-Eating Worm Li the Third encouraged him wholeheartedly. He brought up the idea, saying, "Let's rebel!" The troops under his command, like tigers and wolves, all roared their agreement.

First they killed the county magistrate, plundered the storehouse, and burned down the city gate. Whenever they encountered anyone on the road, they just killed him, and many who feared being killed simply joined them. The governor-general soon learned of this and ordered infantry and cavalry mustered up and sent out. He promoted Commander Dang to regional military commissioner and put him in command of two thousand troops with orders to advance on and destroy the rebels.

In a little over over ten days, Commander Nan had assembled six or seven thousand men and horses, but although his men were numerous, the majority were actually refugees. During the day they set about plundering, but at night they feared the army might be catching up to them. Because they couldn't sleep day or night, they were all exhausted. How could they possibly face Commissioner Dang's fierce, brave advance? But there were also well-trained soldiers and cavalry in Dang's command, and they set off together along small roads.

When the two sides met, there was heavy fighting, with 60 to 70 percent of Commander Nan's troops and cavalry killed. Wounded and soundly defeated, he ordered his remaining troops to retreat deep into the mountains to hide, where they went hungry for seven whole days.

Who would have thought that when Li the Third rose in rebellion he would first raid the county's military supplies, stealing many mules and horses? These he took with him as his personal property and went to throw in his lot at the encampment of the roving bandit Old Muslim. When he heard that Commander Nan had been defeated by government troops and was hiding in the mountains, he immediately requested that five thousand members of the bandit gang move out and relieve him. When Commander Nan received the reinforcements who broke the tight siege, he went over to the rebel camp, where he became a forward commander.

Commissioner Dang had achieved a huge victory, and the governor-general was extremely pleased. As they were resting, there was a report that rebel troops had already reached their boundaries, so the commissioner put his armor back on and led his troops to meet the enemy. He saw that there were only a little more than a thousand rebel troops out in front enticing him into battle. Commissioner Dang didn't realize it was a trap and pursued them with all his strength. As they turned toward a place deep in the woods, they found that all four sides were filled with chopped-down tree branches, which blocked the way out, so he desperately turned his army around, but rebel troops were coming at him from everywhere, as far as the eye could see. Relying on his manly might, Commissioner Dang dashed left and broke through on the right, resisted on the east and held off on the west. But even though he killed many men, fighting from mid-morning until early evening, in the end even his strength had limits.

While they were fighting at close quarters in a mountain cleft, his horse's hoof slipped, and he fell off a cliff. From out of the thick grass, enemy soldiers reached out for him with restraining hooks on poles. They tied up Commissioner Dang and took him away, escorting him to the camp, where the Old Muslim had just entered his tent. From a distance he saw Commissioner Dang being escorted in. Immediately he stepped down from his seat and personally untied his bonds, exclaiming loudly, "Elder Brother! Please forgive your younger brother!"

Now Commissioner Dang was naturally loyal and violent. With fury in his eyes he bared his teeth and cursed the Old Muslim loudly, saying, "Rebel! Traitor! What did the dynasty ever do to you, that you should rebel like this? Worse yet, why give protection to this lecherous thief and, for no reason at all, wreak havoc all around? The great army will exterminate you in a matter of days—you don't even realize your death awaits!" And he clenched his fists, ready to fight, but was pinned down by runners who came forward from both sides. Commissioner Dang gave a twist and knocked down several of them with his elbow.

Alarmed, the Old Muslim said, "Men, tie him up for me as before. Send him to the flaying pavilion, and have Commander Nan take good care of him."

To Commander Nan, hearing these words was like receiving an imperial edict. He changed into a red robe and ordered his servants to put his camp chair in place. Two groups of jailers shouted loudly for the court to convene, and they led Commissioner Dang into the camp. There they wanted him to kneel, but Commissioner Dang straightened his back and cursed them continuously.

Commander Nan swaggered in, looking completely pleased with himself, and came forward to scold him. Commissioner Dang bit off his own tongue, chewed it into pieces, and spat them at Commander Nan's face. Commander Nan covered his face and went back to his seat, cursing him, saying, "You're so fierce in nature, but today even if you had wings, you could not escape, so you'll just have to accept my grinding and breaking!" But before he had finished speaking, Commissioner Dang's last breath caught in his throat, his anger not yet relieved.

The men reported, "Commissioner Dang is already dead. His hands and feet are like ice." Commander Nan walked forward slowly and examined and touched him all over, and sure enough, he was dead. He immediately called his attendants to prepare several tables for a wine feast and invited many of his comrades to drink toasts of victory to their hearts' content. At the same time, he called for someone to capture the horse that Dang had ridden and lead it over. He had them place the corpse astride the horse and then stuck Dang's goose-feather sword into his bosom. And then the great horns and drums began to play.

With a wine cup in his hand, Commander Nan walked toward Commissioner Dang's corpse and cursed him, saying, "Bandit Dang, Bandit Dang, where is your heroism of the past? Today you have died at my hands!" He threw the wine in Dang's face and turned back to take his seat. But though his mouth was speaking, his mind was not on guard. Suddenly, Dang's horse leaped up and tossed his mane with a loud neigh. Commissioner Dang's eyebrows stood straight up, and he grasped the sword with one hand and pulled it out of his bosom.

Everybody on both sides cried out, "Commissioner Dang is alive! Commissioner Dang is alive!"

Commander Nan quickly turned his head to look, but that snow-white sword tip moved up in a flash, and before anyone realized it, Commander Nan's head had fallen to the ground. Everyone was shocked. Commissioner Dang's rigid corpse then fell forward onto the ground.

The horse suddenly sprang to its feet and dashed out through the gate of the camp just as Li the Third was riding his horse back in. Facing him straight on, the horse seized Li the Third with its teeth, flipped him to the ground, and kicked him in the heart several times. Seeing that Li the Third was dead, the horse reared several times and dropped dead as well.

Everyone exclaimed, "The spirit of a loyal subject and a righteous minister doesn't change, even in death. We said he was dead, but he could still take revenge on his enemy as a heroic spirit. This man was much more determined than those who just die and turn into malicious ghosts to kill rebels."

When the Old Muslim saw that this heroic spirit was so fierce, he immediately withdrew his soldiers and left. Now that the world is at peace and tranquil, Commissioner Dang's spirit has manifested itself over and over again, so that to this day the burning of incense in his shrine never ceases.

I started out by telling of a living person being dead—this story was about a dead man being alive. We can see that in a chaotic and desolate world, strange events are especially plentiful. By now those who witnessed that chaotic world have all been killed, and those still alive have never seen it. So it has been buried, and no one speaks of it. Only I, with just a few breaths left in me, can still talk idly about it here under the bean arbor. This is not just by chance. Gentlemen, take advantage of these tranquil times, and hasten to cultivate your virtues!

As they all finished listening, each sighed fearfully and dispersed.

General Comments

If people are able to be vigilant in times of peace, and live in an ordered society that defends against chaos, then even if changes bring unforeseen events one day, they won't be taken by surprise and find themselves with no support. During the Ming period the roving bandits were savage, and livers and brains littered the ground. If you haven't personally experienced these feelings of suffering and misery and such fantastic and terrifying circumstances, you ought not to talk about them casually.

As for promiscuity and lust and loyalty and righteousness, in the end each had its own karmic result. Commander Nan plotted rebellion because he indulged in lust, and Commissioner Dang was captured as a result of a bloody battle, and in their cases, evil and uprightness are clearly distinguished. Commissioner Dang never thought when the two enemies met on a narrow road that he'd fall into the hands of his enemy. To satisfy his ambitions, the petty villain Commander Nan wanted to get revenge through his pursuit of new pleasures. But who knew that Commissioner Dang's spirit would flicker on and use his dead body at that moment to proclaim Commander Nan's sins, then rise up after making a living head die? This was Heaven rewarding the loyal and punishing the evil. Heaven is indeed extremely accurate! From this story we know that the world is full of strange occurrences, but people are like the frog in a well.[14] This detailed narrative will surely open the world's deaf ears and blind eyes!

Translated by Lindsey Waldrop

In Detail, Rector Chen Discourses on the Cosmos

As for the affairs of this world, big or small, if you don't want people knowing your business, then just don't do it. It is just like the pods growing on the bean arbor—sooner or later, people will pick some to eat, and they'll sell some to other people, in large amounts or small. Since bean arbors don't need much labor or space, farm families can earn a little income from the beans, even if it doesn't add up to much. Yet because nobody had planted them in the past, no one realized that they could build a bean arbor to escape from the summer heat in its cool shade, and that it would attract people to gather there for idle gossip. Once this particular bean arbor was erected and a good number of stories had been told here, listeners spread word of it in all directions, so that it gradually began to draw crowds in the afternoons. Nor did they diminish, any more than do the crowds around the storytellers' tables in the courtyards of shrines and temples.

Yesterday the old gent told of a headless man who could still weave mats and a dead man who was able to kill another fellow, stories that all the listeners felt were as weird as they could be. After we went home to bed, we saw in our dreams many who were dead or wounded in battle, or bared fangs and slashing claws, or who bore cudgels and spears, with no place to hide from them. When we woke up, our hearts pounding with alarm, the thought of listening to the storytellers again was even stronger than in days past. This is how most of the people under the bean arbor felt today.

No one would have thought that word of this storytelling would travel so far. But unexpectedly, word of it did reach the ears of a certain person in the city, and as soon as he heard that someone was telling stories here, outside the city, he slipped on his scholar's robe, donned his square cap, and traveled all this way until he reached a nearby village to ask about it. But what he'd originally heard was not quite right, because he didn't ask about stories from the bean arbor. Instead he mistakenly asked about "Brother Dou" who was telling stories in the village, saying that he'd come especially to "beg for instruction" from this person.[1] He asked in nearby villages west and east of the city, but no one knew anything about this Mr. Dou. Then he asked in front of this village and behind it, until one person laughed at him and said, "Your Honor got it all wrong. There's no 'Brother Dou' here who can tell stories. But in our village they happened to put up a bean arbor where a few friends who have some spare time get together to gossip and tell tales about things old and new. These are just things seen or heard that you might learn about in a country school, nothing worthy of sullying your refined ears."

Then that fellow began to laugh as well, saying, "'Twas indeed a grand misapprehension!" Thereupon he walked into the village, where, sure enough, he did see a number of people sitting under a bean arbor and squeezed himself right in among them.

When one of the people sitting there saw this person squeezing under the arbor, he got up and nudged another man and, with his mouth close to the man's ear, said, "This old fellow is a Confucian rector who lives in the city. His name is Chen Gang (Unbending Chen) , his informal name is Wuyu (No Desires), and his nickname is Chen Wugui (No Ghosts Chen).[2] He has a rigid and conservative disposition, and he's biased and obstinate in everything he says. He's already more than fifty, and he's read every book in existence. I've heard him lecture back and forth about all the principles of Heaven and Earth, his words flowing like a waterfall, with no letting up.[3] There's not a soul in the whole country who could beat him in a debate. I wonder what could have dragged him out here to our village?"

He had not yet finished speaking when the rector saluted everyone and began to talk. "I've heard that a brother of considerable learning has been lecturing hereabouts on the principles behind events past and present. With no concern for the distance, I've come here to humbly beg his instruction."

The audience all looked at one another, without the slightest inkling of where he had gotten that idea. Only the old fellow who had told the story yesterday said, "We humble folk have taken advantage of the cool breezes to share a little idle talk, but these were just things we've seen and heard, things that happened along the roads—nothing to do with classics or histories or any kind of moral principles—just such things as can be found in those 'tracts for reforming the world.'[4] Luckily it's still early in the day, and so our friends haven't made a crowd yet. We had no notice that you'd be coming, sir, so if we took the liberty of telling some nonsense here, I fear that we might insult Your Honor's ears or even make you so amazed that you might spit out your early morning breakfast."

"Be not so apologetic, my good sir," Rector Chen said. "I came not to meddle in your affairs. Because the Confucian Way is in decline, and the Neo-Confucian School of Principle is daily becoming more obscure, I realized that if I cannot personally expound upon the Way of Yao, Shun, Wen, and Wu before the imperial court, nor transmit the essence of the Way of Zhou, the Chengs, Zhang, and Zhu to my own associates,[5] then I would be allowing heretical teachings to run wild, human hearts to be corrupted, and the age-old school of the True Teachings to disappear without a trace!"

"Today we are blessed by your presence, Your Honor," the old gentleman said. "This is truly the chance meeting of a lifetime. If you, sir, don't disdain this old, dried-up arbor, please ascend our head seat and bestow a lesson or two upon us to remove the mental obstacles of this crowd. Given your abundant compassion for the world, Your Honor, surely you wouldn't begrudge us your teachings."

Hearing the old man speak in this manner, as quick as if irritated by a rash or a boil, the rector said with the next breath, "How could I rightly be 'disputatious' on this matter?[6] Indeed, I must do so." Saluting the crowd, he went over and sat down on the central chair, saying, "Where should I begin, good sir?"

"How about beginning with before there was a Heaven and an Earth?" replied the crowd.

THE RECTOR'S LECTURE

Before there was a Heaven and an Earth, in the midst of the Infinite Great Vacuity there was an Energy (Qi), all confused, which then became the Limitless. The Energy of Emptiness of the Limitless was none other than the Energy of Principle of the Great Ultimate, and the Energy of Principle of the Great Ultimate was the root of Heaven and Earth.[7] The root of Heaven and Earth transformed and gave birth to people and things, all of which in the beginning belonged to Creation. Once they had been given life, those beings that were created became fewer, and those that were physically born became more numerous. It is like worms that are born in wood and lice that are born on the human body—these things are given life by the process of creation. If there were no sweat energy on the human body, or decay energy in wood, what could their origin be? Thus the Great Ultimate's Energy of Principle is the origin of Heaven and Earth.

But perhaps what I have said is not yet clear. Bring me a sheet of paper, and I will draw a diagram for you all to look at.

At that, some of the fun-loving young men went to fetch a writing brush, others to borrow an inkstone. They placed them neatly on the table. The rector took a sheet of paper and drew a diagram, which he showed to the crowd.

An illustration of when Heaven and Earth first separated.

When the Great Ultimate separated, the Yang Energy was light and pure, and it circled all around the outside.

Rector Chen's first diagram, from Aina, *Doupeng xianhua, Zhaoshi bei*, 155.

The Yin Energy was heavy and turgid, and it concentrated in the middle.

All around is Empty Energy.

The crowd asked, "How did the Energy of the Principle of the Great Ultimate come to include Yin and Yang, sun and moon, and stars and constellations?"

The essence of Yang is the sun, and the essence of Yin is the moon. The stars float across the heavens, to gather into the images of constellations. Yin Energy condensed in the center and became Earth. The Five Agents and the Ten Thousand Things are all borne by Earth, and they gather into forms.[8] Think of the breath in a person's nose as an example. What is exhaled rises and is warm—thus it belongs to the Yang. What is inhaled is constricted and is cold—thus it belongs to the Yin. Yin condenses in the middle, and thus mud congeals in water, thereby completing the Five Agents. Yang floats away to cover the outside, swirling high and low, its form like that of a chicken's egg. Earth is the yolk—it precipitates into the center and does not move. Heaven is like the egg white—it moves around the outside without ceasing. The movements of Heaven are constant and strong.[9] They never pause for even a moment.

Spring, Summer, Autumn, and Winter, wind and clouds, thunder and rain, and humanity and things all transform and are transformed, give birth and are born by following the movements of Energy—all happen naturally, and the world is thereby rendered complete. When the refined Energy of Heaven and Earth overflows in its completeness, it produces of itself a Sage who will assist Creation with what is not yet complete. Thus the saying "The Sage makes a Great Triad with Heaven and Earth" refers precisely to this. But perhaps this is not yet clear. Allow me to draw another diagram for you to examine.

An illustration of Heaven's Clarity and Earth's Turbidity. All around is Energy.

Wherever the sun reaches, there is time. Then the sun reaches the zenith, then it is noon. The other times occur in similar fashion.

Rector Chen's second diagram, from Aina, *Doupeng xianhua, Zhaoshi bei*, 156.

When Heaven embraces Earth and spins to the left, there is north and south, but there is no east or west, or up or down.

Sun is the ultimate manifestation of Yang. When it reaches the precise center of *zi*, then the sun begins to ascend, as do all the Yang Energies, and so this [half of the day] belongs to Yang. When it reaches the precise center of *wu*, the sun begins to decline. Then the Yang Energies all decline, and the Yin Energies rise, and so this [half of the day] belongs to Yin.[10]

The crowd asked, "If the body of Heaven is all light and pure, where is the Great Jade Emperor? Likewise, if the body of the Earth is heavy and turgid, where are King Yanluo and the Prison of the Ghosts?"

The body of Heaven is light and pure, but it moves from hour to hour. How could it admit any thing? If things are not admitted, how could it admit the gods to abide there? When morning is on the top, night must gradually revolve around to the bottom in accordance with the sequence of the hours. When night is at the bottom, morning must gradually revolve around to the top in accordance with the sequence of hours. If in fact the Jade Emperor and other gods were in Heaven, they, too, would have to revolve around in accordance with the sequence of time. How could the gods do otherwise? Even though the body of the Earth is very thick, below its surface are water and mud and dirt and rocks, layer upon layer, all piled up on top of each other. If there were a King Yanluo and a Prison for Ghosts, they, too, would have to be there in the midst of the water, the mud, the dirt, and the rocks. How could they be elsewhere?

Interruption from the crowd: "You say that the Sage stands together with Heaven and Earth to make a Triad, and that if Heaven and Earth exist, then the Sage must continually exist as well. So how could such sages as Emperor Fuxi, Yao, Shun, and Confucius all pass away with the passage of time?"

Before the Sage was born, this Principle and this Energy existed in Heaven and Earth. Once the Sage was born, this Principle and this Energy exist in the Sage. Even though a Sage may grow old and die, that morality, those teachings, are passed on for ten thousand generations to come, enduring as long as Heaven and Earth themselves. Thus even though the body of the Sage may pass away, that Principle and that Dao are returned to Heaven and Earth as before. Heaven and Earth endure forever. So, too, does the Sage.

Interruption from the crowd, "Since Confucius was a Sage and yet went to beg instruction from the Old Lord of the Most High, might this be because he feared death?"

Laozi was a petty man who was covetous of life. In his teachings he placed value on emptiness, nonbeing, and the yielding.[11] Consider how he trained his disciples—"Observe my tongue: Does the existence of my tongue not depend on its yielding? Observe my teeth: Is losing my teeth not because of their being hard?" Of the things that have been produced by Heaven and Earth, what ought to be hard is naturally hard and what ought to be yielding is naturally yielding. If we were to cause the teeth in a man's mouth to be as soft and yielding as his tongue, then he could not even eat his rice. How could he live long in this world? Like the metals that come in five colors—there is yellow gold, white silver, black iron, and copper and tin. If we were to say that it is the nature of gold and silver to be yielding and valuable, then gold and silver would be good only for beating into ornaments, utensils, objects for amusement, and the like. But iron is hard and can be used for plows, and thus we have grains to eat to preserve our lives. Used in the kitchen, it serves in cooking and chopping. Used by soldiers, it can pacify the people and prevent thievery. There are too many others to mention, but in summary, the usefulness of metals depends on their hardness.

In man's covetousness of sex he inevitably feels fondness because of the woman's yielding. In his covetousness of wealth, he covers up his contrivances by being yielding. Petty people inevitably are those who are yielding in order to pursue profit and avoid harm. If a woman were to be unyielding by nature, who would dare to flirt with her? If she had a fiery temper, who would dare to play around with her? In Fuxi's classic, the principles of change emphasize the word "hard," but Laozi spoke of "yielding," demonstrating that he had scorned the Sagely classic and the Way of Heaven. Furthermore, human life does not exceed one hundred years, and yet Laozi was covetous of living more than a hundred. Likewise he wanted his Yang essence not to decline and thus stole the Energy of Creation.[12] Thus his placing high value on Emptiness and Nonbeing was in fact his covetousness of Being. His placing high value on the yielding was in fact his desire to surmount the hard. Is this not greatly contrary to the Orthodox Principle of Heaven and Earth?

Through my research, I have learned that Laozi was born at the end of the Zhou period in a place that is now Lingbao County in Henan Prefecture. His father, a poor man from the countryside, was named Guang. He worked as a hired hand for a wealthy family in his youth, but even after he reached the age of seventy, he had not married. Laozi's mother was likewise an uneducated country woman who had not yet married, although she was over forty. By chance they had an illicit coupling in the mountains and obtained the Numinous Energy of Heaven and Earth. She was pregnant for eighty months. Disgusted that she had been pregnant for so long, her master would no longer tolerate her in the household. With no alternative, she walked over to a large plum tree on a broad plain, where she gave birth to a son with white hair and white eyebrows. Because his mother did not know what Guang's family name was, she took the name of the tree, *li* (plum), as his surname. When she saw how big his ears were, she named him Li Er ("Ears" Li). When other people saw his white hair, they called him Laozi, "the Old Guy." When he grew up, he managed the library for the Zhou king as a petty official. Thus he came to know a great deal about ancient events and ancient rituals.

This is why Confucius came to ask about rituals and offices. In his old age Laozi perceived that the Zhou was about to descend into chaos, so he mounted his black ox and headed west through the Hangu Pass. There he encountered the commandant in charge of the pass named Xi, who treated the old man as his teacher. Thus Laozi wrote out the five thousand words of the *Daode jing* at Zhouzhi County in Qinchuan. Thereafter he died in that place, and his tomb mound was raised there. This is the beginning and the end of Laozi. During his lifetime, he was not able to rescue the Zhou royal house from chaos, nor did he leave the slightest benefit for the world. How could it be that upon his death he would return to Heaven to become one of the Three Purities?

Another interruption from the crowd, "How about the teachings of the Buddha that came from the West?"

The Buddha, too, was a petty man who coveted long life. In his teachings he placed high value on emptiness and maintained that people should abandon and ignore all the affairs of the worldly life. Furthermore, he wanted to cut off and extinguish all thought, leaving the mind forever empty with no sense of self. To render eyes and ears forever empty, one must extinguish all that one sees and hears with eyes and ears. One must control one's mouth, body, hands, feet—the whole Yin-Yang form—so that they are still, causing one's entire being to be empty. He strives for making the Essence (Jing), the Breath (Qi), and the Spirit (Shen) complete, to form one unity, in order that one's natural disposition and consciousness should not perish but constantly exist in the world.[13] Because in his heart he was covetous of life and Being, he takes the True Emptiness to complete his true reality. He steals the spiritual essence of Heaven and Earth and is unwilling to return it to Heaven and Earth. Thus he is the greatest thief between Heaven and Earth. How could he claim that this is True Emptiness?

My research reveals that before the Buddha was born, his mother dreamed of a white elephant entering her body, and from this moment she was pregnant. He grew bigger day by day until her belly could no longer hold him. When he was born, he split his mother's belly—she died as he was being born. Because this anomalous man would bring chaos to the universe, he began by killing his mother.[14] All the foul things of this world—owls, scorpions, and poisonous snakes—can be born only when their mothers die. Why should the birth of the Buddha be like that of those foul creatures? People of the world fast and carry out ritual purifications and in a hundred ways pray for good fortune for their mothers because we cause harm to our mothers at birth, yet this Buddha did not protect his own mother. How could he then turn around and protect other people's mothers?!

My research has further revealed that as the prince of an Indian state in the Western Regions, he had a beautiful wife and a beautiful concubine, and he was called a "bodhisattva." He had treasures of all kinds, but even though his state was prosperous, its influence was weak, its area being small. All the surrounding states were strong and fierce and frequently invaded his state. The army and cavalry of the Buddha's state were weak and few, unable to withstand the enemy. Consequently, he abandoned his country and fled. With no alternative, he could only propose a theory of self-cultivation and love of virtue. He also established theories about the Four Types of Births and the Six Paths of rebirth, retribution, and transmigration in order to make fools of the neighboring states. His ideas could be stated simply, "You lot have slaughtered my people, stolen our goods. In future lives you will be changed into dogs and horses to repay us for our losses."

As a consequence, within twelve years the neighboring states had all become foolishly misled, and Buddha returned to his state to rejoin his wife and children. His state regained its prosperity, with later generations living in security. By using a wise strategy to propagate True Emptiness, he attained considerable concrete advantage instead. He did not originally convert our China by using strategy. It was only because the teachings of China's sages were not working, and people were being overcome by their desires, that their deluded minds won out.[15] They dared not seek clarification of moral principles from Yao, Shun, the Duke of Zhou, or Confucius—they simply begged for blessings from the Buddha. The Sages taught people to be without desires and taught men to distance themselves from ghosts and gods in order to fulfill the dictates of the Way of Humanity. The Buddha was concerned only about himself and put out of mind all the states under Heaven, thinking of them all as a sea of suffering, totally beyond consideration. What he took as True Emptiness was in fact things that could not be empty. He misled people into being covetous of desires—he misled people into wild pursuits and turning away from the proper Way of Humanity. All this is a result of his single-minded pursuit of Emptiness.

One among the crowd said, "The Four Great Elements are all empty, the Yang spirit does not decline, the theories of neither the Buddha nor Laozi are concerned about anything other than the preservation of our True Nature, which will lead to a long, eternal life.[16] This is also the Orthodox Principle of Heaven and Man. Why is Your Honor so biased against them in what you say?"

Laozi coveted life and lived to be more than a hundred, and yet he also desired that his Yang spirit would not be extinguished.[17] The Buddha coveted life, but he lived only sixty-three years and still wanted his True Nature to exist forever. The lifetimes of people in this world are all fixed, and yet the Buddha and Laozi alone wanted longer lives. Every living being is extinguished at death, and yet the Buddha and Laozi alone wanted to exist forever. They claimed that beyond this body both the Yang spirit and the True Nature are numinous. Therefore the Buddha has one body but three forms, and Laozi has one body that he changed into the Three Purities.[18] This is precisely like a willow tree on the ground changing into a willow spirit and a fox in a cave changing into a fox spirit. If one Buddha or one Laozi can divide his body when he leaves this world, how can he be any different from trees or beasts that can become spirits or demons? Not only this, but I will explain the heretical teachings of Buddhism and Daoism. The people of this world have been greatly deluded and confused—they are lost and are unable to wake up. I will point out these delusions one by one, with a total of ten points. You should all heed my words.

Item: The theory of *śarīras* from the Buddhist sutras.[19] They take this body as a temporary dwelling for the spirit and consciousness that exist permanently and transmigrate from lifetime to lifetime. They drink mother's milk as if it were the inexhaustible water of a river and thereby even treat their parents as a dwelling, a dwelling they borrow in order to transmigrate. This is to show disrespect for their own physical bodies, as if they were earth or wood, inciting the myriad generations ever after to commit the crime of filial disrespect. This great delusion, which violates innate human nature—this is the first hateful thing.

Item: The Buddhist scriptures consider the body a temporary dwelling and have no regard for it. Thus those who seek blessings and benefits and are not satisfied in this life wish to enjoy them in the next life. To that end they go on pilgrimages to the mountains, where they cast away their lives, throwing themselves off towering cliffs, smashing bones and body. Likewise, consider the wastrel and the prostitute, the lecherous man and the reckless youth. If their feelings are so deep and their love so strong that they are unable to cut off their relationships, they all too often hang themselves or throw themselves into a river together. They say that if they cannot be together in this life, they pray that they can be husband and wife in the life to come. This is the fallacy of believing in transmigration: on any given day one may lightly cast off this body. The great delusion that leads people to committing suicide rashly—this is the second hateful thing.

Item: When people of this world regard their bodies as temporary dwellings and do not recognize how precious they are, if they believe that the body is a mere inn, then it matters not at all when women who believe in the gods or make offerings to the Buddha are debauched and cheated by the lechers among the monks and priests, Buddhist or Daoist. Thus a woman may often have sexual intercourse with men in order to commune with some "dragon's vein" or to join with some "Buddha root," believing her female form of this life will be reborn as a man's body in the next.[20] All too often when women of good families and wealthy households are debauched, they willingly bear their shame and keep silent about it for the rest of their lives. This great delusion, which leads to the debauching of the Inner Quarters—this is the third hateful thing.

Item: Because people of this world are fascinated by the theory of retribution, bandits and ruffians can seize people's wealth and property by force, saying, "In your previous life you owed me a debt, and now I've come to collect!" They either force people to have sex with them or cajole them with clever words into participating in illicit sex, saying, "We were fated to spend the night together, and that is why you met me in this life." Other such evil "debts" can also be explained away as conditioned by a previous life. Moreover, those who want to learn how to refine the immortals' elixir of long life are regularly robbed of their silver by those priests. The great delusion of claiming justification for adultery and theft from the beyond—this is the fourth hateful thing.

Item: People of the world are misled by the Buddhist scriptures into believing that they should repent for their crimes and misdeeds. Thus in broad daylight believers in the Buddha go around committing all kinds of evil acts, leaving no place untouched—then at night they burn incense and recite scriptures, praying to be forgiven for their crimes and to obtain blessings. Day after day they commit evil acts—night after night they repent. At its worst, there was a thief who slipped into the Meridian Gate tower of the Imperial Palace, where he was apprehended by the eunuchs. When they stripped off his clothing to search him, his whole body was covered with Buddhist scriptures. He wore them because he so fervently believed that Buddhist scriptures could help him avoid calamity and achieve transcendence, and thereby help him be a successful thief. This grand delusion, which causes the destruction of normal human affairs—this is the fifth hateful thing.

Item: Bewitched by the idea of honoring the Buddha and respecting the Daoist deities, people of the world go on pilgrimages. Each month they exert themselves to scrape together some money and collect some rice, totally without regard for whether their parents are cold and hungry or lacking food and clothing. Moreover, every family sets up an altar to make offerings to the Buddha, the Immortals, or the other deities, even though their own lineages, clans, and earlier generations have no shrines or ancestral halls. This is the great delusion of destroying family feelings and turning one's back on the clan—this is the sixth hateful thing.

Item: Misled by the theories of purity, suffering, and emptiness, people of the world suppose that those who cultivate immortality or study Buddhism must absolutely not have wives or children, homes, or property. Do they not know that humans are beings made of blood, breath, bones, and flesh? How could we have no desire for sexual intercourse, as if we were earth, wood, water, or stone? Even though the Buddhists and Daoists advocate theories of purity and emptiness, when were they ever without wives and concubines, sons and grandsons, wealth and property? After the false proclamation of this prohibitive loop,[21] people of later ages adhered to it earnestly, but eventually the prohibitions can no longer hold, and as before, desire takes control with a vengeance. These people stop at nothing. They fornicate with their disciples and humiliate women of good families. They are content to behave like birds of prey and beasts, disregarding everything else. This great delusion destroys the human sense of shame—this is the seventh hateful thing.

Item: The Buddha and Laozi advocated strange theories that cheat the world so that all people of later ages are misled into begging for blessings with no regard for the things people should do. Thus in the past when bandit soldiers were besieging the capital, the ruler and his ministers still donned the simple Buddhist clothing of barbarian horsemen to listen to a lecture on the *Laozi* or Buddhist teachings. Such cases are too numerous to be counted. Not only did Emperor Wu of the Liang starve to death, Emperor Huizong of the Song was taken as a captive into the desert, and the Tang emperor Xuanzong was forced to flee along the road to Shu.[22] Their great delusions that cheat rulers and mislead their states—this is the eighth hateful thing.

Item: By their fake magic and techniques for immortality, the Buddhists and Daoists burn incense and assemble crowds. First they invite people to look into a basin of water and see themselves as sick and impoverished beggars, and they renounce all their family wealth as a result. When others look into the basin, the men see themselves as nobles, generals, or ministers and the women as empresses or imperial concubines with their crowns, their robes, and their jade pendants. Before long they raise armies and rebel, slaughtering cities and smashing battle formations. Among others, think of Zhang Ling and Zhang Jiao of the Han, Han Lin'er and Xu Zengshou of the Yuan, and Tang Sai'er, Zhao Guyuan, and Xu Hongru during the Ming.[23] They were a curse on the whole world, killing many tens of thousands. Even when fettered on the execution ground, both teachers and disciples were still declaring, "We're all bound for the Western Paradise," and, until the end, never woke up to the truth. This great delusion of subjecting the world to destruction and killing—this is the ninth hateful thing.

Item: Scholars, farmers, craftsmen, and merchants—each and every one must practice a trade or profession to provide for his clothing, food, and lodging and to fulfill the human relationships required by morality. No one is immune from these needs. Those Buddhists and Daoists advocate fallacies. Their monks and nuns, priests and Daoist sisters—all four groups—loiter about and eat like parasites, cheating people out of money and living in peace while carrying out their licentious and improper affairs. Above they rebel against Heavenly standards—below they abandon human affairs. They waste the wealth of the world just like pigs, sheep, fish, and turtles. Thus when Bodhidharma came from the West, he meditated on a blank wall for nine years, peacefully enjoying the clothing and food of the world for the sake of his self-cultivation.[24] Supposing that all of the world's people meditated facing a wall for nine years and abandoned their professions, who would be willing to go till the fields? No one would be producing food and clothing, and all the world's people would freeze and starve to death. How could this be the proper way of the Creator of the world? Furthermore, they build temples and shrines, adorn images with gold, offer sacrifices and conduct rituals, wasting money without limit. This great delusion of abandoning the professions and gobbling up wealth—this is the tenth hateful thing.

Now I have enumerated just ten items. There are countless other matters, too many to mention, but you could extrapolate from these. Because those Buddhists and Daoists can persuade the ignorant populace with their gods and immortals, I have taken great pains, using these ten items, to explain the nefarious ways they defy the True Teachings. However, there are certain things that I have seen and heard in my own life that delude the world and mislead the people, waste money and confound morality—these are deeply detestable. If you, good people, were to personally investigate these matters, then you would know that I simply have no alternative. My sense of mission to dispel three thousand years of delusions is greater than Mencius's burden of carrying on after Yao, Shun, the Duke of Zhou, and Confucius!

One among the crowd remarked, "If it is as you have said, Your Honor, that neither Buddhism nor Daoism offers anything worth having, then Heaven, Hell, ghosts and spirits—you've wiped them all out, too."

People who hold these common views live lives of constant befuddlement. The people of the world are surrounded by tales of gods and ghosts—they are unable to extricate themselves. Their confusion all stems from coveting benefits and blessings. The Buddhists and Daoists seize on these confused views and fabricate a Heaven, a Hell, gods of the watery world and others, and even ghosts and monsters, long life and blessings, and the like in order to cheat people out of their wealth, delude them, and confound their moral standards, all in order to compete with the teachings of Yao, Shun, the Duke of Zhou, and Confucius. They preach that in Heaven there is the Jade Emperor and his immortal officials, that there are gods enfeoffed to send down the rain and who reward the virtuous and punish the evil, all at the command of the Jade Emperor.

The *Jade Emperor Scripture* says that there was a king in the West, Pure Virtue by name, who had reached the age of forty without having a son. Queen Precious Moon and her lord prayed to the Old Lord of the Three Purities. The Old Lord sent them a son, who then became the Jade Emperor. The *Dark Warrior Scripture* says there was a kingdom in the West called "Pure Joy." Its ruler had no son and prayed to the Old Lord. The Old Lord sent him a son—this was the Patriarch Dark Warrior. The Buddhist scriptures say that in the kingdom of Pure Goodness in the West, the crown prince was named

Buddha. He married a woman of the Yetuo clan, and they produced a son named Muhūrta.[25] Later he left the family for twelve years, during which time he was enlightened and became a buddha. From this perspective, the line of Buddhist monks began seven hundred years after the Zhou dynasty. What was past is present—what is present was the past. How could what does not exist in the present have existed in the past?

Nowadays if you examine the West, it is all foreigners who have a rank odor, like sheep. How could you call them "pure"? Since no one nowadays has ever seen people with three heads and six arms, four eyes and eight hands, how can we believe that they are the divine generals of the Heavenly King? Likewise, since there are no people who are two or three hundred years old, how can we believe in long life without getting old?

A member of the crowd said, "The Jade Emperor is the Lord on High. It says in the books that King Wuding dreamed that the Lord on High presented him with Fu Yue.[26] And Mencius talked about fasting and cleansing himself in preparation for sacrifices to the Lord on High. Clearly there *is* a Lord on High."

People were already deluded by tales of ghosts and gods even in the time of Tang and Yu, and so they transmitted the image of the Lord on High.[27] Wuding prized the virtuous. So extreme was his sincerity that when he saw the appearance of Fu Yue in his dream and did not know his name, he sent people to find him using his painted image. Although people might never have seen a live dragon or a living phoenix, they often see them in dreams at night. Or they are able to visualize them in dreams because they have seen the painted images of them.

In talk about the Lord on High, there will be strings of jade pieces, crowns, and robes. But since the Yellow Emperor created clothing top and bottom, you can see that the Lord on High was born after the Yellow Emperor.[28] There was no Lord on High before the Yellow Emperor. If you say that he existed before the Yellow Emperor, he must have appeared naked, getting clothes only at the time of the Yellow Emperor. What we call "Emperors" are those who rule over Heaven, Earth, and the Myriad Creatures. That's the reason we call them "emperors." One refers to the Lord on High as the one who embodies the Great Ultimate. But if the Great Ultimate were the same as the Lord on High, what appearance could he have that would be visible? One who has the pure and clean heart needed to face Heaven on High can offer sacrifices to the Lord on High.

"Yanluo in Hell is in charge of life and death," a member of the crowd said. "When a person is born, a ghost sends him along, and when he dies, a ghost summons him back down, and if he has committed wrongs, the ghosts will torture him. If a person has done good deeds, he'll be reborn with wealth and high position. Animals who have done good deeds may be reborn as people, and a person who has committed evil deeds will be reborn as a bird or a beast. When animals have committed evil deeds, their spirits and consciousness will be extinguished.[29] Isn't this the way it really is?"

As a way of teaching stupid and vulgar people, this is all right, but in reality this is not true. When a man and a woman copulate, the father's sperm and the mother's blood coalesce to form a fetus. The mother produces life within her own belly. If a soul comes to lodge in it by the time it becomes a fetus, I know not whether it enters through the pregnant woman's mouth or from below the pregnant woman's waist. After a while the blood clot in the belly begins moving noticeably, but what is this thing then? For a person to have a body there must be a combination of form and energy, and only then can he know pain.[30] Now a person who is paralyzed in half his body can feel the pain of neither moxibustion nor acupuncture. If a person's form and energy separate after he dies, what he was must all become dust, to evaporate into a cold wind. What sort of corporeal shell, what form and substance could be left to suffer the infernal punishments of mountains of knives or trees of swords, boiling oil, or being ground to bits? Even supposing that the black Northern Dipper Wind could gather together the scattered souls of evil persons so that they might be punished again, those ghostly judges from the Netherworld would have no such delicate skills.

One among the crowd asked, "Could it be that the ghost judges of King Yanluo record when a person is to be born and the time until that person is to die, and such matters as his wife and children, his wealth and position, his failures and successes, and that all of this is written down and fixed in an account book that cannot be changed?"

The Biography of the Dark Warrior says that demons ate countless human beings, but Xuanwu caught them all to rid humanity of this source of harm. If indeed they ate countless human beings, then King Yama did not record their ages at death. If it were written down that they should be eaten, then this would reflect the laws of proper retribution. But if the Dark Warrior had exerted himself to save them, to the contrary, this would contradict the theory that birth and death are predetermined.

It is also said that Pengzu, who lived eight hundred years, married seventy-two wives. As his seventy-second was about to die, she asked Pengzu, "Why is it that you have enjoyed such long life? Aren't you in King Yama's registers?'"

"The judges twisted my name into a paper spill to tack their ledger together."

When Pengzu's wife saw King Yama, King Yama asked her, "How could Pengzu have so many wives?"

"His name had been twisted into a paper spill," she told him. King Yama opened his register, saw this, and went off at once to summon Pengzu.

If we look at it this way, Pengzu's wife was also born randomly, not determined by King Yama. If the food and clothing, successes and failures for Pengzu's whole life were not predetermined, how could other people's lives be predetermined? It is said that in the time of Confucius and Mencius there was no paper to write on. Bamboo strips and wooden boards were used instead. Now this Hell is still down below the water and the mud, the earth and the rocks. Where could they find there a store of paper for their ledgers? This story is just too ridiculous!

"City Gods and local earth gods are to be found everywhere," said a person in the crowd. "Surely you have something contrary to say about them?"

In the age of Tang and Yu, there were not yet any city walls or moats. It was only later, during the time of the Xia and the Shang, that walls were constructed and moats dug to defend against bandits. Men of later times thus erected City God temples and offered sacrifices to the City Gods and the local earth gods, referring to them collectively in general as the deities of the earth. They saw them as the mothers of humanity and of all things in the world. Separately, in the fields they were seen as beneficial in producing the five grains and were offered sacrifices as the gods of the community, in rural villages and on market streets they were seen as beneficial to respect and tranquility and were offered sacrifices as local gods, in a family's residence and courtyard they were seen as beneficial to the carrying on of family lines and generations and were offered sacrifices as gods of the household, in the mountains and peaks of a region they were seen as beneficial to the production of all goods and were offered sacrifices as gods of the mountains and marchmounts, in walled and moated communities they were seen as beneficial in preventing theft and staving off calamities and were offered sacrifices as the City Gods—all manifestations of the same earth.

From the perspective of the people, they are all motivated to think about the source of water when they take a drink, to express gratitude for blessings and repay favors. How could they make male images for the front shrine rooms, make female images for the rear halls, and in addition make an old man image for the whole family?[31] Clearly they made small statues in human form that they then falsely interpreted as the true gods of Heaven, Earth, and Nature. This theory is even more ridiculous!

"But the City God and the earth gods often manifest their divinity, and in fact they appear as living human figures," one among the crowd said. "Why do you refer to them all as just 'made of clay'?"

There is a principle behind the manifestations of divinity. When the heroes and martyrs of this world die bearing grudges or are wrongfully killed, or if they die violently in their youth before having children, the energy of their noble souls does not scatter but instead manifests itself at temples. For example, Wen Tianxiang, who was killed during the Yuan, and Yu Zhongsu, who was killed during the Ming, are both said to be the City Gods of the capital now.[32] They were born into this world as righteous men—at death they became righteous energy. The souls of such righteous spirits became the gods of rivers and mountains, hills and streams. This happens naturally,[33] not because of imperial proclamation or because people molded them out of clay. This is all due to the mysterious movements of the righteous principle of Creation. Yet in fact the particular gods and spirits of mountains and rivers or the locality cannot be identified as a particular person who became a particular god.

One among the crowd said, "Indeed, righteous men are known for their spiritual energy. But between Heaven and Earth, weird people and strange events can appear, even if not very often. I spent a number of years in Zhongzhou, where I saw a willow tree sprout a human figure two inches tall. In Jiangxi, Heaven rained down black rice, and in Xuzhou little beans with the shape of human heads fell from the sky, complete with eyes, mouths, and noses. It's true that strange events and weird creatures do occur in this world."

Confucius did not speak of "prodigies, force, disorder, and gods,"[34] and yet he knew that extraordinary changes do appear in the world from time to time as omens of impending disaster. The Sage follows only the Upright Path and is not willing to believe in using such weird events to invoke delusions among the people. The Buddhists and Daoists rely exclusively on just these in order to frighten people, and this is what makes their teachings heretical. When the world is about to change, all things may die in war's destruction—thus the Five Agents take on monstrous proportions, producing not only willow trees but even stones, foxes, and monkeys as well. Among the people, only those who are righteous and have cultivated the virtues will be able to dispel them.

One among the crowd said, "Magic and uncanny events are something that only gods and immortals can create. During the Chenghua reign period of the Ming,[35] in Yanshi County in Henan, there was a commoner named Zhu Tianbao who died. Three days after he was buried, his wife Sancui'er went to offer sacrifices of food and drink. As she crossed over a high ridge, she saw a large stone some twenty feet tall. Just as she came up beside it, there was a loud, clear sound and the rock fell over, revealing a stone box. Sancui'er came closer to look and saw that the box was open a crack, revealing a precious sword and a book of magic spells. Sancui'er secretly took them away, and after she practiced reciting the spells for several days she could tell what the future would bring. The people of that area recognized her exceptional powers and revered her as a Buddha Mother. In less than a year she had about ten thousand followers and devotees. She had powerful magic—when she blew her breath on them, sprouts in the fields would turn into swords and spears, plank benches became tigers and leopards, and cloth scarves turned into walls and moats. One morning she raised a rebellion, and imperial forces were sent to suppress her. Many were killed and wounded on both sides, but finally they were able to capture her. They locked her up in a jail, and after three days the cangue and fetters were still there, but nobody knew where Sancui'er had gone.[36] If this kind of magic was not done by an immortal who had divine skills, then such miraculous things could never have happened."

Conjurors are in the category of gods and immortals. They steal some of the craft of creation from Heaven and Earth to make their magic, and then they hide in the mountains. When the state of the world is fated to change, the people will experience disasters—when the fate of the world is left to conjurors, they only aid in creating chaos. At such times countless people are slain, starve to death, or die wrongfully. Even though this is brought about by the destiny of Heaven and Earth, myriad living beings must experience it. Even though it was caused by gods and immortals, the crime of rebelling against Heaven would be unforgivable. Belief in the gods is not only of no value to the world—in fact it harms the world.

One among the crowd said, "When the Jin ruler crossed the Yangzi, the water didn't come up to his horse's belly. The crown prince of the Yuan fled north, and when he got to the Great River there was no boat, but a golden bridge appeared in midair on which he crossed over. Weren't these miraculous events?"

The creative energies of Heaven and Earth supplement that which is insufficient and reduce that which has surplus. During the Xia and the Shang, human beings were very few in number, and so Heavenly destiny produced numerous sages and worthies in order to give life and nourishment to humanity. After eight hundred years of peace under the Zhou house, humanity had become extremely numerous, and the wicked and violent were also numerous, the good and virtuous being extremely few. The Way of Heaven despises wicked people being so numerous and consequently produced men who were good at killing and who would make war on them. For example, it gave birth to Bai Qi, who buried four hundred thousand soldiers from Zhao, and it allowed Bandit Zhi to "rampage back and forth across the empire" and yet die at home of old age. Heaven helped the Jin ruler cross the river in order to strike chaos into the Central Plain and presented a golden bridge to the Yuan crown prince in order to preserve his progeny. It is not as if the Way of Heaven acts blindly. These events occurred because Heaven was depleting that which was excessive. Since Heaven intended to restore the Han enterprise, ice miraculously formed and Guangwu was able to cross. When the Way of Heaven is exhausted, then there will be a major change in the succession. Weird and uncanny affairs may happen from time to time, but one may not discuss them from only one perspective.

One among the crowd said, "What you have said exhausts the wellsprings and probes the sources, Your Honor, in your efforts to awaken us all from our confusions. We've never heard before what we've heard here today, and it has cleared away all our mental obstacles. But Buddhism and Daoism are everywhere in this world—they've long since seeped into people's hearts. You, sir, have refuted the popular views with your unique perspectives even more thoroughly than the 'Memorial on the Bone of the Buddha' or 'Discussion on There Being No Ghosts.'[37] Yet since those who support these heretical teachings are so numerous, Your Honor's lips and tongue have their limits. It may not be possible for you to bring these blessings to the people of the world. Instead, the people of the world truly can constitute a disaster for you, Your Honor."

Feeling that the convictions of the crowd were impossible to refute, the rector then said, "Evening approaches. I must repair to my cart and reenter the city."

The elder escorted him across the bridge over the creek, then returned to say to the owner of the bean arbor, "It was I who worked up a fad for this idle talk. Now people in all four directions have heard of us, and our crowd increases every day. Nowadays the government's prohibitions are so strict, and, worse yet, the mind of man is unfathomable. Even if we all agree with what Rector Chen advocates, if somebody outside who doesn't know better just says that I've been flapping my lips and banging my tongue here, advocating some heresy to delude people's minds, then this bean arbor might well become a meeting place for brewing up disaster. Now autumn is coming to an end—first frost is almost upon us, and the beans stems are drying out."

"What you say is insightful, Uncle," one in the crowd said, "and extremely cautious." Without thinking, he leaned on a post with his arm, and it gave way at the base, bringing down the entire arbor and all its posts. Everyone had a good laugh over this. The owner broke the bean vines off the bamboo rods and the wooden frame and walked off with them bundled up in his arms.

"Too bad that old pedant had to hold forth with such nonsensical theories and sweep away all the tales of the Buddha and Laozi and the ghosts and gods in the world," the people in the crowd said. "We put up this bean arbor for idle talk to encourage people to fast and recite the name of the Buddha, but now we've lost interest in all that."

"Far more things in this world have been destroyed by such old nonsense than just this one bean arbor!" the old man remarked.

GENERAL COMMENTS

How fluently his words have flowed! He brought up original chaos, the rise and fall of states, feelings and things, and their principles, from the overarching to the detailed, from the crude to the refined. He analyzed them all, forgetting nothing. Even if one had brought back Confucius, Laozi, and Śakyamuni the Buddha to the same hall to talk, their lectures would still lack the coherence and breadth manifested here. Moreover, the Han glosses and the Song commentaries are meant only for outstanding Confucian scholars of the School of Principle. One cannot use such abstract discourse and empty actions to indoctrinate the hearts and enter the ears of the average man. Moreover, since even the village women and untamed youths who sat on the sides also nodded their heads in agreement at certain parts, even if he had assembled rocks, he still could have preached this Dharma to them.[38] In those several passages that refute Buddhism and Daoism, he exerted himself to oppose their erroneous activities and dispel their confusing concepts with vigor.

Aina has said, "You know that I have no alternative. My sense of mission to dispel the three thousand years of delusions is greater than Mencius's obligation to carry on the traditions of Yao, Shun, the Duke of Zhou, and Confucius."[39] How can you not believe him? Writing books and establishing their theories are the means by which the sages and worthies expressed their resentment,[40] but their texts require skillful reading by scholars of later times. Not reading skillfully makes it inevitable that people like Mr. Wang Jiefu would bring calamity down on the realm in the name of classical learning.[41]

In the case of fiction, in something as extraordinary as the Outlaws of the Marsh, tales of stalwart martial heroes could be misunderstood as espousing banditry if they are not read skillfully. In the case of the "Life of Ximen," one could mistake stylishness as mere venery if it is not read skillfully.[42] Their cautionary elements are presented ironically or subtly—their brooding sadness and lamentation are embedded in extreme joy and licentiousness and may not be immediately recognized by men of the world. These effects must all wait upon a skillful reading in order to detect the authors' deeply hidden meanings. Yet in order to have a greater effect on the world, I suppose it would be better if these messages were clear and simple enough that a person could understand them as he reads, like achieving sudden enlightenment from a shout or a blow.[43]

Aina, the Man of Dao, has digested ten thousand volumes. His words flow like a waterfall.[44] Once he puts pen to paper, no one can stop him. Whatever idea he takes up, he will treat it exhaustively. Once published, his numerous poetry collections and his plays have been a tasty treat for the world. At the height of summer, as a way of passing the time, he completed Idle Talk under the Bean Arbor in only a few days. While rocks melted and molten metals flowed, with everyone's sweat raining down, only Aina the Man of Dao sat comfortably at his northern window, fanning himself as he plotted out his tales. Whether recalling something he heard or presenting his own views, alternately creating and deleting back and forth, his discussions stirring a breeze that cooled both mind and body, always smiling and exuberant without being abusive.

When we read these stories, it matters little whether or not we read skillfully. If we have eyes, we will reach some understanding using our eyes—if we have ears, we will reach some understanding through our ears. There is not one heretical phrase here, nor a single biased statement. For whatever you find unclear in the classics, their commentaries, the philosophers, or the histories, you might find something helpful when perusing these stories. Whatever topics your father and mother, your teachers and friends have not elucidated for you, you might just be enlightened about by hearing these stories. Thus everyone will be reading them skillfully. This first collection is presented to the public complete in twelve sessions. A continuation would be similarly welcome, now that he has begun this splendid writing.[45]

Translated by Robert E. Hegel

Afterthoughts on Stories

Translating Aina's tales generated a lot of discussion among the translators and others. What follows here are ideas that came to us as we reflected on both overt and implicit meanings in the stories and how they might reflect Aina's times and his sense of the art of writing fiction. We present them here to stimulate the reader's further reflections as well.

The Introduction

Although several details about the collection may not be crucial to an appreciation of Aina's tales, they are striking in that they distinguish his creative spirit from what had become conventional in the late Ming period in stories by Feng Menglong and Ling Mengchu.

The Narrative Frame

Aina's frame tale seems to be unique among vernacular short fiction collections. His model may have been Buddhist scriptures written in the form of sermons built around a series of parables.[1] Although some sutras include dialogues involving the speaker, usually the Buddha, and members of his audience, they are limited to points of doctrine, and the Buddhist anecdotes have no unifying image parallel to the beans here. Lengthy romantic *chuanqi* plays of the time often did rely on an object (a fan, for example) to unify the many scenes of their rambling narratives, but their separate stories all combine at the end of the plays.

The Writerly Mode

It has been observed that a writerly mode and a greater emphasis on philosophical engagement characterize early Qing short fiction.[2] In this it contrasts sharply with Feng Menglong's *Three Words* (Sanyan) and other late Ming collections published only about forty years earlier. The exaggerated argumentation presented here appears intended to make fun of their conventional structure as well. Compared to other early Qing story collections, Aina's tales are much darker in tone, more cynical, and far more obvious in their ironic inversions of conventions of plot and characterization.

Robert E. Hegel

PREFACE AND FOREWORD

It is a commonplace for fictional or dramatic works in the late imperial period to be prefaced with an introductory piece in parallel prose, which may be seen as a subgenre in itself. As a virtuoso performance on the part of its author, it serves as an introduction to the particular work and writer and as an advertisement for the work. Such prefaces are often signed using pen names. If the authorship of numerous works of fiction is enigmatic, then the authorship of such prefatory materials can be even more tantalizing—although in many cases the writers could have been none other than the authors of the fiction.

The preface here has all the characteristics of such writings. It is deliberately recondite and allusive, full of hyperbole: the author "is blessed with the talents of ten thousand individuals, like those who composed poems while walking seven steps or while folding their arms eight times." In spite of his talents, he was not successful in the civil service examination and had to prove his worth in other areas. He is "unable to sell his bellyful of '*The Classic of Poetry* states . . .' or 'So said Confucius. . . .'" It seems that he participated in activities in literary or political associations and societies, but not wholeheartedly, perhaps harboring serious reservations: "Despite having a multitude of brothers and comrades in associations and groups, why should he join them in their farcical activities?" The piece also touches on the purport of the collection in memorable lines: "He hastened through old legends, replacing one name with another, quietly righting the wrongs of history." This is followed by statements about how skilled the author is and how powerful the effect of reading such tales could be. Parts of this piece are problematic; for instance, the derogatory terms used to describe Aina's "brothers and comrades" in literary or political societies, the paeans heaped on him, and the eerie familiarity with the method of composition in the collection, among others. All this suggests that Aina penned the preface himself, at least in part playfully.

The foreword is signed using the author's pen name. Here Aina mentions his inspiration, a collection of poems on a bean arbor by one Xu Jutan; these tales may be seen as a supplement. However, both Xu Jutan and his poem are unidentifiable.[3] The poem was adapted from a regulated verse titled "The Western Garden" (Xiyuan) or "The Western Garden in Summer" (Xiari xiyuan) by the Buddhist monk Dexiang:

> I have just added a small thatched cottage in the Western Garden.
> Nowhere can I find a cool place to escape from the summer heat.
> In the sixth month, the ponds are always shallow;
> In the woods, the saplings of three years ago have not yet grown tall.
> I constantly sweep the floor—to cleanse my body and mind.
> Keeping the windows and doors ajar constantly, I do not burn incense.
> For evening breeze, there are only willows south of the rivulet.
> But I fear the cicadas shrieking in the twilight.[4]

The monk Dexiang (14th century), a native of Qiantang (Hangzhou), was a renowned poet and calligrapher. Qian Qianyi's (1582–1664) compendium of Ming poetry *Collected Poems from Several Reigns* (Liechao shiji) includes 172 of his poems, while Zhu Yizun's (1629–1709) *Compendium of Ming Poems* (Ming shi zong) contains 25. Certain scholars have asserted that his "Western Garden" poem incurred censure from the first Ming emperor. Lang Ying's (1487–1566) *Notes on Seven Subjects* (Qixiu leigao) states in no uncertain terms that he died before his time as a result.[5] Certain Buddhist records also mention that the emperor was offended by his poem. *Lives of Eminent Monks, Continued, with Supplements* (Bu Xu Gaoseng zhuan), *juan* 25, states that he barely escaped punishment, an assertion mentioned in the notes on his *Tongyu Collection* (Tongyu ji) in the imperial Qing bibliographic guide *Summaries of the Contents of the Complete Works of the Four Treasuries* (Siku quanshu zongmu tiyao), *juan* 175.[6] But according to *Collected Poems from Several Reigns*, he was still alive after 1403.[7] *Lives of Eminent Monks, Continued, with Supplements* also records that he died of natural causes in a monastery, in front of all the monks gathered to witness his passing. His biographical sketch in *More Records of Pointing at the Moon* (Xu zhiyue lu) contains more details about how he died: "He . . . was highly regarded by the worthies of his time. One day as he was approaching *nirvāna*, the group of monks asked him for a *gātha*. Abruptly he leaned back on the seat and said, 'You wine-drinking sots—what can I do about you?' And thereupon he hastened into stillness."[8]

Aina made certain changes (he confessed that writing poetry was not his passion) to Dexiang's "Western Garden" poem, making it fit the occasion of the bean arbor gathering and attributing it to an eminent scholar from his home area. "Xu Jutan" was surely not Dexiang's name before he took the tonsure because his secular name was not Xu. Was "Xu Jutan" meant to be fictitious? Aina himself confessed that he "hastened through old legends, replacing one name with another, quietly righting the wrongs of history." If so, this poem might serve as an instance of his "replacing one name with another" and putting the hat of one person on a different head.

Li Qiancheng

SESSION 1

The collection begins with a double frame: the storyteller under the bean arbor tells the story of another group of men telling stories to one another under another bean arbor. Among that second group, two elderly gents carry on a storytelling duel with great zeal, tense action, and rich description. Because telling stories about female jealousy is presented as a duel, exaggeration is required, and the homicide/suicide plot serves the purpose.

Discrepancies between intention and result and situational absurdities abound in this session. The far-sighted editor of *A Mirror of Jealousy*, who acquired great merit for his book, intended to warn men and women about the dangers of jealousy, but he failed to foresee the result—that his female readers would be inspired to greater jealousy. When Jie Zhitui goes missing, the duke absurdly orders the least likely person, an impatient warrior, to look for him. Wei Chou then sets the fire that inspires Jie Zhitui's own conflagration. Similarly, when the session commentator compares the beginning of Aina's story collection to the *Classic of Poetry* and *Documents of Antiquity*, because both of these classics start with stories about male-female relationships, doing so does not elevate the status of Aina's collection but rather points to the fictitious image of harmonious family relationships in canonized works.

Mei Chun and Lane J. Harris

Session 2

The second story and the first are sometimes considered a pair, as both tell femme fatale stories by debunking historical anecdotes and satirizing exemplary figures. While female jealousy is the central theme in the first story, the second turns to ridiculing moral models such as Xi Shi and Fan Li, and at the same time challenging the validity of the historical record. Not only did Aina turn the story of Xi Shi inside out, he even goes further to provide "evidence" by referring to local legends and re-interpreting famous poems by Li Bai and Su Shi. By doing so, Aina is able to instill a sense of skepticism among his audiences, inviting them to question the reliability of history and the reality of exemplary figures. The questioning of authoritative accounts and skepticism echoes what Patrick Hanan (*Chinese Vernacular Story*, 195) has identified as "the luxury of ambiguity" one can sense throughout the collection. Yet from the aesthetic point of view, it also highlights the potential of storytelling to re-construct a "new" reality through debunking legends and re-interpreting historical sources.

Li Fang-yu

Session 3

As in other sessions of this collection, the military chaos that accompanied the seventh-century fall of the Sui and rise of the Tang also comments on Aina's lifetime. Some read Liu Cong's military movements in the southeast as a veiled reference to the Ming loyalist Zheng Chenggong (Coxinga) or to his father, the pirate Zheng Zhilong.[9] Either way, the storyteller-narrator has evidently taken a fairly minor historical episode and radically transformed it with elements of popular narrative: inventing Liu Cong (perhaps as an allusion to Qiuran, or "Curly Beard," a Tang literary figure who moves overseas to found his own kingdom), injecting the "three brocade sacks containing stratagems" episode from the novel *Romance of the Three Kingdoms*, and likening Wang Hua to the son of Squire Jiao from the novel *The Three Sui Quash the Demons' Revolt* (Pingyao zhuan). His historical unreliability as a narrator thus becomes a significant element in the construction of the session.

By embedding the narrator within the story world and imbuing him with a clear personality and some suggestion of a backstory, the frame narrative of *Idle Talk under the Bean Arbor* enabled Aina to open up space for a kind of unreliable narration not often seen in premodern Chinese literature.

Alexander Wille

SESSION 4

Forming a pair with session 3, this session is also about a wastrel who unexpectedly attains wealth and fame in the end. Yet rather than emphasizing the hidden talent of a seemingly unintelligent man, as in session 3, this session emphasizes moral actions and their predictable outcome, using the Buddhist karmic cycle (*yinguo baoying*) and Daoist idea of "the changing course of the Cosmos" (*Tian Di zaohua*). These two ideas are introduced at the beginning of the session, in which the narrator uses the process of growing beans to emphasize the link between cause and effect (a parallel to the biblical "Whatsoever a man soweth, that shall he also reap"),[10] citing Sima Guang's teaching on strengthening the importance of accumulating merit through one's moral action.

Yet despite setting the moral tone from the beginning, the story seems to develop more around the unavoidable consequences of all actions regardless of one's intentions. The "hidden merit" (*yinde*) the young master accumulates has a two-sided karmic outcome, neither of them predictable. In this sense, human agency seems to have its limitations, while the "changing course of the Cosmos," viewed within a wider span of history, takes control of the events of individual lives. This echoes the collection's overall view of recent political events: dynastic change is more a natural process of change than specific karmic punishment (*baoying*) for certain people's actions.

Li Fang-yu

SESSION 5

Aina and his contemporary short story writers, such as Li Yu, show a peculiar interest in rewriting the familiar story of an altruistic beggar who either returns lost money to its original owner or rescues a girl in trouble, or both, and ends up being generously rewarded with official recognition and, in most cases, with a good marriage that produces successful sons. What distinguishes Aina's Ding'er from other fictional beggars is Aina's promotion of the philosophy of survival to his audience, which included survivors of the fall of the Ming. Aina makes little effort to romanticize Ding'er's marriage to a "fallen" woman. Eventually Ding'er's family history will be glorified through his extraordinarily successful sons, and so will the dynastic history. By rewriting a clichéd theme as satire and by misquoting or distorting references to classical or historical texts, Aina gives more complexity to this didactic story than appears on its surface.

Zhang Jing

SESSION 6

This story might pass as tritely anti-Buddhist if not for Aina's handling of its savagery. Torture and mutilation, inflicted on human bodies both alive and dead, abound here. Aina's narrative exploits the reader's sensory imagination of pain by presenting it through the hearing, touch, and sight of a passerby. More horrifying than the monk's awful death is the factual, dispassionate tone of a female victim explaining to the magistrate why women's leg bones are favored and how they are made into chopsticks that look like ivory. Equally disturbing is the collective silence among the locals concerning the monks' atrocities. This mass reticence indicates the reception of violence as normal, powerfully evoking Aina's contemporary readers' recent memories of the violent dynastic transition. The lack of moral responsibility in this silence again suggests Aina's uneasy position as a survivor under the new regime. Violence here mimics the practice of Buddhist transcendence, indicating a strong sense of spiritual crisis. The fact that the historical Tang general Li Baozhen died from an overdose of immortality pills, a death by delusion, ironically groups him with the gullible laity deceived by the exalted monks.

Last, on Aina's embedded narrative, the exalted monks giving lectures intended to deceive their audiences in the main story both parallel and contrast the frame story of storytelling under the bean arbor, cautioning Aina's readers against superficial reading and pointing to his philosophical pursuit in fiction writing.

Zhang Jing

SESSION 7

Aina and scholars like him embraced Shuqi's conundrum because they found themselves in a similar situation. It slowly dawns on Shuqi that the Shang has lost the hearts of the people, an ironic comment by Aina on Shuqi's acceptance of the Zhou notion of the Mandate of Heaven. The Ming dynasty had fallen with the suicide of the Chongzhen emperor (r. 1627–44), but various pretenders to the throne continued to hold out against the Manchus in what is known as the Southern Ming resistance (1644–62). Should scholars remain loyal to the pathetic remnants of the Ming royal family or shift their loyalty to the powerful new Qing dynasty? Aina never defines a "right" course of action but uses the Master of Making Things Equal, a deity conjured by Shuqi in his dream (also Aina's original creation), to suggest that transferring one's loyalty to a new dynasty is acceptable because, like the change of seasons, such dynastic transitions accord with the fluctuations of celestial time.

Mei Chun and Lane Harris

SESSION 8

Here *Idle Talk* gives us a parable of irony, cynicism, and disappointment as a meditation on the chaotic era during which it was composed. For instance, references to dynastic change appear even on the level of wordplay: when a divine lectures Master Wei by saying, "By curing all of them of their blindness, you prevent the stipulations of divine punishment from being applied," the phrase "curing all of them of their blindness" might be rendered more literally as "giving them a bit of *ming* (brightness)" where *ming* is the name of the recently fallen dynasty.

The central conceit of the primary story—that mortal life is a vile, filthy trudge—lies unavoidably at the heart of Buddhist teachings; this is hardly the only work of late imperial Chinese literature to comment on it. Kong Shangren's 1690s play *The Peach Blossom Fan* (Taohua shan) ends with his hero and heroine abandoning their love for each other in favor of contemplation in separate religious communities. Nevertheless, few works of the period can match Aina's for their potent mixture of dripping cynicism and dry wit.

Alexander Wille

SESSION 9

The episodes in session 9 belong to the past of living memory, a traumatized memory of the fall of the Ming hastened by the failure of the country's rulers to quell widespread banditry. The text falls into three sections: an opening treatise on poverty as the root cause of both individual theft and large-scale banditry; an account of a corrupt law enforcement practice described by a deputy of the imperial police forces; and the story of hapless Liu Bao, the spoiled son of a disgraced official whose benighted attempt at armed robbery necessitates his rescue by a real highwayman. Each section offers parallel contrasts between the minor and the major criminal. While the small-scale thief driven by hunger and cold presents an object of pity, or, in Liu Bao's case, the subject of a painful joke, no mercy is spared for the greater criminals. Aina's dispensation of punishment in the fictional realm revels in the ambiguity between an inevitable working out of retribution (*bao*) and the implementation of justice through legal means. Justice miscarries in all cases presented, from the execution of the apprentice thieves who are really only police plants, the preemptive beheading of Huang Xiong, and the deaths in jail of bandits accused of the wrong crime, to the extrajudicial murder of the unnamed bandit leader. Yet, on a cosmic level, all these incidents suggest the Way of Heaven inevitably finding its mark, sooner or later, and dealing out retribution with a very heavy hand. A criminal punished for a crime he did not commit, in this moral worldview, merits retribution for some other crime he either did commit or intended to commit. Retribution arrives seemingly by chance to clean up what the legal system overlooks, a comforting prospect amid chaos. The ultimate question would seem to be whether or not Aina means us to take the narrator at his word when he marvels at "the artfulness of the Way of Heaven in levying retribution."

Annelise Finegan Wasmoen

SESSION 10

This session begins with the old man's recitation from a medical text on a kind of bean; this occasions sarcastic comments about a locally grown variety, which leads to gossip about Suzhou customs. Responses from the crowd then introduce the several stories concerning the small-time hustlers of Tiger Hill in Suzhou. They dramatize the daily life of a place; they portray one-dimensional and yet recognizable characters; they comically parody human foibles while expressing sympathy for those who embody them. Aina's reflections seem to represent early Qing period Suzhou, when the locals were poorer and more abject in their needs than during the late Ming.

The stories reveal broad familiarity with customs and terminology used in Tiger Hill entertainments; apparently Aina had firsthand knowledge of Suzhou diversions as well—and the risks they presented.

The ragtag assemblage of freeloaders, pimps, traffickers in children, and confidence men described here invites comparison with groupings and their motivations in more polite society.[11] As the commentator observes, "there are deep meanings to be found hidden within Aina's words"; certainly these characters are meant to be cautionary. Yet it seems unlikely—as the commentator hints—that the story's message has relevance only for visitors to Tiger Hill. Surely pretense and hustlers were to be found in the postwar social and political circles of Aina's day and most likely were easily identified by his first generation of readers.

Robert E. Hegel

SESSION 11

The lighter humor of the tenth story takes a harsh turn toward the dark realities of the fall of the Ming dynasty in the penultimate session under the bean arbor. The collection departs from its claims of telling leisurely stories and confronts in this session the terror that overwhelmed the country when the Ming fell to the rebels. The narrator's personal account seems detached but detailed, focused on the violence and cruelty of the rebels. The intensity and detail of his dark narrative is unique for the genre, which generally favored humor and happier endings.

This fictional account describes a loyal commander's fight to avenge his dynasty and his martyred sister. As readers of the time would likely have expected, it has a happy ending. Yet the ending feels hollow and unsatisfying because the audience is left with the haunting knowledge that it is mere fiction, especially since the story is directly opposed to the narrator's own story, which is decidedly unhappy. Indeed, audience members respond to the story not with praise for the hero but with fear. They retreat to nightmare-filled slumber before returning for what becomes the final session under the bean arbor. The depiction of the fall of the Ming in this story begins a series of questions about greater cosmic order that ends only with the collapse of the bean arbor itself at their final gathering.

Lindsey Waldrop

The teacher's sermon seems to be based on the Neo-Confucian School of Principle's (Lixue) rejection of Daoism and Buddhism even as it adapts some of their concepts, such as retribution. Certain ideas here reflect the writings of Zhou Dunyi (1017–1073) concerning the origins of the material world;[12] however, the rector's use of Qi as a kind of material force echoes Zhou's contemporary Zhang Zai (1020–1077) as well.[13] Ideas about Principle (Li, especially as Tian Li, the Principle of Heaven) appear to be drawn from Cheng Hao (1032–1085), Zhang Zai's nephew and a student of Zhou Dunyi's. In addition, the commentary suggests that these tales must be read carefully, "skillfully," in order to apprehend Aina's subtle uses of irony and satire. Probably nowhere is this more so than when he deliberately mistakes facts and substitutes legends and what seem to be fanciful fabrications for historical persons and events, as he does throughout the collection.[14] These misrepresentations come from voices in the crowd as well as from the grandiose lecture presented by this self-righteous Confucian teacher. On the surface, the common people, who have enjoyed this "idle talk" up to this point, seem anxious to debunk the pedant's rant. Yet the story's final lines, about closed minds, follow hard on a statement by one audience member whose interest has soured on didacticism in general. Here, as so many times throughout this collection, Aina leaves us with ambiguities that can only have been created knowingly.

Finally, this concluding session brings together previous references to karma, in particular the insight that purposeful words, thoughts, and deeds all have consequences. The scholar explains carefully his reasons for coming and why he takes the positions that he does, but then these self-serving rationalizations form an ironic contrast to the political interpretation offered by the old gentleman, the host for the gathering, whom readers have come to know through these tales. Since this outsider had so misunderstood whatever gossip he had heard about the bean arbor sessions, others could misread their intentions as well, putting both storytellers and listeners in jeopardy. The bean arbor had to come down, even if it had not collapsed. Probably too much had already been said there; the challenge is for us readers to seek out the true meaning of these sessions, whether conventional stories or otherwise.

Robert E. Hegel

Historical and Cultural References

Aina

Patrick Hanan (*Vernacular Story*, 191–92, 240nn2, 3) and Chen Dakang, ("Doupeng xianhua kaozheng," 1–2) compile what factual data exists about Aina and the conclusions that might safely be drawn about his life. Hanan joins Hu Shi and others in identifying Aina with the obscure Hangzhou writer Wang Mengji, who revised a novel about the eccentric Buddhist monk and knight-errant Ji Dian (Crazy Ji). Chen, agreeing with Hu Shiying (*Huaben xiaoshuo gailun*), speculates that he was a different Hangzhou dramatist, Fan Xizhe, eight of whose plays survive. Zhang Feifei ("*Doupeng xianhua* fayin," 17–41) carefully sorts through available evidence and suggests that Ming loyalist writer Huang Zhouxing (1611–1680) was Aina. Little solid evidence for these claims is to be found, although surely these writers were Aina's contemporaries; Hanan (240n3) notes that a poem on an illustration in the Ji Dian novel is signed "Aina," but with a character for *na* other than the one in this collection.

Bai Qi

Bai Qi was a highly successful Qin commander of troops during the Warring States period. After defeating the Qin's primary rival, Zhao, he massacred the Zhao army, reportedly by burying them alive. Later he fell afoul of his ruler and was allowed to commit suicide in prison.

Bamboo strips and nap boards

In a comment on paper lanterns, *denglong* (*Guazhi'er*, juan 8, "Yongbu"), Feng Menglong observes that the term *miepian* (lit., "bamboo strip") derives from a vulgar joke referring to the stiffening material a man had employed in order to perform sexually; from that, it came to mean one who arranges liaisons with sex workers or other types of crass commercial exchanges. In the Wu dialects, it is homophonous with such terms as *mipian* 覓騙 and *miepian* 滅騙, suggesting cheating. We are grateful to Daniel Youd for bringing this reference to our attention; the term appears as a pejorative in other sessions as well. *Huban*, translated here as "nap boards," has also been interpreted as *hubiban* 忽壁板, that which sticks to the boards of the partitions (presumably of the bedrooms in a brothel), indicating a sponger who arranges sex for a male client. Both terms are synonyms for "freeloaders." These figures are central to session 10, but the term—and the character type—appear in session 9 as well.

Bandit Zhi

Bandit Zhi is by legend one of the great villains of Chinese history. He and his nine thousand men roamed throughout Zhou territory pillaging and plundering, terrorizing the population, and kidnapping women. *The Zhuangzi* creates a famous exchange between the bandit and Confucius in which Zhi successfully argues the Daoist perspective on conventional values. See Zhuangzi, *Complete Works*, 323–31.

Beheaded Brook (*Duantou Xiaohe*)

In the entry "Two Beggars" (Ergai) in the collection of classical tales *Huadangge congtan*, edited by Xu Fuzuo (1560–1629), a likely source for Aina's story, a beggar refuses to give some hooligans the money he has found, saying, "You can cut off my head, but you won't get the money!" (Wu tou ke duan, jin bu ke de!). The phrase "a boat in a dead-end swamp" (*chuan jin duantou bang*) is an allegorical saying (*xiehouyu*) meaning "no way out." The name suggests that this incident is to be read metaphorically.

Bodhidharma

By legend, the basic teachings of Chan Buddhism were brought from India by Bodhidharma, who arrived in South China in 527, held discussions with Emperor Wu of the Liang, a Buddhist, then traveled north. His reputation as a teacher began with his achieving enlightenment during his nine years of meditation facing a blank wall in a cave on Mount Song (Songshan) near the Shaolin Temple. He reportedly died at the age of 150, having taught the principles for quieting the mind and teaching beyond the written word.

BOPI

Ji Bopi was a high minister of the state of Wu later in Fuchai's reign. After fleeing from Chu, he fawned on Fuchai and took bribes. Wu Zixu warned against an invasion by Yue, but Bopi arranged to have him executed for opposing his king. During the war with Yue, Bopi accepted Fan Li's bribe and persuaded the Wu king Fuchai to spare the Yue king Goujian's life after he had surrendered. Later, when Wu waged war against Qi, King Goujian took the opportunity to attack and conquer the state of Wu. According to *Records of the Grand Historian* (Shiji), King Goujian executed Bopi for disloyalty and corruption in 473 BCE when Wu fell to the state of Yue, yet in *Zuo's Commentaries* (Zuozhuan), Bopi became a high-ranking official in the court of Yue. The expression describing his behavior in session 10 parallels the vulgar colloquial phrase "kissed ass."

CAO CAO AND HIS SONS

Cao Cao (155–220) gradually emerged as one of the most powerful warlords at the end of the Han dynasty and was named Duke of Wei by the declining court. Shortly after Cao's death, his eldest son, Cao Pi (187–226), forced the last Han emperor to abdicate and proclaimed himself Emperor of Wei. His brother Cao Zhang (d. 223), a notable military figure who served under their father, died under mysterious circumstances while visiting Cao Pi in 223. Cao Zhi, a rather eccentric figure known for his bouts of heavy drinking, fought to inherit from his father but was passed over in favor of Cao Pi. The legends about the younger brother's skill in versification regularly recount his witty response to Cao Pi's threats on his life.

CHEN, RECTOR CHEN (CHEN ZHAIZHANG)

The name Rector Chen in session 12 would most likely remind alert readers of a character in the famous romantic *chuanqi* play by Tang Xianzu (1550–1616), *The Peony Pavilion* (Mudan ting) of 1599. That Rector Chen failed the civil service examinations but supposedly excels in virtue. However, he is intellectually inferior to a clever maid as he tries to tutor the pampered daughter of an official family. Although not performed by a *chou*, or clown actor, he is generally presented as an impractical fool throughout the play.

This Rector Chen's proper name and informal name, mentioned later in the story, form the adage "The absence of desire makes a man strong." *Lunyu* 5.11: "The Master said, 'I have never met anyone who is truly unbending (*gang*).' Someone said, 'What about Shen Cheng?' The Master said, 'Cheng is full of desires. How can he be unbending?'" (Confucius, *Confucius*, 39–41). His nickname Chen Wugui (No Ghosts Chen) becomes more significant toward the end of the session, in particular when the tract that denies the existence of ghosts is mentioned. The titular character in *The Zhuangzi*, chap. 24, is Xu Wugui (No Ghosts Xu); see Zhuangzi, *Complete Works*, 261–79.

CHILDLIKE INNOCENCE

The concept of *chizi zhi xin* (infant heart/mind) mentioned in session 5 refers to the Confucian philosopher Mencius's (371–289?) theory that human nature is fundamentally good. This passage refers to the interpretation of the moral nature of knowledge (*liangzhi*) supported by Wang Yangming (1472–1529), founder of the Neo-Confucian School of Mind (Xinxue), as "intuitive knowledge." In this, he critiqued the rigidity and dogmatism of the Cheng-Zhu school of Neo-Confucianism, the School of Principle. Li Zhi (1527–1602) elaborated Wang's interpretation in his essay "On the Child Mind" (Tongxin shuo). For the importance of this term and its associated concepts among late Ming intellectuals, see Lee, *Li Zhi*, 45–68.

COXINGA

Zheng Chenggong (1624–1662) is known to Westerners as Coxinga (the Dutch pronunciation of "Guoxingye" [Lord with the Imperial Surname]), a title based on his surname Zhu, which was granted to him by the last Ming emperor. After being ennobled by the Southern Ming court, he battled the new Manchu government until his death. Liu Cong in session 3 is more likely modeled on his father, the pirate Zheng Zhilong (1604–1661), who switched his loyalties to the Qing in 1646, seeing no hope for the rump Ming regime. See *ECCP*, 108–11; Zhang Feifei, "*Doupeng xianhua* fayin," 10.

Hanan (*Chinese Vernacular Story*, 191–92, and esp. 240n1) dates the Hanhailou edition to the middle of the eighteenth century. However, Chen Dakang, "Doupeng xianhua kaozheng," 6, and *Zhongguo guji shanben shumu (Zibu)*, 17.17a, list these two editions as "Early Qing," the Shuyetang *keben* edition as Qianlong 46 (1781), and the Sandetang edition as Qianlong 60 (1795). In his foreword ("Qianyan") to the Nanjing Jiangsu Guji edition, Zhang Daoqin states confidently that the Hanhailou version is older, because the Shuyetang edition simplifies certain difficult passages. For example, *Xihu jiahua, Doupeng xianhua*, 136n2, notes that the Shuyetang edition substitutes *bingcheng* for the Hanhailou edition's *can*, thus eliding the philosophical concept intended. See Aina, *Doupeng xianhua, Zhaoshi bei (he kan)*, 156.

The reign in which a book was printed can sometimes be determined by the characters that it does *not* use—those proscribed by the emperor because they appear in his own name or in honorary names for his predecessors. The character *xuan* appears several times here; it was banned during the Kangxi reign period (1661–1722), although the ban was not enforced until some years into the reign. See Chen Dakang, "*Doupeng xianhua* kaozheng," 6.

According to Ōtsuka (*Zōho Chūgoku*, 27–28), the earliest extant edition may be the Hanhailou edition published early in the Kangxi reign period, that is, after 1662 but before 1700. Its illustrations certainly follow late seventeenth-century conventions. The National Library of China copy was photoreprinted as volume 184 in *Guben xiaoshuo jicheng*. The National Library of China (at website http://www.nlc.gov.cn/newen/) and Nanjing Library have copies of the Shuyetang edition, dated 1781. Other reprints and editions in Beijing include the Sandetang edition of 1795, the Baoningtang edition of 1798, the Zhihetang edition of 1805, and several other undated block-printed editions; see http://opac.nlc.cn/F/6C2NYEPHUQBJRQCMKFALAXVGD4US KU76IPF166G7MY1K5EAQHG-14222?func=short-jump&jump=51. According to this list (accessed August 11, 2015), there have been at least twenty new editions published in the People's Republic of China in 2000 and after.

"Dew on the Shallots"

"Dew on the Shallots" (Xielu) is a funeral song dating from the Han period. According to tradition, the song was composed by the followers of Tian Heng, the King of Qi, who committed suicide out of shame when defeated by Liu Bang, the Han founder. A century later, Han Wudi's court musician Li Yannian divided the song into "Dew on the Shallots" to mourn the deaths of nobles and "In the Tomb" (Houli) for officials and commoners; see Guo Maoqian, *Yuefu shiji*, 396. See also Sima Qian, *Records*, 1:201–2.

DISPUTATIOUS, ON BEING

Mengzi 3B.9: "Gongdu Zi said, 'Outsiders all say that you, Master, are fond of disputation. May I ask why?' 'I am not fond of disputation,' answered Mencius. 'I have no alternative'" (Mencius, *Mencius*, 127). This begins Mencius's lengthy disquisition on the alternation of good and bad rule and the decline of morality into chaos that he fears. Rector Chen in session 12 avers that he is not "disputatious."

DOCUMENTS OF ANTIQUITY

The *Documents of Antiquity* (Shangshu) is a collection of statements attributed to sage-kings and others of high antiquity; it became a central text in the Ming-Qing civil service examination system. In session 5, Aina reverses the voices of the kings and the ministers on giving commendations, hence indicating the political chaos of his time. For an example, see Legge, *Chinese Classics*, 3:53–54.

DOU AND TIAN

Dou Yin is mentioned in session 2. He was the nephew of Queen Dou and lived during the Western Han period. He and Guan Fu supported one royal offspring as heir apparent; Tian Fen, the uncle of the Han emperor Wu, supported another. Guan Fu was sentenced to death first because he insulted Tian Fen in public. Dou Yin was beheaded later as a result of Tian Fen's plot against him. The spring following Dou Yin's death, Tian Fen died of a severe illness caused, it was said, by the ghosts of Dou Yin and Guan Fu.

DU HALDE, JEAN-BAPTISTE

Jean-Baptiste Du Halde's massive survey was printed in four volumes in French in 1735 and 1736 (Paris: P. G. Lemercier, 1735; A La Haye: Chez Henri Scheurleer, 1736); English translations appeared in 1736 (London: J Watts),

1738 (London: T. Gardner in Bartholomew-Close, for Edward Cave, at St. John's Gate), and 1741 (printed for J. Watts and sold by B. Dod at the Bible and Key in Ave-Mary Lane, near Stationers-Hall), among other editions. See "A Dialogue, Wherein Tchin, a modern Chinese Philosopher, declares his Opinion concerning the Origin and State of the World," in Du Halde, *The General History of China: Containing a geographical, historical, chronological, political and physical description of the empire of China* (London: J. Watts, 1736), 3:257–92. For European responses to Chinese thought at that time, see Mungello, *Great Encounter*, esp. 83–90.

Du Zichun

Du Zichun, mentioned in session 4, is the central character in a Tang *chuanqi* story about a wastrel who goes to Mount Kunshan with a foreign conjuror—who had paid off his debts—to practice internal alchemy after he repents. He went through several trials to remain silent, including mental torture and physical pain, but later fails because he cannot bear watching what appears to be the death of his son. Some believe the source text is from *Record of the Mysterious and the Strange* (Xuanguai lu), but there is no agreement on its author. The story was adapted from a Buddhist tale in Xuanzang's *Great Tang Records on the Western Regions* (Da Tang xiyu ji) and was later adapted by both Chinese and Japanese writers.

Duke of Zhou

The Duke of Zhou—mentioned several times by Rector Chen in session 12—was regent to the first king to rule over Zhou in the eleventh century BCE. The duke was "the architect of the Zhou feudal system" (Confucius, *Confucius*, xv) and by legend a man of highest ethical principles, especially applied to hierarchically organized government.

Fan Li's son

According to *Records of the Grand Historian* (Shiji) 41, Fan Li, a minister of Yue (and a central character in session 2), had three sons. When the second committed murder in the kingdom of Chu and was in jail awaiting execution, Fan sent his first son with a letter and a huge amount of gold to his friend Zhuang Sheng, who held a high position at the Chu court. Zhuang accepted the gold and persuaded the King of Chu to grant amnesty to all prisoners. Fan's first son thought the amnesty was merely a coincidence and asked Zhuang to return the gold. Zhuang was offended and talked the King of Chu into killing Fan Li's second son after all.

FENG MENGLONG

A prolific author of fiction of all sorts, Feng's vernacular story collections are *Stories Old and New* (Gujin xiaoshuo), 1621; *Stories to Caution the World* (Jingshi tongyan), around 1624; and *Stories to Awaken the World* (Xingshi hengyan), 1627. The other major story collections of the late Ming are Ling Mengchu's *Slapping the Table in Amazement* (Pai'an jingqi), 1628, and *Slapping the Table, Second Collection* (Erke Pai'an jingqi), 1632.

FOUR TYPES OF BIRTHS, SIX PATHS OF REBIRTH

According to Buddhist teachings mentioned in session 12, all sentient beings come into existence in one of four ways: born from a fetus, born from an egg, born from water, or born through transformation. The Six Paths (Dao) of Rebirth are rebirth into Heaven, rebirth as a human, rebirth as an *asura* (demon), rebirth as a hungry ghost, rebirth as an animal, and rebirth into Hell. The account given here does not match the usual legends of the historical Buddha's life.

FUXI

By legend, Fuxi (trad. 2953–2838 BCE) was an ancient sage-king and cultural hero who taught the human race to hunt and cook food. He is also credited with creating the hexagrams in the ancient divination text *Classic of Changes* (Yijing). He is one of the many ancient behavioral models mentioned in the lecture in session 12.

GAMES

Popular gambling games of the seventeenth century mentioned in session 10 include cards, *pupai*; throwing dice or *zhishai*; and "struggles and jabs," *doushuo*.

"Gentleman"

As the narrator notes in session 3, "Chaofenglang" (rendered there as "Gentleman Official") originally denoted a government position. In time, *chaofeng* gradually came to be a courteous term of address for a wealthy person, something akin to "squire" in English. It sometimes refers specifically to pawnbrokers like Wang Xingge in session 3.

Guan, Lord

Guan Di, the historical general Guan Yu (160–219), the patron god of merchants and performers, is always represented with a bright red face in temple images, an indication of his fierce loyalty. In session 10 red-faced drunks are likened to images of the god.

Guangwu, Emperor, of Han

Liu Xiu, the Guangwu emperor (r. 25–56 CE), restored the Han dynasty after the short-lived Xin dynasty of Wang Mang (9–23 CE). The references in session 12 to the Jin (Jurchen) and Yuan (Mongol) rulers suggest parallels with the Manchu conquest just two decades or so before this collection was compiled. Patrick Hanan (*Chinese Vernacular Story*, 198) suggests that the reference to Emperor Guangwu in session 12 might indicate the author's hope for a Han restoration of the Ming, which never materialized.

Han Lin'er and Xu Zengshou

Han Lin'er was the son of Han Shantong (d. 1351), who plotted the Red Scarves (Hong Jin) rebellion against the Yuan (1351–68). The younger Han then became a leader; although lauded as the "Little Ming King," he may have died at the hands of the Ming founder, Zhu Yuanzhang, who consolidated Han's forces under his command. "Xu Zengshou" may be an error for "Xu Shouhui," an important founder of the Red Scarves army. This mistake may have been deliberate on Aina's part; it reflects the shaky hold that session 12's Rector Chen has on both history and philosophy.

HAN SHAN

"Han Shan" is the name of a mountain near Hangzhou that several Tang period poets took as a pen name. The lines quoted in session 11 are not in any standard collection of Han Shan poems, most of which express a negative view of normal social life and promote withdrawal to the mountains for the practice of meditation. Instead of the joys of autumn, many address the difficulties of the life of self-denial. See Henricks, *Poetry of Hanshan*.

HAN YU'S (HAN CHANGLI'S) ESSAYS

References in session 6 and 12 include "The Origins of Dao" (Yuan Dao), a defense of the Confucian principles of humanity and ethical behavior against the claims of Daoism and Buddhism in their focus on inactivity and transcendence of this-worldly responsibilities. In "Proclamation on Driving Off the Crocodiles" ("Qu e'yu wen"), rationalistic Han Yu relies on his temporal authority in ordering the crocodiles of Chaozhou to be gone and stop plaguing the people in his jurisdiction, an effort that may not have been entirely sincere. See also "Memorial on the Bone of the Buddha."

HUIZONG, EMPEROR OF SONG

In 1127 the Song emperor Huizong and his son and successor, Qinzong, were captured by invaders from the Jurchen state of Jin and taken north into the barren lands of Central Asia. Both died many years later of exposure and disease. Huizong is often used as an example of a poor administrator, as he is in session 12.

IMPERIAL BODYGUARDS AND SECRET SERVICE

The Imperial Bodyguards mentioned in session 9 were a Ming period unit, the Jinyiwei: "embroidered-uniform guard unit . . . the most prestigious and influential of the Imperial Guards; functioned as the personal bodyguard of the Emperor; cooperated with influential eunuchs in maintaining an empire-wide, irregular police and judicial service" (Hucker, *Dictionary of Official Titles*, 166). Secret Service: Dongchang, the "Eastern Depot, a palace eunuch agency created in 1420 to investigate treasonable offenses of any kind, gradually becoming a kind of imperial secret service headquarters not subject to the control of any regular governmental organization, and greatly feared" (ibid., 551).

INCENSE

The two types of incense referred to in session 10: According to Li Shizhen's *Materia Medica, huangshu* incense is made from the heartwood and knots of the aloeswood tree. The part that floats when the wood is soaked in water is made into *huangshu* incense; the heavier wood is ground into another variety of incense.

Ompa is also a type of incense, presumably imported from Southeast Asia. The syllables of the term might also have been taken from the Chinese transliteration of "*Om* mani *padme* hūm," the chanted prayer of Tibetan Lamaist Buddhism. Either way, exoticism is for sale here.

JADE EMPEROR SCRIPTURE AND DARK WARRIOR SCRIPTURE

The title *Jade Emperor Scripture*, one of many texts referred to in session 12, may be a shortened reference to the *Acts of the Jade Emperor Scripture* (Yuhuang benxing jing), an alternative title for *A Collection of the Acts of the Most High Jade Emperor* (Gaoshang Yuhuang benxing jijing) in the Daoist canon. The title *Dark Warrior Scripture* may refer to *Miraculous Scripture Told by the Most High about the Divine Spells of Zhenwu, Great Lord of the Dark Heavens* (Taishangshuo Xuantian Dadi Zhenwu benzhuan shenzhou miaojing) and/or *Scripture of Zhenwu's Repayment of Virtuous Acts* (Zhenwu bao'en jing) in the Daoist canon, although this is not a standard reference. Xuanwu or Zhenwu is one of the more powerful Daoist deities identified with the direction north.

JIN RULER AND CROWN PRINCE OF THE YUAN

In 1161 Wanyan Liang, the emperor of Jin (known later as Prince of Hailing), mounted a large-scale invasion of the Southern Song. After failing to cross the Yangzi near present-day Nanjing, he was murdered by his generals near Yangzhou as he prepared for a second attempt. By that time he had been replaced on the Jin throne by a rebellion among the Wanyan imperial family. See Mote, *Imperial China*, 232–35.

The account in session 12 totally contradicts the historical record. In 1388 the Ming general Lan Yu (executed 1393) inflicted a heavy defeat on the

Mongol forces of Toghus Temür (1342–1389) at Lake Büyür, north of the Gobi Desert, although the Mongol leader and his son Tianbaonu escaped (*DMB*, 1293–94). There seems to be little correspondence between these facts and the anecdote recounted in session 12, which Rector Chen apparently knows nothing about. His subsequent mention of centuries of peace during the Zhou is similarly incorrect.

JUDICIAL PROCEDURES

For more on the judicial procedures and review, interrogation, and crime reports mentioned in session 9, see Hegel, *True Crimes*, 12: "Investigation of the more serious cases required approval from successively higher levels, where cases were retried as they passed upward through the judicial review system. Each stage produced standardized written reports presenting all the facts and outlining all administrative procedures followed—proving that the process had been conducted properly—and included recommendations as to the appropriate punishment for each individual offender." Military procedures were similar, but simpler.

JUPITER

The planet Jupiter (Taisui xing), with its period of twelve years, apparently was the origin of the twelve "earthly branches" that were used since high antiquity along with the ten "celestial stems" to keep track of time (days, months, and years). Jupiter came to represent the passage of time and therefore life's transience. Temple images of Jupiter often include representations with a string of skulls around his neck, hence the nickname for the rowdy young man in session 11.

LAOZI

The life of Laozi as recounted in session 12 is based on legends recorded in *Records of the Grand Historian* 63: Confucius visited him to consult about ritual matters (see Confucius, *Confucius*, 227–28). Zhouzhi County is in present-day Shaanxi. By later legend, Laozi ascended to heaven upon his death, to become Old Lord of the Most High (Taishang Laojun), one of the heavenly manifestations, the Three Purities, of Daoist religion. The wag in the crowd in session 12 refers to the philosopher by the name given him in Daoist religion and then pushes the joke further by associating this deity with the search for an elixir of long life associated with Daoist alchemy. This alchemical "external elixir" (*waidan*) trend had been supplanted by the "internal elixir" (*neidan*) practices of meditation and self-purification since around the year 1000.

According to chapter 10 in *Garden of Tales* (Shuoyuan) by Liu Xiang (ca. 77–6 BCE), when Chang Cong, Laozi's teacher, was on his deathbed, Laozi went to see him, hoping to hear his final instructions. Chang Cong "opened his mouth and showed it to Laozi: 'Is my tongue still there?' 'Yes,' said Laozi. 'Are my teeth still there?' 'They are gone.' 'Do you know why?' asked Chang Cong. 'The tongue remained,' replied Laozi; 'isn't it because it is soft? The teeth are gone; isn't it because they are hard?' Chang Cong said, 'Ah, you are right. You have exhausted [the reality concerning] all things under Heaven. What more do I need to say to you?'"

"Layman" and its Biographical Implications

Aina's self-proclaimed title "layman," or *jushi*, ostensibly refers to one who follows the precepts of Buddhist practice, although many used it to mean simply that they were living in retirement. Shengshui (Sagely Waters) is the name of a river. The *Classic of Rivers* (Shuijing) notes that this is a name for Liulihe in the area of Beijing where Aina may have resided for a time; however, most scholars identify Aina as being from the lower Yangzi area, Jiangnan. One of the old names of the West Lake in Hangzhou is "Mingshenghu"; from this and other evidence, several scholars, including Patrick Hanan and Hu Shi, have concluded that the author of this collection was a native of Hangzhou.

Lü Mengzheng and Old Governor Cai

Both Lü Mengzheng and Old Governor Cai, referred to in session 10, are figures from operas current at that time, Lü Mengzheng in the short *zaju The Broken Kiln* (Poyao ji) and Old Governor Cai in the lengthy *chuanqi* play *The Lute* (Pipa ji).

Zheng Yuanhe was the male lead in a series of romantic operas based on the Tang period tale "The Tale of Li Wa" (Li Wa zhuan) in which Zheng squanders his wealth on the courtesan Li Wa and is cast into poverty by his outraged father, only to be nursed back to health and guided to scholastic honors under her tender care.

The "gutter" in which the old freebooter's corpse will be abandoned is an allusion to *Mencius* 1B.12, in which the philosopher chides the ruler of a small state for abandoning the weak and the aged in times of famine. See Mencius, *Mencius*, 44–45.

LUOYANG

The specific identification of the place from which the dead and wounded soldiers in session 7 came suggests a topical reference for Aina's contemporaries. Luoyang had been the home of a particularly extravagant Ming noble, the Prince of Fu, who was widely hated for expropriating land from local farmers. In 1640 the rebel Li Zicheng captured the city of Luoyang, butchered the prince, drank his blood, and fed his cooked remains to his troops. See Wakeman, *Great Enterprise*, 337–39, 339n65.

"MEMORIAL ON THE BONE OF THE BUDDHA"

In 819 the poet and minister Han Yu (768–824) wrote his "Memorial on the Bone of the Buddha" to the emperor, chiding him, in a jocular tone, for the elaborate ceremony planned to welcome a relic of the historical Buddha. The emperor was displeased, and Han Yu barely escaped with his life. In 507, during the Liang period, Fan Zhen (450–510) wrote an essay titled "On the Extinction of the Spirit after Life" (Shen mie lun), critiquing belief in the religion of the time. Wang Chong (27–97) also denied the existence of ghosts. *See* "Han Yu's essays." Aina uses these references to discredit the pontification of the rector in session 12.

MR. PEACEMAKER

The historical Mr. Peacemaker referred to in session 5, Hejing Xiansheng, is Lin Bu (967–1029). A well-known poet, Lin led a reclusive life in Gushan, Hangzhou, and received the posthumous title Hejing from the Song emperor Renzong (r. 1022–63) even though he never served in officialdom. For Lin's life, see "Gushan," in Zhang Dai, *Xihu mengxun*, 165–69.

OGRES AS TEMPLE DECORATIONS

The ogres referred to in session 1 are *taotie*, faces made up of animal parts that were cast onto bronze ritual vessels of the Shang and Zhou periods in high antiquity. Often interpreted as ravenous, they seem to represent the infinite and the afterlife.

OUTLAWS OF THE MARSH AND "LIFE OF XIMEN"

Outlaws of the Marsh (Shuihu zhuan) mentioned in sessions 11 and 12, also known as *Water Margin*, is a compilation of the adventures of many bandit heroes and their collective exploits. "Tales of Ximen" in session 11 is a reference to the late sixteenth-century novel *Plum in the Golden Vase* (Jin Ping Mei), which narrates the sensuous life of Ximen Qing, his six wives, and his many associates and lovers. Although venery is a central concern for the novel, it also records daily activities in a wealthy merchant household in remarkable detail.

PLUMS

In *Mengzi* 3B.10, Mencius and Kuangzhang debate moral integrity. Kuangzhang sees Chen Zhongzi as a paragon of integrity because he chose to eat spoiled foods rather than share in his brother's ill-gotten gains. Mengzi sees Zhongzi as impractical. See Mencius, *Mencius*, 133. In the reference in session 5, we see Aina's ambivalence about martyrdom. The phrase "plums eaten by larvae" (*cao shi zhi li*) comes from a popular riddle in Qing China (What is a plum eaten by larvae?), quoted in Duoduofu, *Another Night's Conversation—More Elegant Riddles* (You yixi hua—xu yami); see Gao Boyu, *Zhonghua mishu jicheng*, 246. Its answer, "the plum's remains" (*li yu*) is a clever pun on the key words *li* (with the meaning of both "plum" and the surname Li) and *yu* ("remains" or "surplus"): Li Yu is the name of a famous filial son from the Three Kingdoms period (220–65). For his biography, see Chang Qu, *Huayang guozhi*, 10B.16a.

"ROTATING HANDS"

The "rotating hands" (*fanzi shou*) described in session 9 were government-employed runners serving in rotation who specialized in the arrest of bandits and thieves. For more on the role of runners, see also Reed, *Talons and Teeth*.

SCHOOL OF PRINCIPLE (LIXUE)

The School of Principle was the dominant school of Neo-Confucianism from the Song through the Qing, roughly seven hundred years. Its primary thinkers are referred to in session 12: Zhou Dunyi (1017–1073), the brothers Cheng Hao (1032–1085) and Cheng Yi (1033–1107), Zhang Zai (1020–1077), and the most influential by far, Zhu Xi (1130–1200). See "Session 12" in "Afterthoughts on the Stories."

SHANTANG RIVER BRIDGE

This Suzhou bridge crosses the Shantang River to reach Shantang Road, which runs for seven *li* (approx. 3.5 kilometers, or 2.2 miles) along the north bank from the Chang Gate (Changmen), in the northwestern section of the old walled city, to Tiger Hill. By tradition it was built when the poet Bai Juyi (772–846) held office in Suzhou. It is still lined with small shops catering to the tourist trade, similar to its description in session 10.

SHENGGONG

Master Zhudaosheng (Shenggong) was a fifth-century monk who was said to have preached the Nirvāṇa Sutra at Tiger Hill Temple in Suzhou. At first, no one was convinced. Then he gathered some rocks as his audience, and the rocks nodded with conviction while listening to his sermon. The title of a slightly earlier collection of vernacular short fiction, *Rocks Nod Their Heads* (Shi dian tou), and its preface, written by Feng Menglong (1754–1646), refer to this anecdote.

SHI YOU'S WIND

The character Shi You in session 1 has a complicated textual history. The poem referred to at the end of the tale is by the Tang poet Sikong Shu (ca. 766), titled "Farewell to Lu Qinqing" (Liu Lu Qinqing); it is quoted in Hong Mai, *Random Notes from Rong Studio* (Rongzhai suibi), *juan* 3. The phrase "Shi You's wind" derives from a tale in Feng Menglong's late Ming classical story collection *The Anatomy of Love* (Qingshi leilue), in which a merchant's wife who fails to dissuade her husband from leaving on a business trip dies in desolation and becomes the kind of whirlwind or strong headwind that obstructs the departure of other merchants' boats. A similar entry in Chu Renhuo's *Strong Gourds, Second Collection* (Jianhu ji, erji) from later in the seventeenth century presents Shi You as a kind of insect living in the river. When the Shi You worms come out, there would be heavy winds.

STONE STEPS

The number fifty-three in the stone steps on Tiger Hill mentioned in session 10 may refer to the number of wise teachers encountered by Sudhana in his quest for enlightenment in the final chapter, "Entry into the Realm of Reality" (Gandavyuha ["Ru fajie pin" in Chinese]), of the Avatamsaka Sutra, known in Chinese as *Huayan jing* (Flower garland sutra). Alternatively, it may refer to the number of incarnations of the Buddha in the past, a list that varies with the scriptural source. During the seventeenth century, there were several albums with images of fifty-three incarnations of the bodhisattva Guanyin. See McLoughlin, *Image and Appropriation*, esp. 160–61.

SU QIN

A well-known story from the Warring States Period has Su Qin tie his hair to the rafters and periodically stab himself in the leg so that he would stay awake while studying. The expression "hang from the rafters, stab in the thigh" (*xuan liang ci gu*) came to signify diligence in scholarship. In session 9, Liu Bao misinterprets the phrase to suggest that he will hang himself.

SU SHI

Su Shi (Su Dongpo, 1037–1101), mentioned in the original preface and in sessions 2, 3, 4, and 12, was a polymath who excelled at painting and calligraphy, as well as prose and *ci* and *shi* poetry. His barely veiled criticisms of Grand Councilor Wang Anshi (1021–1086) and the emperor brought imperial censure and exile on several occasions. For a comment by Zhaoyun, one of his female attendants, on his irreverent perspectives, see note 9 in the preface.

TANG SAI'ER

The account of Sancui'er in session 12 seems to be an abbreviated version of the exploits of the historical Tang Sai'er, who reportedly was a Buddhist laywoman and may have become a nun after her husband's death. By legend, she discovered a divine book on military tactics in a stone box while visiting her husband's grave; she may also have found a sword there. She rebelled in 1420, calling herself "Buddha Mother." Using the magic spells from the book, she could see both past and future; she could also convert paper cutouts into soldiers and cavalry as other White Lotus (Bailianjiao) leaders reportedly did. Her force numbered only about five hundred, however, and before long they were captured. Yet she somehow escaped from prison, leaving a cangue and fetters behind, and was never apprehended. Her exploits became the basis for the eighteenth-century novel *The Heretical History of a Female Immortal* (Nüxian waishi). See *DMB*, 1251–52, and Haar, *White Lotus*, 138–39.

THREE BODIES OF THE BUDDHA

The three forms of the Buddha, or Three Bodies (Sanshen), referred to in session 12 are the Dharmakāya (his essential nature, identical with the Ultimate Reality), the Sambhogakāya (his body of bliss as a deity in Paradise), and the Nirmāṇakāya (his transformation body, by which he can appear in any form as an expedient for saving others).

THREE FESTIVALS

The three important festivals mentioned in session 10 are Qingming, or Memorial Day, and the Dragon Boat (Duanwu) and Mid-Autumn (Zhongqiu) festivals.

Zhu Sanxing's nickname refers first to his inflated sense of himself as a young man. The word *jie*, "time" or "festival," is a homophone for *jie*, "accepted," as is *jie*, the three "portions" of his life, and *jie*, "joints" later, making many puns in his name simultaneously.

THREE PURITIES

The Three Purities (Sanqing) mentioned in session 12 are heavenly manifestations of the Dao in Daoist religion. All three were participants in the creation of the universe, and each oversees a particular heaven, but for ease of comprehension they are represented as enthroned elders. On Laozi as one of them, see "Laozi": scriptures vary on whether he took human form to reveal the *Daode jing* to humanity or became one of these deities after a lifetime on Earth.

WANG JIEFU

"Wang Jiefu," mentioned in the commentary on session 12, was the informal name of the Song minister Wang Anshi (1021–1086), whose radical fiscal reform measures were inspired by his reading of the policies of China's ancient sages. These measures were strongly opposed by many officials and scholars, including historian Sima Guang (1019–86) and Su Shi (see "Su Shi"). The latter was exiled until Wang's schemes were brought to a close and the status quo ante reestablished.

WEN TIANXIANG AND YU ZHONGSU

Two figures mentioned in session 12 were considered to have become deities after death because of their unshakable virtue. Wen Tianxiang (1236–1283) was a commander of Song loyalist troops who repeatedly suffered defeat at the hands of the Mongol invaders. Ultimately he was taken captive and executed because he refused to renounce his allegiance to the defeated state.

Yu Zhongsu was the Ming's Minister of War Yu Qian (1398–1457), who greatly admired Wen Tianxiang. Yu was decisive in maintaining the Ming capital in Beijing despite an invasion by Mongols; his reorganization of the armed forces was central in pacifying the northern regions. In the end, his enemies accused him of treason and had him executed. Within a decade a shrine in his honor was constructed in eastern Beijing, however. See *DMB*, 1608–11.

WU, EMPEROR OF LIANG (LIANG WUDI)

Among the rulers who failed because of their religious beliefs mentioned in session 12, Xiao Yan, Emperor Wu of Liang, starved to death at Taicheng in 549 during the rebellion begun by Hou Jing the preceding year. He was deeply engaged in Buddhist teachings; by legend, he considered himself an enlightened monk and appears as a character in several Ming period religious novels.

Wu, King

King Wu (Wu Wang), discussed in sessions 2 and 7, was the conquering founder of the Zhou dynasty, although King Wen, his father, was nominally considered the first Zhou ruler; doing so was a filial act on King Wu's part. King Wu was considered a moral paragon and model ruler, despite his historical military conquest of Shang.

Wu Zixu

The central figure in numerous prose and dramatic narratives, and mentioned in sessions 3, 4, and 10 here, Wu Zixu was a fifth-century BCE minister of the Wu Kingdom. His father, Wu She, was the tutor of Prince Jian of Chu. A second tutor, Fei Wuji, slandered Wu She and convinced King Ping of Chu that Wu She and the prince were planning a rebellion against him. The king ordered Wu She killed and tried to trick Wu's two sons, Wu Shang and Wu Zixu, into joining their father in Chu. Wu Zixu refused and so survived. He hid his identity for years, awaiting a chance to avenge the deaths of his father and brother. He became a high minister of Wu and led the kingdom to great prosperity, after which it devastated the Chu armies. After entering the capital, Wu Zixu exhumed the former king's corpse and gave it three hundred lashes to avenge his father.

Wuding, King

Wuding (1238–1180) was a ruler of the Shang, who made the builder Fu Yue a high minister after dreaming about him. The reference to Mencius that follows this comment in session 12 is abridged from *Mengzi* 4B.25: "If the beauty Xi Shi is covered with filth, then people will hold their noses when they pass her. But should an ugly man fast and cleanse himself, he would be fit to offer sacrifices to [the Lord on High]" (Mencius, *Mencius*, 167, 169). Both references are meant, not seriously, to confirm the existence of a supreme deity.

Wuxing (Five Agents)

The references in sessions 1, 9, and 12 reveal aspects of this complex term: Although *wuxing* is generally translated as "five phases" when it refers to stages of development, philosophers often use it in the sense of "agents." The term refers to aspects of a situation or a person, not to the constituent elements. The five agents are wood, fire, earth, metal, and water.

XIAN, DUKE, AND CHONG'ER

Duke Xian, mentioned in session 1, ruled the state of Jin in 676–51 BCE and expanded its grasp. Early in his rule he decided to massacre most of his extended family so that only his direct descendants would ever rule the state. After his concubine Li Ji gave birth to a son, however, Duke Xian wanted this son to replace his older son Shensheng as his heir. The ensuing conflict led to a war, known historically as "Li Ji's Unrest" (657–51 BCE), in which Duke Xian fought Shensheng and his brother, Chong'er; the latter became a much more common subject of legend and story.

XIANG YU

Readers of sessions 6 and 9 generally would know that Xiang Yu (232–202), the Hegemon King of Chu, and his troops were surrounded by Han forces led by Liu Bang at the battle of Gaixia in 202 BCE. At night the Han soldiers began to sing Chu songs, which aroused the Chu soldiers' longing for home, causing most of them to desert the battlefield. Xiang Yu's subsequent suicide, recorded in *Records of the Grand Historian* 7, has been immortalized in numerous legends and retellings, including the Beijing opera *Hegemon King Bids Farewell to His Concubine* (Bawang bie ji). See Sima Qian, *Records*, 1:37–74.

XUANZONG, EMPEROR OF TANG

In 755 the border general An Lushan rebelled and led his armies against the Tang capital. The Tang emperor Xuanzong, also known as Minghuang, fled, but his guard rebelled along the way, and he was forced to allow Prime Minister Yang Guozhong and his favorite, Yang Yuhuan, the Guifei, or "Precious Consort," to be executed. These events have been immortalized in numerous poems, plays, and novels, hence the reference in sessions 6 and 12 .

YAMA KINGS

See "Yanluo, King Yanluo."

Yamen

A general term for an administrative center used in sessions 3, 4, 8, 9, and 11, in particular the court where the official (magistrate, prefect, provincial governor, etc.) heard cases and pronounced judgments in civil and criminal cases. Such halls were open to the street, making it possible for bystanders to witness all proceedings.

Yanluo, King Yanluo

In traditional beliefs based in part on Buddhist teachings, King Yanluo (Yanluowang; Yama in Sanskrit) rules over the Underworld, a place of punishment where sinners undergo horrendous tortures after death, some of which are mentioned in session 12. The Ten Judges of the Dead are collectively called "Yama Kings," or Yanwang, as in session 4.

Yao and Shun

Among the behavioral exemplars mentioned in sessions 2, 5, 7, 8, and 12, by tradition the ancient sage-kings Yao (r. 2357–2255 BCE?) and Shun (r. 2255–2205 BCE?), were models of benevolent rule. The sage Confucius lived long afterward, from 551 to 479 BCE, but he, too, took these ancient rulers as models.

Zhang Ling and Zhang Jiao

Zhang Ling (34–156), also known as Zhang Daoling, was the founder of the Celestial Masters (Tianshi) line of religious Daoism, and Zhang Jiao (d. 184) originated its Taiping sect. Their followers, numbering in the hundreds of thousands, were major components of the Yellow Scarves (Huang Jin) rebellion against the Han (184–205). In session 12, Rector Chen lists them as examples of dangerous heretical teachers.

Zhao Guyuan and Xu Hongru

Zhao Guyuan, mentioned in session 12, was a White Lotus (Bailianjiao) rebel leader during the late sixteenth century. Another leader, Xu Hongru (d. 1622), reportedly attracted followers with his magic skills, including the ability to induce people to see themselves reflected in basins of water dressed as royalty and high ministers; see *DMB*, 587–89.

ZHURONG

In early Chinese mythology, Zhurong is the fire god and god of the south, as in session 4 and elsewhere. In session 1, he appears as a guardian figure found just outside the main sanctuary of a traditional temple.

THE ZHUANGZI PARABLES

Kun is a type of gigantic fish that turns into an enormous bird called the Peng in the opening chapter "Free and Easy Wandering" (Xiaoyaoyou) of the Daoist philosophical text *The Zhuangzi*; its perspective is necessarily larger than that of smaller creatures, Zhuangzi argues.

In chapter 20, "The Mountain Tree" (Shanmu), Zhuangzi talks about how a tree was spared by a woodcutter because it was considered useless and a goose that sings was able to live longer than the one that did not sing because it was considered useful. When his disciple asked if he would prefer to be useful or useless, he replied that he would rather be in between useful and useless. These stories illustrate the relativity of conventional value judgments.

Chapter 3, "The Secret of Caring for Life" (Yangsheng zhu), relates how Cook Ding demonstrated his extraordinary skill in cutting up an ox. The cook then explained the intuitive process he followed, and the ruler considered it a lesson for the nurturing of life.

In chapter 13, "The Way of Heaven" (Tiandao), an experienced wheelwright explains that his intuitive techniques for making wheels cannot be taught through words; likewise, Duke Huan will not be able to understand the sages' thoughts through reading their words, because the real meaning cannot be expressed in conventional words.

NOTES

INTRODUCTION: GOSSIP AND EXAGGERATION

1   Studies of the classical-language narrative tradition include Campany, *Strange Writing*; Schafer, *Divine Woman*; Lin Chen, *Shenguai xiaoshuo shi*; Zeitlin, *Historian of the Strange*; and Zeitlin, *Phantom Heroine*. The best survey of the vernacular tradition is Hanan, *Chinese Vernacular Story.*

2   On the use of ambiguity, see Yenna Wu, "Bean Arbor Frame," pp. 12–19, 24.

3   See "Feng Menglong" in "Historical and Cultural References."

4   I am grateful to Wang Wei for this suggestion. On text and illustrations in various seventeenth-century narratives, see Wang Wei's forthcoming dissertation, "The Lure of Visualization," at Washington University.

5   See Lu Hsun (Lu Xun), *Brief History of Chinese Fiction*, chaps. 12–13, 21.

6   This line appears on the *fengmian*, or cover page, of Feng Menglong's first collection of stories, *Stories Old and New* (Gujin xiaoshuo), published in 1621. For a translation, see Hanan, *Chinese Vernacular Story*, 22.

7   Aina's contemporary and likely friend Li Yu (1610/11–1680) also deliberately deviated from the standard *huaben* form in his story collections.

8   See "The Writerly Mode" in "Afterthoughts on Stories." Session 8 offers another alternative, although this, too, seems to be in jest.

9   Zeitlin discusses the doomed palace lady as symbolic of a fallen state in *Phantom Heroine*, 92–97. For an exploration of the range of women characters in early Qing period postwar writings, see Wai-yee Li, *Women and National Trauma*, esp. chaps. 4–6.

10 For further reading on this period, see Mote, *Imperial China*; Brook, *Confusions of Pleasure*; and Wakeman, *Great Enterprise.*

11 See Hegel, "Dreaming the Past."

12 See Wai-yee Li, "Early Qing to 1723," 201.

13 The most thorough and compelling study of this author is Hanan, *Invention of Li Yu*. See also Hegel, "Inventing Li Yu." For examples of his stories, see Li Yu, *Tower.*

14 Wai-yee Li, "Early Qing to 1723," 201.

15 In some editions and other writings, his name is given with a different second character. For more information on the author, see "Aina" in "Historical and Cultural References."

16 See Zhang Daopin, *Qianyan*, 1. The foreword mentions ingredients in his nostrums, but this is a metaphor for his use of common themes in his tales, not evidence that he practiced medicine.

17 Zheng Zhenduo, *Zhongguo wenxue yanjiu*, in *Zheng Zhenduo quanji*, 424, endorses the idea that Aina was a Ming loyalist and compares his writing with that of Dong Tuo (1620–1686), whose given name is often read "Yue." Zheng supposes that Dong Tuo was the author of *Augmented Journey to the West* (Xiyou bu), the 1641 sequel to *Journey to the West* (Xiyou ji), although Dong was probably only the editor of the novel written by his father, Dong Sizhang (1587–1628).

18 Hanan (*Chinese Vernacular Story*, 196–98) discusses this session in some detail, concluding that Aina blamed Confucian dogma for the fall of the Ming dynasty.

19 Hu Shi ("Xu") opined that the commentaries were written by Aina himself; Hanan and others assume that they were written by a friend.

20 The commentary on session 3 advises Aina to make the story into a play. Indeed, somewhat after these stories appeared, a writer produced *Idle Plays under the Bean Arbor* (Doupeng xianxi). This is said to have been edited by Li Yu. Li's name is also on this play, probably to enhance its commercial appeal. The three plays adapt stories that debunk historical incidents described in sessions 1, 2, and 7, but not 3. See Hanan, *Chinese Vernacular Story*, 240n5.

21 *Honglou meng* originally bore the title *Shitou ji*, or *Story of the Stone*, which is the title of the excellent English translation by David Hawkes and John Minford. The most important English-language study of fiction commentary is Rolston, *Traditional Chinese Fiction*.

22 See Hanan, *Chinese Vernacular Story*, 194. Zhang Daoqin notes the tremendous frustrations recorded so clearly in these stories; see his "Qianyan," 1.

23 See "Dating the text and its editions" in "Historical and Cultural References." In her doctoral dissertation, "The Lure of Visualization," Wang Wei explores the relationships between text and illustration in this and other contemporary publications.

24 See editions at Mengyuan shucheng, http://www.my285.com/gdwx/xs/bj/dpxh/; Weiji wenku, https://zh.wikisource.org/zh-hant/豆棚閒話; and Project Gutenberg, https://www.gutenberg.org/ebooks/25328.

25 I am grateful to an anonymous reader for the University of Washington

Press for bringing this information to my attention. See "Du Halde" in "Historical and Cultural References."

26　For a French translation, see Lebeaupin, *Propos oisifs*; for the translation by Yenna Wu, see Aina, "Jie Zhitui." Session 1 was translated afresh for this volume, although the translators acknowledge that Wu's translation saved them from misunderstanding the text in several places. Lebeaupin's rendition was also very helpful in clarifying translation questions in several sessions.

27　See "Feng Menglong" in "Historical and Cultural References."

28　The collections by Feng and Ling were discovered in Japanese libraries— only portions of volumes remained in China by 1900. See Sun Kaidi, *Riben Dongjing*, 10–11; Sun Kaidi, *Zhongguo*, 91–94; and Ōtsuka, *Zōho Chūgoku*, 9–16.

29　Zeng Yandong, *Xiao doupeng*. For more on Aina's later influences, see Waldrop, "Tension and Trauma."

30　This anonymous novel is *Qilou chongmeng*, also known as *Honglou xumeng*. I am grateful to Li Qiancheng for pointing this out to me. For the online Open-Lit text, see http://open-lit.com/bookindex.php?gbid=428, accessed August 9, 2015.

Preface

1　That is, a proud man unrestrained by any social prohibitions.

2　To save his life, Cao Zhi (192–232) once composed a poem while taking seven steps in response to a challenge from his murderous older brother (see session 1). By legend, Wen Tingyun (ca. 812–ca. 866), a gifted poet, would often fold and unfold his arms eight times when composing a poem.

3　The man with three ears is blessed with great intellectual gifts. Legend has it that Dong Shen was made a functionary in the Underworld. He appointed as his clerk Zhang Shentong, a Changzhou scholar who had passed the lower civil service examination. Dong had him adjudicate a case and sent a report to the administration in Heaven. A yellow-robed man came, bringing Heaven's decision that the verdict was not appropriate. Angered, Dong Shen sealed one of Zhang's ears with a piece of meat. Zhang presided over the case for the second time. After some time, a document was sent from Heaven, saying the verdict was handled appropriately. Delighted, Dong Shen had others take out the meat. He had a child mold it like an ear and had it put on Zhang's forehead, saying, "I sealed one of your ears. Now I give you a third ear. Could this compensate you?" After some time Zhang Shentong came back to life. He felt an irresistible itch on his forehead, and another ear had grown there. More intelligent now, Zhang's contemporaries laughed over the matter, saying, "In the air flying there are the nine-headed birds—on earth we have a three-eared scholar." See, among others, Li Fang et al., *Taiping guangji, juan* 296, which cites *Xuanguai lu* as its source.

4   In Master Zhiyi's (538–597) *On Lines from the Lotus Sutra* (Miaofa lianhua jing wenju), eight varieties of pride are associated with eight kinds of birds. Pride in one's appearance is associated with the dove. See *Miaofa lianhua jing wenju*, 75.

5   Aina's "belly" is filled with quotations from the Confucian classics, which applicants were tested on in the civil service examinations. But apparently he did not proceed very far up this ladder to success. Among the literary and political associations active before the fall of the Ming, the best known is the Fushe (Revival society), which was suppressed in 1652 for its anti-Manchu positions. Aina's contemporary, the well-known literatus Wu Weiye (1609–1671), tried to revive such organizations in the 1650s, but they were banned by the new Qing regime. See Yenna Wu, "Bean Arbor Frame," 7–8.

6   See the "Wudu" chapter in Han Fei, *Han Fei Tzu*, 97.

7   *Zhuangzi* 24. "Medicines will serve as an example. There are monkshood, balloonflower, cockscomb, and chinaroot—each has a time when it is the sovereign remedy, though the individual cases are too numerous to describe"; Zhuangzi, *Complete Works*, 277. This implies that something insignificant can find its use at the appropriate time.

8   Upon biting an olive, one initially notices its bitter taste, but after chewing a while, one may perceive a sweet aftertaste.

9   Legend has it that Su Shi (Su Dongpo, 1037–1101), the doyen of letters of his age, asked those near him what was in his belly. Zhaoyun, one of his female attendants, said that it was full of thoughts that were out of keeping with his times. Amused, Su agreed.

10   Dongfang Shuo (154–93 BCE) became a legendary comical immortal.

11   *Zhiyue lu* 23, a Chan classic: Master Fadeng, when he was among the monks, "was bold, unconventional, and uninhibited. He did not have anything to do. He was looked down upon by the multitude, but only Fayan looked up to him. One day, Fayan asked the multitude, 'Who can untie the metal bell on the neck of the tiger?' No one was able to reply. When Master Fadeng entered the room, Fayan asked the same question of him. The Master replied, 'He who tied it to the tiger in the first place.' Master Fayan said, 'You cannot afford to neglect him.'"

12   Legend has it that on the advice of some weaving girls, Confucius attached a thread to an ant, which pulled it through the minuscule pores of the pearls when the ends of the pearls were covered with honey.

13   Qian Yu (Song dynasty) compiled a collection of medical prescriptions in the name of Sun Simiao (581–682), the legendary Tang dynasty physician, titled

Recipes of the Immortal Sun across the Sea (Sun Zhenren haishang fang). Daoist immortals are said to live on isles in the sea.

14   By legend, the Bamboo Grove was originally a park that was given to the Buddha Śākyamuni as a residence. Later, the term came to indicate any place where Buddhism was preached, whether actually associated with bamboo or not.

15   Zai Wo, or Zai Yu (522–458 BCE), was a disciple of Confucius. *Lunyu* (5.10): "Zai Yu was in bed in the daytime. The Master said, 'A piece of rotten wood cannot be carved, nor can a wall of dried dung be troweled. As far as Yu is concerned, what is the use of condemning him?'" (Confucius, *Analects*, 77).

16   Yanluo (Yama in Sanskrit) is the ruler of the Underworld in popular religious beliefs. See "Yanluo" in "Historical and Cultural References."

FOREWORD

"Layman Aina": For a discussion of the title Layman, see "'Layman' and its biographical implications" in "Historical and Cultural References." "Ziran the Eccentric Wanderer from Yuanhu": "Ziran" refers to a beard of dark, purplish color, and "Kuangke" means "Eccentric (or 'Mad') Wanderer"; neither provides any help in identifying this person. Yuanhu (Duck Lake) has been identified with Nanhu at Jiaxing in Zhejiang. In place of this pen name, another edition has Bailan Daoren (The Man in Pursuit of Dao Who Neglects All Else) of Suzhou.

1   For notes on Xu Jutan and the poetry collection, see "Preface and Foreword" in "Afterthoughts on Stories."

SESSION 1: JIE ZHITUI SETS FIRE TO HIS JEALOUS WIFE

1   Goat's-eye beans are also known as white hyacinth beans (*Dolichos lablab alba*).

2   Tripitaka, the Sanskrit name of the Buddhist monk known in China as Xuanzang (ca. 602–664), traveled widely in Central Asia and northern India collecting sutras to bring back to the Tang empire, for which he is said to have earned untold merit. In this context, "the West" refers to India.

3   *Notes on the Strange* (Shuyi ji) is attributed to Zu Chongzhi (429–500), a famous mathematician of the late Six Dynasties period (222–589).

4   The first reign period of Sima Yan (236–290) is known as the Taishi period (266–274). The Jin, or Western Jin, lasted from 265 to 420.

5   Cao Zijian (192–232), better known as Cao Zhi, is considered one of China's greatest early poets.

6   Translation from Knechtges, *Rhapsodies*, 359.

7   The "Southern Bough" dream refers to a famous classical-language story of the Tang period in which a young man dreamed that he had a splendid career and happy marriage only to see it all fall into ruins. When he awoke, he gave up his grandiose plans.

8   For these images, see "Ogres as temple decorations" and "Zhurong" in "Historical and Cultural References."

9   The state of Jin lasted approximately from the eleventh century BCE to 453 BCE, when it was split into three new states—Han, Zhao, and Wei—which ended the historical era called the Spring and Autumn Period. Jin was located in present-day Shanxi.

10   See "Xian, Duke, and Chong'er" in "Historical and Cultural References."

11   In 206 BCE, during the revolts against the Qin dynasty, the aristocrat Xiang Yu, leader of the Chu forces, burned the capital city Xianyang to the ground. Its palaces smoldered for more than three months.

12   The Qingming Festival is also known as the Tomb-Sweeping Festival.

13   Cold food is eaten during the Cold Food Festival, which begins the day before the Tomb-Sweeping Festival and lasts for three days, during which time no one eats hot food in honor of Jie Zhitui's giving his flesh to Chong'er.

14   *Śarīras* are mineral-like relics of varying sizes and colors left behind after the cremation of a Buddhist monk or nun of great spiritual purity.

15   See "Shi You's wind" in "Historical and Cultural References."

16   *The Extensive Records* (Taiping guangji) is a compendium of unofficial histories and fiction imperially commissioned during the Taiping reign (976–983). Compiled under the supervision of Li Fang (925–996), it is considered the most important source of early fiction. See "*Wuxing*" in "Historical and Cultural Background."

17   A line from the *Classic of Changes* (Yijing), hexagram 11.

18   "Fair, Fair, Cry the Ospreys" (Guanju) is the first poem in the *Classic of Poetry* (Shijing) that, despite metaphorical interpretations, ostensibly celebrates the approaching marriage of a young man and a young woman. "Marrying Down" (Lijiang) is the first story in *The Documents of Antiquity* (Shang shu) and refers to Emperor Yao's decision to marry two of his daughters to the commoner Shun in order to test the latter's qualifications to become emperor. If Shun could maintain a peaceful household with two sisters as his wives, it was assumed he could be a great emperor. And, by legend, he was.

1   This aphorism appears in several plays in the Yuan, Ming, and Qing dynasties, including Yang Xian's (14th cent.?) *Journey to the West* (Xiyou ji), book 5, act 19; Gao Ming's (1305–1359) *The Lute* (Pipa ji), act 31; and Hong Sheng's (1645–1704) *The Palace of Eternal Life* (Changshengdian), act 28.

2   This mention of stories told by professionals refers specifically to *pinghua*, a form of professional oral storytelling specializing in romantic tales of love and heroism that is still very popular in Yangzhou.

3   Three Sovereigns and Five Emperors (Sanhuang Wudi) refers to a group of mythological rulers of ancient China who preceded the legendary Xia dynasty. Shang is the earliest historical dynasty.

4   Shiniu was located in what is now Wenchuan County, Sichuan.

5   These poems are in the fifth-century BCE *Classic of Poetry* (Shijing), nos. 1 and 11. The first poem describes a young nobleman's pursuit of a fair and virtuous maiden; the latter extols the glories of royal offspring. The Duke of Zhou (Zhou Gong) referred to here is the brother of King Wu of the Zhōu dynasty (both sons of King Wen), not the "King Zhòu" of Shang mentioned earlier.

6   King You (r. 782–70 BCE) was the last ruler of the Western Zhou dynasty.

7   *Washing Silk* (Huansha ji), of 1577, with music by Wei Liangfu and libretto by Liang Chenyu (1520–1580), was probably the first in the soon-to-be-famous *kunqu* operatic form.

8   See "Bopi" in "Historical and Cultural References."

9   This common expression appears in the *Intrigues of the Warring States* (Zhanguo ce) and other ancient texts in anecdotes about historical figures of that time.

10 By tasting his feces, Fuchai, the King of Wu, diagnosed the King of Yue's illness and thereby won his trust. See "Bopi" in "Historical and Cultural References."

11 Suzhou is in the old Wu region; the city is considered the cradle of Wu culture.

12 This description of King Yue is recorded in *Chronicles of Wu and Yue* (Wu Yue chunqiu), written by Zhao Ye during the Han dynasty.

13 Historically, "Sir Taozhu" (Taozhu gong) was written with surnames that do not have specific meanings. The narrator here substitutes homophones so as to exaggerate Fan Li's character.

14 In Chinese mythology, the Crystal Palace is the palace of the Dragon King, ruler of the sea.

15 These are the last two lines from Tang poet Li Bai's "At Su Terrace Viewing the Past" (Sutai huaigu); translation from Watson, *Columbia Book of Chinese Poetry*, 208, with modifications.

16 These titles are fanciful. There are no such books.

17 Xishi's arm is lotus root, and her breast is blowfish belly. References to both can be found in Ye Jiaoran's (b. 1614) *Poetry Collection of Longxing Hall* (Longxingtang shihua). Xishi's tongues are a type of clam, possibly mussels, mentioned in Li Yu's *Random Lodgings for My Idle Feelings* (Xianqing ouji).

18 See "Su Shi" in "Historical and Cultural References." The poem is "Drinking by the Lake: Clear Sky at First, Then Rain" (Yin Hushang, chuqing houyu). For an alternative translation, see Fuller, *Road to East Slope*, 167.

19 Hu Lai means "Running Wild."

20 A *sheng* is an ancient wind instrument with some pipes that are played with the fingers and other pipes that serve as drones. The reference here is to music in the pleasure quarters. Mulberry trees and hemp are cash crops, the trees for leaves to feed silkworms and the hemp for rope, chair seats, and other uses.

21 See *The Zhuangzi* parables" in "Historical and Cultural References."

22 See "Dou and Tian" in "Historical and Cultural References."

23 See "Fan Li's son" in "Historical and Cultural References."

SESSION 3: A COURT-APPOINTED GENTLEMAN SQUANDERS HIS WEALTH BUT TAKES POWER

With special thanks to Li Fang-yu and Xu Yunjing for their considerable help.

1 On Su Dongpo, see "Su Shi" in "Historical and Cultural References."

2 The 1069 CE Green Sprouts Policy (Qingmiao Fa) took advantage of grain surpluses to provide loans to farmers, one of many fiscal and revenue reforms promoted by Wang Anshi during his tenure as Grand Councilor.

3 The poem, as it appears here, is a slightly modified version of the historical Su Dongpo's poem "Playfully Written on Bathing My Son" (Xi er xi zuo).

4 Kong Rong (zi Wenju, 153–208) was an official of the Later (Eastern) Han whose opposition to the policies of Cao Cao led to his execution. Cao Pi (187–226) named him one of the so-called Seven Masters of the Jian'an Era (Jian'an qizi) in recognition of his refined poetry.

5 The Sui dynasty fell, and the Tang arose in 618 CE.

6 Wang Hua was indeed a military leader of the early seventh century, but Aina's storyteller takes major liberties with his life story (as he himself later acknowledges).

7 On this title, see "Gentleman" in "Historical and Cultural References."

8 Squire Jiao and Hu Yong'er are characters in the novel *The Three Sui Quash the Demons' Revolt* (San Sui Pingyao zhuan), of around 1610. Feng Menglong later

adapted it into a much longer novel with the same title. Yong'er's husband is severely mentally handicapped.

9   Pingjiang is present-day Suzhou.

10 The phrase *shi dui he* (ten boxes) is a play on words with *dui he* (profit or interest equal to the principal capital). The two are homophones, hence the implication that ten boxes would serve as an omen of future profit.

11 The reference is to a parable in chapter 2 of *The Zhuangzi*, in which Zhuang Zhou is uncertain whether he was dreaming he was butterfly or is a butterfly dreaming he is a man. See Zhuangzi, *Complete Works*, 49.

12 The full name of the outcropping is the Rock for Fishing for Ao, the Great Turtle of Legend (Diao Ao ji).

13 Zhong Kui is a fearsome figure from mythology famed as a killer of demons.

14 An arhat is an enlightened individual who, having achieved *nirvāna*, is no longer subject to reincarnation. In this context, "the West" refers to India.

15 In imperial China, the period from sunset to sunrise was divided equally into fives watches, with the third watch centering on midnight.

16 This might refer to the Six Commanderies of the state of Wu during the Three Kingdoms period; however, the historical Wang Hua seized control of six departments (*liu zhou*), so this may be a reference to those departments.

17 This plays on the historical Yellow Scarves (Huangjin) and Red Scarves (Hongjin) rebellions at the end of the Han and Yuan dynasties, which played major roles in the change of dynasties.

18 Liu Cong is not mentioned in either of the standard dynastic histories of the Tang. He was most likely invented by Aina, inspired by the historical Wang Hua.

19 Artillery using gunpowder had not yet been invented at the time in which this story is set. It is difficult to say whether this is deliberate anachronism on Aina's part.

20 This is an echo of chapter 54 of the novel *Romance of the Three Kingdoms* (Sanguo zhi yanyi) in which the brilliant Zhuge Liang gives Zhao Zilong (also known as Zhao Yun) three brocade sacks containing notes outlining stratagems that will subsequently be of great value.

21 To say the bandits did not respect the Chinese calendar is to say that they did not respect imperial suzerainty.

22 For a likely historical reference here, see "Coxinga" in "Historical and Cultural References."

23 Literally, to accept the Chinese calendar; see note 21.

24 Qian Wusu was founder of the Kingdom of Wu-Yue during the Five Dynasties period in the tenth century.

25 Qiuran (Curly Beard) is the central character of the Tang dynasty classical-

language story "The Man with the Curly Beard" (Qiuranke zhuan). In it, he flees the chaos of the Sui-Tang transition and founds his own kingdom in a distant land, having realized that Li Shimin is better qualified than he to found a new dynasty in China.

26 Xu Zhigao is a previous name for Li Bian (889–943), founder of the Southern Tang state during the Five Dynasties period.

27 Song Qiqiu (887–959) was Xu Zhigao's chief strategist.

Session 4: The Commissioner's Son Wastes His Patrimony to Revive the Family

1 This is the first half of the third of five poems in the series *Returning to the Fields to Dwell* (Gui yuantian ju) by Tao Qian (Tao Yuanming, 365–427); see Hightower, *Poetry of T'ao Ch'ien*, 52.

2 The proverb is perhaps elaborated from a similar line in the Mahayana Mahaparinirvana Sutra, but this version appears as the central theme in story 12 in *Stories Old and New* (Gujin xiaoshuo), edited by Feng Menglong.

3 For discussions of Yin and Yang as philosophical concepts, see session 12.

4 This phrase has its source in *The Zhuangzi* 2: "I'm going to try speaking some reckless words, and I want you to listen to them recklessly." See Zhuangzi, *Complete Works*, 47. When Su Shi (see entry in "Historical and Cultural References") was living in deserted places, he frequently invited friends to drink and "speak with reckless words."

5 This teaching from Sima Guang's family instructions (*jiaxun*) is widely quoted.

6 *Rabbit Garden Texts* (Tuyuan ce) is an examination preparation book from the Tang dynasty. Li Yun, one of the sons of Emperor Taizong (Duke Jiang), ordered his assistant Du Sixian to compile a book of questions similar to those on the civil service examinations and to provide answers from the classics.

7 The use of lightning and shadow to convey ephemerality has its source in the final verse of the Buddhist Diamond Sutra (Jin'gangjing): "All conditioned phenomena / Are like dreams, illusions, bubbles, a shadow, / Like the dew and yet like lightning / And must be so regarded."

8 The Wanli period was the reign of Ming emperor Shenzong, from 1573 to 1620.

9 Kunshan County is located in southeastern Jiangsu, close to the present-day city of Shanghai.

10 See "Wu Zixu" in "Historical and Cultural References."

11 The Tomb-Sweeping or Memorial Festival (Qingming Jie) occurs on April 5 or 6 by the Western calendar.

12 *Mai chun* literally means "buying spring." It can refer to two different activities: buying wine or (as here) engaging in a leisure activity in springtime.

13 A name card (*mingtie*) bears one's name to be presented to the host when paying a visit.

14 The man was a *xiucai*, an unofficial reference to all men qualified to participate in provincial-level civil service recruitment examinations, with the real or nominal status of "government student" (*shengyuan*) in Confucian schools at prefectural or lower levels.

15 Li Rusong (1549–1598) was a native of Tieling on the Liaodong peninsula. He was a general during the Wanli period of the Ming dynasty.

16 Liu Fan won the title of *jingkui*, which was given to authors of the five best essays in a provincial examination (*xiangshi*), one for each of the five classical texts in which candidates were allowed to specialize.

17 Zhurong is an ancient official who became the god of fire.

18 Yama Kings (Yanwang) refers to the judges of the dead. The term was used sarcastically to refer to impartial and effective judges. See "Yanluo, King Yanluo" in "Historical and Cultural References."

19 See "Du Zichun" in "Historical and Cultural References."

20 The phrase "clouds arise" alludes to a poem by Wang Wei (701–761), "At My Country Home in Zhongnan" (Zhongnan bieye). See Watson, *Columbia Book*, 202.

SESSION 5: THE LITTLE BEGGAR WHO WAS TRULY FILIAL

1 *Kongzi jiayu*, 4.8b.

2 On this work, see *"Documents of Antiquity"* in "Historical and Cultural References."

3 For the historical reference, see Sima Qian, *Records* 1:174.

4 For details, see under "Childlike innocence" in "Historical and Cultural References."

5 This alludes to poem 260, "Zhengmin," in the *Classic of Poetry* (Shijing): "The people of our race were created by Heaven, / Having from the beginning distinctions and rules. / Our people cling to customs, / and what they admire is seemly behavior." See Waley, *Book of Songs*, 275.

6 This location is in present-day Hubei. This happens to be the hometown of the Ming chief minister Zhang Juzheng (1525–1582). Zhang served as grand secretary during the reigns of the Longqing and Wanli emperors. An extremely influential and controversial figure in the late Ming court,

he was known for his reforms of fiscal measures undertaken to improve the central government's finances and for his luxurious lifestyle, which was exposed after his death.

7   On this name, see "Mr. Peacemaker" in "Historical and Cultural References."

8   See "Plums" in "Historical and Cultural References."

9   Lao Lai was a recluse from the state of Chu during the Spring and Autumn Period. Story 2 in *Twenty-Four Cases of Filial Piety* (Ershisi xiao) says that in his seventies, he put on a five-color costume and danced like a baby to entertain his aged parents.

10   Here the author paraphrases the second couplet of the poem "Drinking on the Qingming Festival" (Qingming ri duijiu) by Gao Zhu (1170–1241). An influential member of the Jiangnan School of poetry, Gao led an entirely reclusive life. He died and was buried by West Lake.

11   On this song, see "'Dew on the Shallots'" in "Historical and Cultural References"

12   On this term, see "Beheaded brook" in "Historical and Cultural References."

13   Yidun was a fabulously rich salt merchant during the Spring and Autumn Period. "Taozhu" was the name taken by Fan Li (see session 2) to disguise himself after he left the service of the King of Yue with his accumulated wealth.

14   Yanluo is the King of the Underworld. See "Yanluo, King Yanluo" in "Historical and Cultural References."

15   By reminding his audience of the possibility of deities passing by and eavesdropping on their storytelling, the author insinuates mention of the intense censorship enforced by the new regime into the story.

16   Zeng Can and Min Ziqian were disciples of Confucius.

17   The line is from the "Great Preface" to the ancient collection the *Classic of Poetry* explaining the origins of poetry in intense feelings also refers to the filial Lao Lai, who danced to please his aged mother (see note 9).

SESSION 6: THE EXALTED MONKS WHO FAKED TRANSCENDENCE

1   The term describing the breezes is from the *Classic of Changes* (Yijing), an ancient Confucian text on divination and cosmology. Here it suggests the unending dangers facing the man of virtue. See Lynn, *Classic of Changes*, 318.

2   This comment paraphrases *Mencius* 3A.3, "Teng is limited in territory. Nevertheless, there will be men in authority and there will be the common people. Without the former, there would be none to rule over the latter—without the latter, there would be none to support the former." See Mencius, *Mencius*, 191.

3   "Regulate the family" and the rest of this list is taken from the first section

of *The Great Learning* (Daxue), a basic Confucian primer. See Legge, *Chinese Classics*, 357.

4   The term "inconceivable" here is frequently used in Buddhist sutras to describe the Ultimate Reality of the Dharma. The Neo-Confucian sense of *qi* and creation is discussed in session 12.

5   Bodhidharma brought the Chan School of Buddhism to China; see "Bodhidharma" in "Historical and Cultural References." On Master Zhudaosheng, see "Shenggong" in "Historical and Cultural References."

6   The term "sweet dew" (*ganlu*) appears in both Buddhist and Daoist writings. See Laozi, *Lao Tzu: Tao Te Ching*, section 32, 91.

7   Shi Le (274–333) founded the Later Zhao dynasty in the Eastern Jin period. "Fotucheng" is the Chinese name She Le gave to the monk Buddhosingha (232–348), who arrived in China from Kucha in 310.

8   The word *rakshasas* (*luocha* in Chinese) is a general term for "demons" in Buddhist writings.

9   "Baldheads" is a disrespectful term for monks, who shave off all their hair at ordination.

10   Presumably, this would take place after cremation, and his ashes would be placed in a vessel.

11   Troublemakers: "Bare sticks," or *guanggun*, is a derogatory term for single males who wandered about the countryside looking for work and getting into trouble. It was also used to refer to Buddhist monks.

12   *Toutuo* (*dhūta* in Sanskrit) are mendicant Buddhist monks.

13   The Kaiyuan period, during Emperor Xuanzong's reign, lasted from 713 to 741.

14   The *Classic of Difficulties* (Nanjing) is a collection of eighty-one questions and answers on medicine attributed to Bian Que (d. 310 BCE), reportedly the man who developed pulse diagnosis techniques. *Shennong's Materia Medica* (Shennong bencaojing) is a standard medical text on agriculture and medicinal plants, attributed to the legendary Shennong (Divine Farmer), also known as Yan Di (Emperor of Fire), who by tradition lived around 2800 BCE.

15   These four sacred Buddhist mountains are Mount Wutai in Shanxi, Mount Jiuhua in Anhui, Mount Putuo in Zhejiang, and Mount Emei in Sichuan.

16   Pugu Huai'en (d. 765) was a Tang general, of Turkic Tiele ancestry. Before his rebellion, he made major contributions to the suppression of the An Lushan rebellion and was made Prince of Daning.

17   For more on this incident, see "Xiang Yu" in "Historical and Cultural References."

18   Han Yu (768–824), also known by his posthumous title Literary Eminence

(Wengong), was an influential poet and prose writer. See "'Memorial on the Bone of the Buddha'" in "Historical and Cultural References."

19   In 446 the Wei emperor Taiwudi proscribed Buddhism, destroying texts, statues, shrines, and temples and executing monks. In 845, the Tang emperor Wuzong carried out a second campaign against Buddhism, destroying 4,600 Buddhist institutions and forcing 260,000 clergy to return to lay life. A few years later, his successor restored Buddhism, which flourished once again.

20   The Tang emperor Taizong (Li Shimin) seems to have originated this aphorism in *Rules for Emperors* (Di fan), his advice to his heir apparent.

21   See "Han Yu's essays" in "Historical and Cultural References."

SESSION 7: ON SHOUYANG MOUNTAIN, SHUQI BECOMES A TURNCOAT

1   This poem, "Seven Steps Poem" (Qibu shi), is usually attributed to Cao Zhi (Cao Zijian, 192–232) but is not found in any ancient collections of his poetry. It first appears in *New Account of Tales of the World* (Shishuo xinyu), a fifth-century compilation of anecdotes.

2   The Three Kingdoms period (220–80) was a time of intense military rivalry between the states of Wei, Shu Han, and Wu, all of which vied to control the empire.

3   On Cao Cao and his sons, see "Cao Cao" in "Historical and Cultural References."

4   The phrase "descendants of Yin" refers to the royal descendants of the Shang dynasty, which the Zhou had overthrown.

5   This may suggest parallels with Aina's own times.

6   In 213 BCE, the First Emperor of Qin purportedly ordered the burning of all books except Legalist texts, medical books, and technical manuals.

7   Versions of the Boyi and Shuqi story appear in many of China's most ancient texts, including the *Analects*, *Mencius*, and *The Zhuangzi*. Sima Qian's *Records of the Grand Historian* provides the fullest early treatment of the story as the first of its biographies.

8   Zhou of Shang is the name of Di Xin (r. 1075–1046 BCE), the last Shang ruler.

9   A great military strategist, Lü Wang, Duke Tai of Qi, better known as Jiang Ziya, led the Zhou armies at the Battle of Muye, which ended the Shang dynasty.

10   Shouyang Mountain, also referred to as "West Mountain" in the story, is near present-day Yongji in Shanxi, near the eastward bend in the Yellow River.

11   This may be a humorous reference to the *Rites of Zhou* (Zhou li): "In the second month of spring, men and women can meet, and they are not prohibited from eloping."

12   *Lunyu* 18.1: "The Viscount of Wei left him (King Zhòu), the Viscount of Ji became a slave on account of him, and Bi Gan lost his life for remonstrating with him. Confucius commented, 'There were three benevolent men in the Yin.'" Confucius, *Confucius*, 183.

13   See "Bandit Zhi" in "Historical and Cultural References."

14   On the city of Luo, see "Luoyang" in "Historical and Cultural References."

15   The deity's name, Master of Making All Things Equal (Qiwuzhu Zhengshi Jinxian), is a reference to chapter 2 of the *The Zhuangzi*, titled "Discussion on Making All Things Equal" (Qiwu lun), in which Zhuangzi argues for the futility and arbitrariness of deciding who wins a dispute. See Zhuangzi, *Complete Works*, 36–49.

16   The original reads "Dai qing shi zuoge kaiguo yuan xun baliao," which, because of its ambiguity, could also be read as "Wait until the time of the Qing, and you shall be its founding ministers."

17   This is another reference to *The Zhuangzi*, "Discussion on Making All Things Equal." Rather than separating right from wrong, the sage illuminates all in the light of Heaven through the use of "clarity" (*ming*), another reference to the fallen Ming dynasty. Zhuangzi, *Complete Works*, 42.

18   On a "Southern Bough" dream, see session 1, n. 7.

19   "Remnant people," or *yimin*, are the supporters of a fallen regime. Many Ming *yimin* took refuge in the mountains or shaved their heads and pretended to be monks. The term *yimin* occurs toward the end of section 18 in the *Analects* (18.8), where both Boyi and Shuqi are listed. The term also occurs as a general reference in *Analects* 20, without specifying names.

20   For details on the ancient beauty Xishi, see session 2. The commentator here points out the essential difference between overturning a legend and condemning disloyalty. But in fact both stories have to do with loyalty and self-deception. The comment probably should not be taken at face value.

21   Sometimes understood as "a dream told *by* a fool," the usual suggestion is that only fools believe in the truth of dreams. The commentator here suggests that we readers would be fools to believe that there is truth in this story, and yet the ironic inversions throughout the story and the commentary suggest just the opposite. This is Aina's commentary on the Ming *yimin*.

SESSION 8: WITH A TRANSPARENT STONE,
MASTER WEI OPENS BLIND EYES

With special thanks to Liang Xia for her assistance.

1   The Ancient Buddha Dīpaṁkara (Randeng Gufo) is the buddha of the epoch preceding that of Śākyamuni. Dīpaṁkara is the first of the three Trikalea

Buddhas (Buddhas of the Past, Present, and Future). He is followed by Śākyamuni and Maitreya. Free-and-Easy (Zizai) is a name taken from a descriptive term in the Daoist text *The Zhuangzi*.

2 In Buddhism, the Western Aparagodānīya (Xi Niuhuozhou) is the western-most of the four great continents in every world.

3 The East Pūrvavideha Continent (Dong Shengshenzhou) is another of Buddhism's four great continents.

4 The name Empty Green is seemingly a pun. The stone is literally translucent, but it is also "empty" of emotions and therefore "transcendent." The term *tongming*, "light throughout," puns on "to pass through the Ming."

5 Nüwa, the sister or consort of Fuxi, the legendary founder of Chinese civilization, is said to have repaired Heaven when it became damaged in early Chinese prehistory.

6 The "pure liquid" is *qingshui*. The name of the Manchu Qing dynasty literally means "pure," taken to contrast with what they saw as Ming decadence. "Blindness" here is the translation of *gumu*. The word *gu* is used figuratively in *Lunyu* 16.6, "to speak without observing the expression on his face is to be blind." Confucius, *Confucius*, 165.

7 During the Five Dynasties period (907–60), he failed to obtain a *jinshi*, the highest degree in the imperial civil service examinations, and lived in seclusion, first on Mount Wudang and later on Mount Hua. Emperor Taizong of the Song dynasty granted him the sobriquet (*hao*) "Master Xiyi." Later he became one of the immortals of legend. His spiritual talents were revealed in his ability to sleep for centuries at a time.

8 "Open our eyes" is the same term, *dianyan*, that indicates the dedication of a god or Buddha statue, when dots are drawn on the eyes, symbolically opening them to the deity's duty of protecting the community.

9 Zhuge Kongming (181–234) is a prescient military strategist in the earliest historical novel, *Romance of the Three Kingdoms* (Sanguo zhi yanyi). His formal name was Zhuge Liang.

10 A story of the rebel Li Zicheng (1605–1645), whose forces overran Beijing in 1644, causing the Ming Chongzhen emperor to commit suicide and his state to fall.

11 The phrase "thoughts and feelings" is literally "lungs and intestines" in the original text, hence the quite visceral purification process that follows.

12 On "natural disposition and consciousness," or *xingling*, see session 12 for a Confucian discussion of the concept.

13 Maitreya is the Buddha of the Future, the third of the three Trikalea Buddhas (of the Past, Present, and Future). The term "great chiliocosmos" refers to the entire Buddhist universe.

14   In Confucian writings, an "upright man" (*zhengren*) is one whose heart/mind has been rectified and thus conforms to orthodox standards. A "true gentleman" (*junzi*) is one who behaves in accordance with the highest moral ideals. Both are important concepts in Confucian writings.

15   According to legend, Du Kang was the inventor of wine in ancient times.

16   "Mysterious" (*xuan*) and "lacking in substance" (*xu*) are two Daoist terms indicating the transcendent and eternal Dao, which brings out the allegorical aspects of the tale.

17   The Three Great Teachings are Confucianism, Daoism, and Buddhism.

18   Liu Ling (ca. 221–300) was one of the eccentric literati of the so-called Seven Sages of the Bamboo Grove (Zhulin Qixian). He drank to excess and carried around a spade, instructing his followers to simply bury him if he should die. Ruan Ji (210–263) was another of the Seven Sages. He would drink to avoid dealing with unpleasant matters, as when he stayed drunk for sixty days in order to avoid discussing the possibility of his daughter marrying the emperor.

SESSION 9: LIU THE BRAVE TESTS A HORSE ON THE YUYANG ROAD

1   Of the five phases/agents (*wuxing*), metal is associated with autumn; of the cardinal directions, it is associated with the west.

2   *Guding*, a nail with a rounded head, also refers to a decorative motif in ceramics, a stud.

3   Jiang Yonglin, *Great Ming Code*, 159; quoted from article 289, "Forcible Robbery."

4   Military terms here are primarily those of the Ming dynasty. See "Imperial Bodyguards and Secret Service" in "Historical and Cultural References."

5   "Rotating hands" (*fanzi shou*) were government-employed runners serving in rotation who specialized in arresting bandits and thieves. For more on runners, see Reed, *Talons and Teeth*.

6   Deadline inspections were official reviews of deputies and similar officers, for the purpose of determining whether they had fulfilled their duties within the stipulated time limits for collecting taxes and arresting criminals. If they had not, they were beaten and required to meet new deadlines.

7   Longyang was a paramour of the King of Wei during the Warring States Period whose name became synonymous with male homosexuality.

8   On the term "freeloaders," or *miepian* (lit., "bamboo strips"), see "Bamboo strips and nap boards" in "Historical and Cultural References."

9   *Mengzi* 7A.36: "A man's surroundings transform his air, just as the food he eats changes his body. Great indeed are a man's surroundings" (Mencius, *Mencius*, 281).

10   See "Su Qin" and "Xiang Yu" in "Historical and Cultural References."

11   Huang Xiong refers here to a legend that Lü Dongbin, one of the Eight
      Immortals of Daoism, could turn things into gold by pointing at them. The
      title Chunyang (Pure Yang), meaning without any Yin, signifies that he has
      attained immortality in the earthly realm.

12   Here "Westerner" refers to a person from the Shanxi-Shaanxi border region.

13   The term "Handan Road" is sometimes an allusion to the Daoist legend of the
      Handan Dream or Yellow Millet Dream, in which a young Lü Dongbin experi-
      ences the vicissitudes of an entire lifetime in the course of a dream while his
      host cooks a meal of yellow millet.

14   During Ming and Qing times, local headmen were appointed to report any-
      thing suspicious or in violation of the laws in their community to the authori-
      ties (magistrates et al.). See "Judicial procedures" in "Historical and Cultural
      References."

15   Silver was not only used in standard, government-issued bars or ingots but
      also circulated by weight: a small amount could be cut off a larger unit. Most
      small traders handled only broken pieces, never full ingots.

16   Earlier in the story, the bandit refuses to give his name, but from this point
      onward, the narrator identifies him as having the surname Li.

17   The metaphor of a mustard seed falling through the eye of a needle seems to
      imply an unlikely phenomenon. However, the narrator may also refer here to
      the frequent pairing of these two items as an image of mutual attraction—as
      in the proverbial phrase "agreeable to each other as mustard and needle"
      (*zhen jie xiang tou*)—because of their magnetic properties when the needle is
      magnetized by iron or the mustard seed is rubbed on amber.

18   The commentator here uses two metonyms for "bandit." The first allusion,
      "drawing lots," or *tanwan*, refers to an episode from the second-century
      History of the [Western] Han (Hanshu) in which a group of young men collude
      to murder officials, drawing lots to determine who would assault whom by
      selecting (*tan*) colored balls (*wan*). The second, "hide in marshes," or *huanfu*,
      originally referred to a marsh but came to stand for the highwaymen who hid
      in dense marshes.

19   *Ou dao* is a blade made by the swordsmith Ou Yezi during the Spring and
      Autumn Period; the term came to stand for an executioner's blade.

SESSION 10: FREELOADER JIA FORMS A LEAGUE ON TIGER HILL

1   White Dew is one of the twenty-four solar periods of the traditional Chinese
      calendar. It begins around September 8 by the Western calendar.

2   A book with the title *Register of Edibles* (Shiwu zhi) can no longer be found;

Aina may have made up both the title and this entry. However, Li Yu mentions this title twice in his *Random Lodgings for My Idle Feelings* (Xianqing ouji), and a medical text with a similar title, *Materia Medica of Curative Foodstuffs* (Shiliao bencao), has been in circulation since the Tang period. See Engelhardt, "Dietetics in Tang China." Aina's description seems to cover several varieties of runner or climbing beans, including hyacinth beans.

3   The *Compendium of Materia Medica* (Bencao gangmu) was compiled by Li Shizhen in 1578. It was printed in Nanjing about twenty years later and became a standard medical reference for the ensuing centuries. This reference book does not include a section devoted to foods as such.

4   This seems to anticipate the final session in this collection.

5   Dong Qichang (1555–1636) was a famous landscape painter from the Shanghai area.

6   This is probably a dish, now rare, made from pig legs and bellies stewed in a thick sauce.

7   Heaven's Lake (Tianchi) is a hill southwest of Tiger Hill near Suzhou. A famous variety of tea was grown at the Tianchi Monastery there; according to Lu Shusheng (1509–1605), Yuan Hongdao (1568–1610), and their contemporaries, Tianchi tea was superior to all others from the region. See Benn, *Tea in China*, 186–88.

8   *Penjing* (commonly known as bonsai from the Japanese pronunciation of the word) are miniature landscapes.

9   See "Incense" in "Historical and Cultural References."

10   "Yellow soup" here is warmed rice wine. The poem could refer either to professional mourners or to nominally bereaved sons—both of whom get drunk after the funeral rites are over.

11   The term *lao baishang* literally means "old 'get-it-for-nothings.'"

12   See "Bamboo strips and nap boards" in "Historical and Cultural References."

13   The seven necessities are fuel, rice, oil, salt, soy sauce, vinegar, and tea.

14   The "Daoist robe" was an outer robe with large sleeves commonly worn for informal occasions by men. Its use originated during the Ming period and had no religious significance.

15   See "Games" in "Historical and Cultural References."

16   The terms for "pledge," *chuantiao* or *chuanmu* ("rafter" or "beam"), seem to indicate a donation toward the temple's building fund.

17   Because of the visitor's unfamiliar dialect, the monks mistook his awkward term *changqu jiang* (professional chanteuse) for *changyu jiang* (butterfish sauce), which reminded them of other types of sauces on the local market.

18   Official speech, Guanhua, or Mandarin, was the spoken language of administration across the empire.

19 See "Stone steps" in "Historical and Cultural References."

20 Ironically, "Fobao" means, more literally, "Protected by the Buddha" and, by punning with 弗保 in the Wu dialect, "Cannot Be Saved."

21 The wordplay here is on *jie*, meaning, depending on context, "festivals," "invitations," "years or stages" of one's life, or "joints" of a bamboo stem.

22 For the significance of these three names and reference to the gutter, see "Lü Mengzheng and Old Governor Cai" in "Historical and Cultural References."

23 There is a visual gag here: "modest talent" is 無貝之才, and "enrich our talent" is 有貝之才, contrasting the homophones "talent" 才, which is something they bring to the encounter, with the "fortune" 財 they hope to take away, the graph for which includes the element 貝, "cowries," or, by extension, "something precious."

24 Weiduo is the guardian figure facing and protecting the main altar in a Buddhist temple.

25 The Buddhist term "form," or *se*, is a synonym or euphemism for "sex" in many contexts, as it is here.

26 Presumably this refers to the occupation by Manchu troops after the conquest in the 1640s.

27 "Dry feet" is a Suzhou colloquialism for "lees" or "dregs" in, for example, a teacup.

28 Qiang She's exclamation puns on "I'll beat you to death!" which accounts for the servant's deliberately misleading interpretation of Qiang She's dismay.

29 Jia Jingshan speaks in Wu (Wuhua), the local language sometimes referred to as a dialect of standard Chinese although it is older than the northern language. Jia's speech is filled with colloquialisms and other words that are recognizable only locally.

30 This phrase parallels the vulgar English-language expression "kissed ass." For explanations of the references to Ji Bopi and Wu Zixu, see "Bopi" in Historical and Cultural References.

31 The rather awkward wordplay on "curio," or *gudong* 古董, splits the word into its constituent syllables and substitutes homophones: *gu* for "old" is replaced by the homophone *gu* 骨 (bone), and the *dong* syllable is replaced by its homophone *dong* 懂 (understand). The minister thus awkwardly "understands them all to the bone."

32 "The Three Dynasties" is "San Dai," and "seventeen or eighteen generations" is *shiqi, ba dai*, using the same term (*dai*) with quite different meanings. In his ignorance, Jingshan not only does not realize the age of the object; he does not understand the historical term (the Three Dynasties) Lord Liu uses. The Three Dynasties are the Xia (ca. 2070–1600 BCE), Shang (ca. 1600–1046 BCE), and Zhou (1046–256 BCE).

33   Zhang Chang lived a thousand years earlier than Jingshan avers, during the Han dynasty, not the Jin (1115–1234). Although Zhang was a strict administrator known for his frank speech, he also painted his wife's eyebrows as a sign of respect for her desire to be attractive.

34   As explained in session 9, note 7, Longyang was a common allusion to a male homosexual lover.

35   This alludes to the minimal gift, a bundle of dried meat, that Confucius expected from his students in payment for instruction (*Lunyu* 7.7). See Confucius, *Confucius*, 57. Obviously the sponger was hoping for payment in silver.

36   Jingkou Station was near Zhenjiang, a city northwest of Suzhou on the banks of the Yangzi. To be exiled to such a relatively close place was a lenient punishment. Minor criminals were often tattooed on the face as a form of public humiliation.

37   Chinese texts printed before the late nineteenth century were seldom punctuated and had to be read carefully in order to get the pauses in the right places. The pastime of deliberately misreading a text was probably enjoyed most when drinking.

38   The commentator here puns on Tiger Hill (Huqiu) and tiger's lair (*huxue*).

39   The phrase "the snow and moon, the breeze and the blooms" refers to more elegant entertainments than those arranged by the spongers on Tiger Hill.

Session 11: In Death, Commander Dang Beheads His Enemy

Special thanks to Ren Chaoyi and Chen Yue for their significant assistance with this translation.

1   The phrase "Let there be autumn" leaves off its obvious complement, "harvest" (*huo*).

2   Zhang Heyang is the poet and calligrapher Zhang Zhihe (730–810), who withdrew from office in the capital to live as a hermit. See "Han Shan" in "Historical and Cultural References."

3   These are sayings derived from a prayer reported in Sima Qian's collective biography of the jesters, *Shiji* 126: "May the crops from the highland fill whole crates! May the crops from the lowland fill whole carts! May grain harvested in abundance fill my house!" (Sima Qian, *Selections*, 404). The prayer is ridiculed because it asks for much after offering little.

4   In 1620, the year the Wanli emperor passed away, the commander of defense for the Liaodong area, Xiong Tingbi (1569–1625), resigned his commission after his colleagues brought multiple impeachment charges against him. His replacement, Yuan Yingtai, committed suicide the next year after he was defeated by the Manchu armies.

5	The eunuch Wei Zhongxian (1568–1627) and the emperor's wet nurse, Madame Ke, held significant power once the teenage Tianqi became emperor. Because he was more interested in other projects, Tianqi left most state and palace matters to Wei, who exercised his power without restraint.

6	In 1629 an economic measure reduced the number of postal attendants by one-third; see Wakeman, *Great Enterprise*, 796. For a succinct and painful overview of those years of natural disasters and the resulting famine and banditry that led to the fall of the Ming, see Brook, *Troubled Empire*, 238–59.

7	Yuan Chonghuan (1584–1630) was a Chinese general assigned to defend Liaodong against the Manchus. He was executed on trumped-up charges of treason, crippling Ming resistance in the region.

8	Mao Wenlong (1579–1629) was a Ming general who helped resist the Manchus but was eventually executed for smuggling by Yuan Chonghuan.

9	The term "borderland" means the Shanxi-Shaanxi border region.

10	This song touched a nerve among eminent modern readers as well. The literary scholar, writer, and translator Qian Zhongshu (1910–1998) mentioned it in his *Limited Views* (Guanzhui bian), in reference to other literary complaints against Heaven; see Qian, *Limited Views*, 346–47. Likewise, the philosopher, essayist, and statesman Hu Shi (1891–1962) was so moved that he sent it to his friend the outstanding linguist Y. R. Chao (Zhao Yuanren, 1892–1982) to set to music. Chao was busy, however, and did not do so for twenty years. A discussion and performance of his 1942 setting are available at the website of the Graduate Institute of Linguistics, Fu Jen Catholic University, Taiwan, http://www.ling.fju.edu.tw/Chao%20Yuan%20Ren/song09.htm.

11	Hanan (*Chinese Vernacular Story*, 199n15) speculates that this tale is based on an anecdote in Feng Menglong's *Survey of Tales Old and New* (Gujin tan'gai).

12	"Great Lord Chai Jin" and "Headquarters Clerk Song Jiang" refer to Chai Jin and Song Jiang, two altruistic heroes in the novel *Outlaws of the Marsh* (Shuihu zhuan).

13	See "Jupiter" in "Historical and Cultural References."

14	The figure of speech "frog in a well" refers to a person who has an overly narrow conception of a situation or of the world as a whole. It derives from a parable in the Daoist text *The Zhuangzi*.

SESSION 12: IN DETAIL, RECTOR CHEN DISCOURSES ON THE COSMOS

1	The wordplay here revolves around Rector Chen mistaking "bean arbor" (*doupeng*) for "Brother Dou" (Dou Pengyou).

2	On Rector Chen, see "Chen, Rector Chen (Chen Zhaizhang)" in "Historical and Cultural References."

3   This is also said of Aina himself. See the "General Comments" section at the end of this session.

4   That is, "lowbrow" writings for the instruction of the general populace, not for the elite.

5   For an explanation of his philosophical sources, see "Session 12" in "Afterthoughts on Stories."

6   For more on the use of the term "disputatious" here, see "Disputatious, on being" in "Historical and Cultural References."

7   Zhang Dainian (*Key Concepts*, 45) warns that the concept of Qi embraces both matter and energy, "*Qi* is both what really exists and what has the ability to become.... *Qi* is the life principle but is also the stuff of inanimate objects."

8   *Wuxing* is often translated as "five phases" because the phases indicate the processes of change. Zhang (*Key Concepts*) gives the translation "Five Agents," which seems more appropriate in this context.

9   This passage is closely modeled after the *Classic of Changes* (Yijing).

10 In traditional timekeeping, the day was divided into twelve segments, or *shi*, each two hours in length and designated by one of the terrestrial branches, or *dizhi*. Noon, *wu*, was the center of the day, and midnight, *zi*, was the center of the night.

11 On Laozi, see his entry in "Historical and Cultural References."

12 The term "Yang essence" (*Yang jing*) here refers to male sexual potency. As in the rector's diagrams (see figs. 12.01, 12.02), it can also refer to the sun, while "Yin spirit" may refer to the moon.

13 Here, *xingling* seems to indicate "natural disposition and consciousness," although in more modern usage, the term refers to the inner world of spirit, thoughts, and feelings.

14 Many of the details given here do not accurately reflect Buddhist sutras. For example, Buddha's mother died seven days after his birth, and his home state was overrun during his lifetime.

15 By saying "our China" (*wo Zhongguo*) and "China's sages" (*Zhongguo shengren*), Aina seems to be drawing a clear distinction between ethnic Han and other ethnicities, probably alluding to China's new Manchu rulers.

16 "True Nature" is given here as "*Zhenxing.*"

17 "Yang Spirit" (*Yang shen*) here can mean either his spiritual essence or his sexual potency; compare "Yang essence" in n. 12.

18 On the Three Purities, see the entry in "Historical and Cultural References."

19 *Śarīras* are mineral-like relics of varying sizes and colors left behind after the cremation of a Buddhist monk or nun of great spiritual purity.

20 In this context, both "dragon's vein" and "Buddha root" seem to have been made up or used inappropriately in order to sound ridiculous.

21   "Prohibitive loop" is the term for the magical hoop the bodhisattva Guanyin puts around the head of the unruly Monkey King to punish him for his misdeeds in the sixteenth-century novel *Journey to the West* (Xiyou ji).

22   Some figures referred to here are historical; others are from legend. See "Huizong, Emperor of Song," "Wu, Emperor of Liang (Liang Wudi)," and "Xuanzong, Emperor of Tang" in "Historical and Cultural References."

23   On these figures, see "Han Lin'er and Xu Zengshou," "Tang Sai'er," "Zhang Ling and Zhang Jiao," and "Zhao Guyuan and Xu Hongru" in "Historical and Cultural References."

24   On Bodhidharma, see his entry in "Historical and Cultural References."

25   The text is incorrect here. The name of Śākyamuni's wife is Yaśodharā (Yeshutuoluo). "Tuoluo" seems to be an abbreviation. The term *mohouluo* (*muhūrta* in Sanskrit) means a period of time, a moment. The name of Śākyamuni's son is Rāhula (Luohouluo).

26   On King Wuding, see "Wuding, King" in "Historical and Cultural References."

27   "Tang" and "Yu" refer to the ancient sage-kings Yao and Shun.

28   The rector here plays on the words "Lord on High" (Shangdi, literally the "earlier" *di*, or "emperor") and "Yellow Emperor" (Huangdi), arguing that the "Earlier Emperor" (Shangdi) must have been naked if he came before the inventor of clothing, the Yellow Emperor, which the audience sees as nonsense.

29   On *xingling* translated as "natural disposition and consciousness," see note 13.

30   "Energy" (Qi) literally means "breath"; here both meanings fit. See also note 7.

31   Presumably Chen includes the Hearth God, Zaoshen, as his last category here.

32   On these two, see "Wen Tianxiang and Yu Zhongsu" in "Historical and Cultural References."

33   "This happens naturally" (*zi ran er ran*) quotes the Daoist classics in describing the Dao. See Laozi, *Lao Tzu*, 82.

34   *Lunyu* 7.21. Quotation from Confucius, *Confucius*, 61.

35   The Chenghua reign period was 1465–87.

36   For the historical figure on whom Sancui'er may have been based, see "Tang Sai'er" in "Historical and Cultural References."

37   See "Han Yu's essays" in "Historical and Cultural References."

38   On the monk who preached to rocks, see "Shenggong" in "Historical and Cultural References."

39   Hanan (*Chinese Vernacular Story*, 241n11) notes "the Confucian zealot Yang Guangxian, famed for his tirades against the Jesuits," used the phrase "having no alternative" in the title of a tract he published in 1665.

40 According to legend, Sima Qian, author of *Records of the Grand Historian* (Shiji), wrote this great history to express his frustration over being inappropriately punished by his emperor. He explains his situation in "Letter to Ren An" ("Bao Ren Shaoqing shu").

41 See "Wang Jiefu" in "Historical and Cultural References."

42 See "*Outlaws of the Marsh* and 'Life of Ximen'" in "Historical and Cultural References."

43 Chan masters used these "sudden enlightenment" teaching techniques to aid their students in achieving the mental breakthrough that is enlightenment.

44 Probably quite deliberately, the commentator uses the same image, words flowing like a waterfall, here and in his first sentence that Aina used in describing the self-righteous scholar parodied in this session (although the storyteller in session 3 is described similarly by the crowd). The term "Man of Dao" used here can refer to any serious seeker of truth in Confucian, Daoist, or Buddhist traditions.

45 There is no evidence that Aina ever wrote more stories, nor have any extant collections of poems or plays been confidently identified as his. Perhaps these comments, too, were intended to be misleading.

AFTERTHOUGHTS ON STORIES

1 Yenna Wu, "Bean Arbor Frame," 4.

2 McMahon, *Causality and Containment*, 133; on the narrator's detachment, see 141.

3 For discussions on this figure and the poem, see Zhang Feifei, "*Doupeng xian-hua* fayin," and Liu Yongqiang, "Fengtu, Renqing, Lishi."

4 Zhu Yizun, *Ming shi zong*, juan 91, 8:4295.

5 Lang Ying, *Qixiu leigao*, 516–17.

6 *Bu Xu Gaoseng zhuan*, 530.

7 Qian Qianyi, *Liechao shiji*, 11:6270.

8 *Xu zhiyue lu*, 8.145. Given his status as a senior Chan monk, his comment was not only a disparaging remark but a subtle teaching, about attachment to identity, at the same time.

9 See "Coxinga" in "Historical and Cultural References."

10 Galatians 6:7.

11 Zhang Feifei ("*Doupeng xianhua* fayin," 58–62) sees this story as castigating the Fushe (Revival society) and other literary-political societies that formed late in the Ming.

12 See his *Explanations of the Diagram of the Great Ultimate* (Taijitu shuo), with selections translated, in Chan, *Source Book in Chinese Philosophy*, 463–65.

13   See Chan, *Source Book in Chinese Philosophy*, 497–98, 502–4.

14   Such fabrications became a regular feature of late Ming romantic comedies in the *chuanqi* dramatic form; Li Yu was to do the same in plays he wrote at about the same time that Aina penned this collection. Note, too, that the commentary following the session uses irony as well, probably intended to undercut the commentator's evaluations of both story and author.

GLOSSARY OF CHINESE CHARACTERS

Aina Jushi 艾衲居士 (Aina 艾納)
An Lushan 安祿山

Bailan Daoren of Suzhou 吳門百懶道人
Bailianjiao 白蓮教
Bandit Zhi 盜跖
bao, baoying 報, 報應
"Bao Ren Shaoqing shu" 報任少卿書
Baoningtang 寶寧堂
Bawang bieji 霸王別姬
Bencao gangmu 本草綱目
Bencaojing 本草經
Bian Que 扁鵲
Bianzhi mode 變徵調
bingcheng 並稱
Bodhidharma 菩提達摩
Bopi 伯嚭
Boyi 伯夷

can 參
Cao Cao 曹操
Cao Pi 曹丕
cao shi zhi li 螬食之李
Cao Zhang 曹彰
Cao Zhi 曹植
Chang Cong 常樅
Changshengdian 長生殿
changqu jiang 唱曲匠
changyu jiang 鯧魚醬
Chao, Y. R. (Zhao Yuanren) 趙元任

chaofeng 朝奉
chaofenglang 朝奉郎
Chen Gang 陳剛
Chen Tuan 陳摶
Chen Wugui 陳無鬼
Chen Wuyu 陳無欲
Chen Zhaizhang 陳齋長
Chen Zhongzi 陳仲子
Cheng Hao 程顥
Chi Xian 遲先
Chi Yi 鴟夷
chizi zhi xin 赤子之心
Chong'er 重耳
Chu Renhuo 褚人穫
Chuan jin duantou bang 船進斷頭浜
chuanqi 傳奇
chuantiao 椽條 or chuanmu 木
Cuoshuo 脞說

Da Tang xiyu ji 大唐西域記
"dai qing shi zuoge kaiguo yuan xun
    baliao" 待清時做個開國元勳罷了
Daxue 大學
denglong 燈籠
Dexiang 德祥
Di fan 帝範
Dianguang zunzhe 電光尊者
dianyan 點眼
Diao Ao ji 釣鼇磯
Dingli 頂禮

dizhi 地支
Dong Qichang 董其昌
Dong Shengshenzhou 東勝神洲
Dong Sizhang 董斯張
Dong Tuo 董説
Dongchang 東廠
Dongfang Shuo 東方朔
Dou Pengyou 竇朋友
Dou Ying 竇嬰
doupeng 豆棚
Doupeng xianhua 豆棚閒話
Doupeng yin 豆棚吟
doushuo 鬥捌
duantou xiaohe 斷頭小河
Duanwu jie 端午節
dui he 對合
Duoduofu 咄咄夫

Emei, Mount 峨嵋山
Ergai 二丐
Erke Pai'an jingqi 二刻拍案驚奇
Ershisi xiao 二十四孝

Fadeng 法燈
Fan Li 范蠡
Fan Xizhe 范希哲
fanzi shou 番子手
Fayan 法眼
Feng Menglong 馮夢龍
fengliu 風流
Fotucheng 佛圖澄
Fu Chai 夫差
Fu Yue 傅説
fumo 副末
Fushe 復社

ganlu 甘露
Gao Ming 高明
Gao Zhu 高簀
Gaoshang Yuhuang benxing jijing 高上玉

皇本行集經
Goujian 句踐
Guan Yu 關羽 (Guan Gong 關公)
guanggun 光棍
Guanhua 官話
"Guanju" 關雎
Guanzhui bian 管錐編
Guazhi'er 掛枝兒
"Gui yuantian ju" 歸園田居
Gui Zhuang 歸莊
Gujin tan'gai 古今譚概
Gujin xiaoshuo 古今小說
gumu 瞽目
Guoxingye 國姓爺
Gushan 孤山

Han Fei zi 韓非子
Han Lin'er 韓林兒
Han Shan 寒山
Han Yu 韓愈 (Changli 昌黎)
Hanhailou 瀚海樓
Hejing xiansheng 和靖先生
Hong Mai 洪邁
Hong Sheng 洪昇
Hongjin 紅巾
Honglou meng 紅樓夢
Honglou xumeng 紅樓續夢
Houli 蒿里
Hu Lai 胡來
Hu Shi 胡適
huaben 話本
Huadangge congtan 花當閣叢談
Hualiyou 滑裡油
Huanfu 萑苻
Huang Zhouxing 黃周星
Huangjin 黃巾
Huansha ji 浣紗記
Huayanjing 華嚴經
huban 忽板
Huizong, Emperor of the Song 宋徽宗

huo (qiu huo) 秋穫
Huqiu 虎丘
Huqiu si 虎丘寺

Ji Dian 濟顛
Jian'an qizi 建安七子
Jiangnan 江南
Jianhu erji 堅瓠二集
jiaxun 家訓
jie 節 (female chastity)
jie 結 (join together)
Jin gu qiguan 今古奇觀
Jin Shengtan 金聖嘆
jing 精
Jin'gangjing 金剛經
jingkui 經魁
Jingshi tongyan 警世通言
Jinyiwei 錦衣衛
Jiu Tang shu 舊唐書
Jiuhua, Mount 九華山
juan 卷
junzi 君子
jushi 居士

kong 空
Kong Rong 孔融 (Wenju 文舉)
Kong Shangren 孔尚任
Kongqing 空青
Kongzi jiayu 孔子家語
Kuangke 狂客
Kuangzhang 匡章
Kunqu 崑曲

Lao Lai 老萊
Li 理 (Principle)
li 李 ("plum" and the surname Li)
Li Bian 李昇
Li Fang 李昉
Li Fang-yu 李方瑜
Li Ji 驪姬

Li Qiancheng 李前程
Li Rusong 李如松
Li Shizhen 李時珍
Li Yu 李漁 (dramatist and writer)
Li Yu 李餘 (paragon of filial respect)
Li Zhi 李贄
Li Zhuang fan Shenjing 李闖犯神京
Li Zicheng 李自成
Liang Chenyu 梁辰魚
liangzhi 良知
Lijiang 麗降
Lin Bu 林逋
Ling Mengchu 凌濛初
Liu Bang 劉邦
Liu Cong 劉琮
Liu Ling 劉伶
"Liu Lu Qinqing" 留盧秦卿
Liu Xiang 劉向
liu zhou 六州
Liulihe 琉璃河
Lixue 理學
Longxingtang shihua 龍性堂詩話
Lu Shusheng 陸樹聲
Lu Xun 魯迅
Luo Rufang 羅汝芳
luocha 羅剎
Luohouluo 羅睺羅
Lü Dongbin 呂洞賓

mai chun 買春
Mao Wenlong 毛文龍
Mei Chun 梅春
Mengyuan shucheng 夢遠書城
miepian 滅騙 (cheat)
miepian 篾片 (bamboo strip)
Ming 明 ("brightness" or "clarity"
    and the name of the Ming
    dynasty)
Mingshenghu 明聖湖
mipian 覓騙 (cheat)

Mohouluo 摩睺羅
Mudan ting 牡丹亭

Nanhu 南湖
Nanjing 難經
neidan 內丹
ni huaben 擬話本
Nüxian waishi 女仙外史

oudao 歐刀

Pai'an jingqi 拍案驚奇
penjing 盆景
pian 騙
pinghua 評話
Pipa ji 琵琶記
Pugu Huai'en 僕固懷恩
pupai 鋪牌
Putuo, Mount 普陀山

Qi 氣 ("Breath" or "Energy")
Qian Qianyi 錢謙益
Qian Wusu 錢武肅
Qian Yu 錢芋
Qian Zhongshu 錢鍾書
Qiantang 錢塘
"Qibu shi" 七步詩
Qilou chongmeng 綺樓重夢
"Qinghua lei" 情化類
qingke 清客
Qingmiao fa 青苗法
"Qingming ri duijiu" 清明日對酒
Qingshi leilue 情史類略
qingshui 清水
Qiuran 虬髯
Qiuranke zhuan 虬髯客傳
"Qiwu lun" 齊物論
Qiwuzhu Zhengshi Jinxian 齊物主證
　　世金仙
"Qu e'yu wen" 驅鱷魚文

Randeng Gufo 燃燈古佛
Rongzhai suibi 容齋隨筆
"Ru fajie pin" 入法界品
Ruan Ji 阮籍

San dai 三代
San Sui Pingyao zhuan 三遂平妖傳
Sandetang 三德堂
Sanhuang wudi 三皇五帝
Sanqing 三清
Sanshen 三身
Sanyan 三言
se 色 ("form" or "sex")
Shangshu 尚書
Shanmu 山木
shen 神
sheng 笙
Sheng gong 生公
Shengshui 聖水
Shennong 神農 (Yandi 炎帝)
Shennong bencaojing 神農本草經
Shensheng 申生
shi 時
Shi dian tou 石點頭
shi dui he 十對盒
Shi You feng 石尤風
Shiji 史記
Shijing 詩經
Shiliao bencao 食療本草
shiqi, ba dai 十七八代
Shishuo xinyu 世說新語
Shitou ji 石頭記
Shuqi 叔齊
Shuijing 水經
Shuoyuan 說苑
Shuyetang keben 書業堂刻本
Shuyi ji 述異記
Sikong Shu 司空曙
Sima Guang 司馬光
Sima Yan 司馬炎

Song Qiqiu 宋齊丘
Su Dongpo 蘇東坡
Su Qin 蘇秦
Su Shi 蘇軾 (Su Dongpo 蘇東坡)
Sun Simiao 孫思邈
Sun Zhenren haishang fang 孫真人海上
方
"Sutai huaigu" 蘇台懷古

Taijitu shuo 太極圖說
Taiping guangji 太平廣記
Taishang laojun 太上老君
*Taishang shuo Xuantian Dadi Zhenwu
benzhuan shenzhou miaojing* 太上說
玄天大帝真武本傳神咒妙經
Taisui xing 太歲星
Tang Xianzu 湯顯祖
tanwan 探丸
tao 逃 (to flee)
Taozhu 陶朱 (Fan Li)
Taohua shan 桃花扇
Tian Di zaohua 天地造化
Tian Fen 田蚡
Tian Heng 田橫
Tianbaonu 天保奴
Tianchi 天池
Tiandao 天道
Tianli 天理
tongming 通明
Tongxin shuo 童心說
Tongyu ji 桐嶼集
toutuo 頭陀
Tripitaka 三藏

waidan 外丹
Wang Anshi 王安石
Wang Mengji 王夢吉
Wang Wei 王蔚
Wang Yangming 王陽明
"Wan'gu chou" 萬古愁

Wanyan Liang 完顏亮
Wei Liangfu 魏良輔
Wei Zhongxian 魏忠賢
Weiji wenku 維基文庫
Wen Tianxiang 文天祥
Wen Tingyun 溫庭筠
Wo Zhongguo 我中國
Wu, Emperor of the Liang 梁武帝
Wu, King of the Zhou 周武王
"Wu tou ke duan, jin bu ke de!" 吾頭可
斷, 金不可得
Wu Weiye 吳偉業
Wu Yue chunqiu 吳越春秋
Wu Zixu 伍子胥
Wuding, King of Shang 商武丁王
"Wudu" 五蠹
Wuhua 吳話
Wutai, Mount 五台山
Wuxing 五行

"Xi er xi zuo" 洗兒戲作
Xi Niuhuozhou 西牛貨洲
Xian, Duke of Jin 晉獻公
xian'er 先兒
Xiang Yu 項羽
Xianqing ouji 閒情偶寄
Xiao doupeng 小豆棚
"Xiaoyaoyou" 逍遙游
"Xiari xiyuan" 夏日西園
xiehouyu 歇後語
"Xielu" 薤露
Xihu mengxun 西湖夢尋
Xin Tang shu 新唐書
Xin xue 心學
xingling 性靈 (basic nature and con-
sciousness)
Xingshi hengyan 醒世恒言
Xinnianjie 新年節
Xiong Tingbi 熊廷弼
Xishi 西施

Xiyi, Master 希夷先生
Xiyou bu 西遊補
Xiyou ji 西遊記
"Xiyuan" 西園
Xu Fuzuo 徐復祚
Xu Hongru 徐鴻儒
Xu Jinlian 徐晉廉
Xu Jutan 徐菊潭
Xu Yunjing 徐允婧
Xu Zengshou 徐增受
Xu Zhigao 徐知誥
xuan 玄
Xuanguai lu 玄怪錄
xuanliang cigu 懸梁刺股
xuanxu 玄虛
Xuanzang 玄奘
Xuanzong, Tang Emperor 唐玄宗
　　(Minghuang 唐明皇)

yamen 衙門
Yang Guozhong 楊國忠
Yang jing 陽精
Yang Xian 楊暹
Yang Yuhuan 楊玉環, the Guifei 楊貴妃
Yangshen 陽神
Yangsheng zhu 養生主
Yanluo 閻羅
Yanwang 閻王
Ye Jiaoran 葉矯然
Ye Zhou 葉晝
Yeshutuoluo 耶輸陀羅
Yidun 猗頓
Yiguang 夷光
Yijing 易經
yimin 逸民
"Yin Hushang, chuqing houyu" 飲湖上
　　初晴後雨
yinde 陰德
yinguo baoying 因果報應
"Yongbu" 詠部

You yixi hua—xu yami 又一夕話—續雅謎
Youlihua 油裡滑
Yu Qian 于謙 (Yu Zhongsu 于忠肅)
Yuan Chonghuan 袁崇煥
"Yuan Dao" 原道
Yuan Hongdao 袁宏道
Yuan Yingtai 袁應泰
Yuanhu 鴛湖
Yuhuang benxing jing 玉皇本行經

Zai Wo 宰我
Zai Yu 宰予
Zhang Chang 張敞
Zhang Dai 張岱
Zhang Daoqin 張道勤
Zhang Heyang 張河陽
Zhang Jiao 張角
Zhang Jing 張靜
Zhang Junfang 張君房
Zhang Juzheng 張居正
Zhang Ling 張陵 (Zhang Daoling 張
　　道陵)
Zhang Zai 張載
Zhang Zhihe 張志和
Zhanguo ce 戰國策
Zhao Guyuan 趙古元
Zhaoyun 朝雲
Zheng Chenggong 鄭成功
Zheng Zhilong 鄭芝龍
"Zhengmin" 烝民
zhengren 正人
Zhenwu bao'en jing 真武報恩經
Zhihetang 致和堂
zhishai 撕色
Zhiyanzhai 脂硯齋
Zhong Kui 鍾馗
Zhongguo shengren 中國聖人
"Zhongnan bieye" 終南別業
Zhongqiujie 中秋節
Zhou, King of Shang 商紂王

Zhou Dunyi 周敦頤
Zhou Gong 周公
Zhou li 周禮
zhu 誅 (execution)
Zhurong 祝融
Zhu Yizun 朱彝尊
Zhuangzi 莊子
Zhudaosheng 竺道生
Zhulin qixian 竹林七賢
Zi ran er ran 自然而然
Ziran 紫髯
Zizai zunzhe 自在尊者
Zuozhuan 左傳

Bibliography

Abbreviations

DMB   L. Carrington Goodrich and Chao-ying Fang, eds., *Dictionary of Ming Biography*.

ECCP   Arthur W. Hummel, ed., *Eminent Chinese of the Ch'ing Period*.

Aina Jushi 艾衲居士. *Doupeng xianhua* 豆棚閑話. In *Guben xiaoshuo jicheng* 古本小說集成. Shanghai: Shanghai Guji Chuban She, 1990. Photo reprint of the Hanhailou 翰海樓 edition.

———. *Doupeng xianhua* 豆棚閑話. In *Xihu jiahua deng sanzhong* 西湖佳話等三種, edited by Zhang Daoqin 張道勤. In *Zhongguo huaben daxi* 中國話本大系. Nanjing: Jiangsu Guji, 1993.

———. *Doupeng xianhua, Zhaoshi bei (he kan)* 豆棚閑話, 照世盃 (合刊). Taipei: Sanmin Shuju, 1998.

———. "Jie Zhitui Traps His Jealous Wife in an Inferno." Translated by Yenna Wu. *Renditions* 44 (Autumn 1995): 17–32.

———. *Propos oisifs sous la tonnelle aux haricots*. Translated by Claire Lebeaupin. Paris: Gallimard, 2010.

Benn, James A. *Tea in China: A Religious and Cultural History*. Honolulu: University of Hawai'i Press, 2015.

Brook, Timothy. *The Confusions of Pleasure: Commerce and Culture in Ming China*. Berkeley: University of California Press, 1998.

———. *The Troubled Empire: China in the Yuan and Ming Dynasties*. Cambridge, Mass.: Harvard University Press, 2010.

Bu Xu Gaoseng zhuan 補續高僧傳. Compiled by Minghe 明河. In *Xu zangjing*, vol. 77, no. 1524.

Campany, Robert F. *Strange Writing: Anomaly Accounts in Early Medieval China*. Albany: State University of New York Press, 1996.

Chan, Wing-tsit, trans. and comp. *A Source Book in Chinese Philosophy*. Princeton, N.J.: Princeton University Press, 1963.

Chang, Kang-I Sun, and Stephen Owen, eds. *The Cambridge History of Chinese Literature*. Vol. 2, *From 1375*. Cambridge and New York: Cambridge University Press, 2010.

Chang Qu 常璩. *Huayang guozhi* 華陽國志. Shanghai: Shangwu Yinshuguan, 1929.

Chen Dakang 陳大康. "*Doupeng xianhua* kaozheng" 考證. In Aina Jushi, *Doupeng xianhua Zhaoshi bei (he kan)*, 1–7.

———. "*Yinyan*" 引言. In Aina Jushi, *Doupeng xianhua Zhaoshi bei (he kan)*, 1–10.

Confucius. *Confucius: The Analects*. Translated by D. C. Lau. 2nd ed. Hong Kong: Chinese University Press, 1992. First published 1979 by Penguin.

Engelhardt, Ute. "Dietetics in Tang China and the First Extant Works of Materia Dietetica." In *Innovation in Chinese Medicine*, ed. Elisabeth Hsu, 173–92. Cambridge: Cambridge University Press, 2001.

Feng Menglong. *Stories Old and New: A Ming Dynasty Collection*. Translated by Yang Shuhui and Yang Yunqin. Seattle: University of Washington Press, 2000.

Fuller, Michael A. *The Road to East Slope: The Development of Su Shi's Poetic Voice*. Stanford, Calif.: Stanford University Press, 1990.

Gao Boyu 高伯瑜. *Zhonghua mishu jicheng* 中華謎書集成. Beijing: Renmin Ribao Chubanshe, 1991.

Goodrich, L. Carrington, and Chao-ying Fang, eds. *Dictionary of Ming Biography*. New York: Columbia University Press, 1976.

Guben xiaoshuo jicheng 古本小說集成. Shanghai: Shanghai Guji, 1990.

Guo Maoqian 郭茂倩, comp. *Yuefushi ji* 樂府詩集. Beijing: Zhonghua Shuju, 1979.

Haar, Barend ter. *The White Lotus Teachings in Chinese Religious History*. Honolulu: University of Hawai'i Press, 1999.

Han Fei. *Han Fei Tzu: Basic Writings*. Translated by Burton Watson. New York: Columbia University Press, 1964.

Hanan, Patrick. *The Chinese Vernacular Story*. Cambridge, Mass.: Harvard University Press, 1981.

———. *The Invention of Li Yu*. Cambridge, Mass.: Harvard University Press, 1988.

Hegel, Robert E. "Dreaming the Past: Memory and Continuity beyond the Ming Fall." In *Trauma and Transcendence in Early Qing Literature*, edited by Wilt Idema, Wai-yee Li, and Ellen Widmer, 345–71. Cambridge, Mass.: Harvard University Asia Studies Center, 2005.

———. "Inventing Li Yu: A Review Article." *Chinese Literature: Essays, Articles, and Reviews* 13 (1991): 95–100.

———. "Niche Marketing for Vernacular Fiction." In *Printing and Book Culture in Late Imperial China*, edited by Cynthia Brokaw and Kai-wing Chow, 235–66. Berkeley: University of California Press, 2005.

———, ed. and trans. *True Crimes in Eighteenth-Century China: Twenty Case Histories*. Seattle: University of Washington Press, 2009.

Henricks, Robert G. *The Poetry of Hanshan: A Complete, Annotated Translation of "Cold Mountain."* Albany: State University of New York Press, 1990.

Hightower, J. R. *The Poetry of T'ao Ch'ien.* Oxford: Clarendon Press, 1970.

Hu Shi 胡適. "Xu" 序. In *Zhaoshi bei, Doupeng xianhua* 照世盃, 豆棚閑話, 1–4. Reprinted in *Hanben Zhongguo tongsu xiaoshuo congkan* 罕本中國通俗小說叢刊, edited by Wang Yizhao 王以昭. Second collection. Taipei: Tianyi, 1974. First published 1961.

Hu Shiying 胡士瑩. *Huaben xiaoshuo gailun* 話本小說概論. Beijing: Zhonghua Shuju, 1980.

Hucker, Charles O. *A Dictionary of Official Titles in Imperial China.* Stanford, Calif.: Stanford University Press, 1985.

Hummel, Arthur W., ed. *Eminent Chinese of the Ch'ing Period.* Washington, D.C.: United States Government Printing Office, 1943.

Jiang Yonglin, trans. *The Great Ming Code (Da Ming lü).* Seattle: University of Washington Press, 2005.

Johnson, David. "The Wu Tzu-hsü *Pien-wen* and Its Sources." *Harvard Journal of Asiatic Studies* 40.1–2 (1980): 93–156 (part 1), 466–505 (part 2).

Knechtges, David R., trans. *Rhapsodies on Natural Phenomena, Birds and Animals, Aspirations and Feelings, Sorrowful Laments, Literature, Music, and Passions.* Vol. 3 of *Wen Xuan, or Selections of Refined Literature.* Princeton, N.J.: Princeton University Press, 1996.

Kogachi Seigi 古勝正義. "Tōhō kanwa no sakusha Ō Mukichi" 豆棚閑話の作者王夢吉. *Kitakyūshū Shiritsu Daigaku Gaikokugo Gakubu kiyou* 北九州市立大学外國語學部紀要 125, no. 2 (2009): 1–20.

Kongzi jiayu 孔子家語. Shanghai: Shangwu Yinshuguan, 1929.

Lang Ying 郎瑛. *Qixiu leigao* 七修類稿. Beijing: Zhonghua, 1961.

Lanselle, R. "*Doupeng xianhua* 豆棚閑話 (Propos oiseux sous la tonnelle aux haricots)." In Chan Hing-ho et al., *Inventaire analytique et critique du conte chinois en langue vulgaire,* vol. 5, 199–242. Paris: Collège de France, Institut des Hautes Études chinoises, 2006.

Laozi. *Lao Tzu: Tao Te Ching.* Translated by D. C. Lau. Hong Kong: Chinese University Press, 1989. First published 1963 by Penguin.

Lee, Pauline Chen. *Li Zhi, Confucianism, and the Virtue of Desire.* Albany: State University of New York Press, 2011.

Legge, James, trans. *The Chinese Classics: With a Translation, Critical and Exegetical Notes, Prolegomena, and Copious Indexes.* 5 vols. Oxford: Oxford University Press, 1893–95.

Li Fang 李昉 et al., eds. *Taiping guangji* 太平廣記. 10 vols. Beijing: Zhonghua, 1961.

Li, Wai-yee 李惠儀. "Early Qing to 1723." In *The Cambridge History of Chinese Literature,* vol. 2, *From 1375,* edited by Kang-I Sun Chang and Stephen Owen, 152–244. Cambridge and New York: Cambridge University Press, 2010.

———. *Women and National Trauma in Late Imperial Chinese Literature*. Cambridge, Mass.: Harvard University Asia Center, 2014.

Li Yu. *Silent Operas*. Edited by Patrick Hanan. Hong Kong: Chinese University of Hong Kong Research Centre for Translation, 1990.

———. *A Tower for the Summer Heat*. Translated by Patrick Hanan. New York: Ballantine Books, 1992.

Lin Chen 林辰. *Shenguai xiaoshuo shi* 神怪小説史. Hangzhou: Zhejiang Guji, 1998.

Ling Mengchu. *Amazing Tales*. Translated by Wen Jingen and Perry Ma. 2 vols. Beijing: Panda Books, 1998.

Liu Yongqiang 劉勇強. "Fengtu, Renqing, Lishi—*Doupeng xianhua* zhongde Jiangnan wenhua yinzi ji shengcheng beijing" 風土,人情,歷史: 豆棚閒話中的江南文化因子及生成背景. *Qinghua daxue xuebao* 清華大學學報, 25.4 (2010): 54–66.

Lu Hsun (Lu Xun). *Brief History of Chinese Fiction*. Translated by Yang Hsien-yi and Gladys Yang. Beijing: Foreign Languages Press, 1959.

Lynn, Richard John, trans. *The Classic of Changes: A New Translation of the "I Ching" as Interpreted by Wang Bi*. New York: Columbia University Press, 1994.

McLoughlin, Kevin. "Image and Appropriation: The Formation of Illustrated Albums of Guanyin in 17th-Century Print Culture." In *The Art of the Book in China*, edited by Ming Wilson and Stacey Pierson, 159–73. London: University of London School of Oriental and African Studies, Percival David Foundation of Chinese Art, 2006.

McMahon, Keith. *Causality and Containment in Seventeenth-Century Chinese Fiction*. Leiden: Brill, 1988.

Mencius. *Mencius*. Translated by D. C. Lau. Rev. ed. Hong Kong: Chinese University Press, 2003. First published in 1970 by Penguin.

Miaofa lianhua jing wenju 妙法蓮華經文句. Compiled by Zhiyi 智顗. *Taishō shinshū Daizōkyō* 34, no. 1718.

Mote, Frederick W. *Imperial China, 900–1800*. Cambridge, Mass.: Harvard University Press, 1999.

Mungello, David E. *The Great Encounter of China and the West, 1500–1800*. Lanham, Md.: Rowman and Littlefield, 1999.

Ōtsuka Hidetaka 大塚秀高, comp. *Zōho Chūgoku tsūzoku shōsetsu shomoku* 增補中國通俗小説書目. Tokyo: Kyūko Shoin, 1987.

Qian Qianyi 錢謙益. *Liechao shiji* 列朝詩集. Beijing: Zhonghua, 2007.

Qian Zhongshu. *Limited Views: Essays on Ideas and Letters*. Translated by Ronald Egan. Cambridge, Mass.: Harvard University Asia Center, 1998.

Rawski, Evelyn. *Early Modern China and Northeast Asia: Cross-Border Perspectives*. Cambridge and New York: Cambridge University Press, 2015.

Reed, Bradly Ward. *Talons and Teeth: County Clerks and Runners in the Qing Dynasty*. Stanford, Calif.: Stanford University Press, 2000.

Rolston, David L. *Traditional Chinese Fiction and Fiction Commentary: Reading and Writing between the Lines*. Stanford, Calif.: Stanford University Press, 1997.

Schafer, Edward H. *The Divine Woman: Dragon Ladies and Rain Maidens in T'ang Literature*. San Francisco: North Point Press, 1973.

Siku quanshu zongmu tiyao 四庫全書總目提要. Compiled by Ji Yun 紀昀 et al. Shanghai: Dagong Shuju, 1926.

Sima Qian (Ssu-ma Ch'ien). *Records of the Grand Historian*. Translated by Burton Watson. 2 vols. New York: Columbia University Press, 1961.

——— (Szuma Chien). *Selections from "Records of the Historian."* Translated by Yang Hsien-yi and Gladys Yang. Beijing: Foreign Languages Press, 1979.

Struve, Lynn, ed. and trans. *Voices from the Ming-Qing Cataclysm: China in Tigers' Jaws*. New Haven, Conn.: Yale University Press, 1993.

Sun Kaidi 孫楷第. *Riben Dongjing suojian xiaoshuo shumu* 日本東京所見小說書目. Beijing: Renmin Wenxue, 1958.

———. *Zhongguo tongsu xiaoshuo shumu* 中國通俗小說書目. Hong Kong: Shiyong Shuju, 1967.

Taishō shinshū Daizōkyō 大正新修大藏經. Edited by Takakusu Junjirō 高楠順次郎 and Watanabe Kaigyoku 渡辺海旭. 48 vols. Tokyo: Taishō Shinshū Daīzōkyō Kankōkai, 1961–78.

Tang Xianzu. *The Peony Pavilion*. Translated by Cyril Birch. Bloomington: Indiana University Press, 1980.

Vitiello, Giovanni. *The Libertine's Friend: Homosexuality and Masculinity in Late Imperial China*. Chicago: University of Chicago Press, 2011.

Wakeman, Frederic. *The Great Enterprise: The Manchu Reconstruction of Imperial Order in Seventeenth-Century China*. 2 vols. Berkeley: University of California Press, 1985.

Waldrop, Lindsey. "Tension and Trauma in *Idle Talk under the Bean Arbor*." PhD diss., University of Oregon, 2016.

Waley, Arthur, trans. *The Book of Songs*. Edited by Joseph R. Allen. Rev. ed. New York: Grove Press, 1996.

Wang Wei 王蔚. "The Lure of Visualization—Narration, Decoration, and Symbolization in the Fiction Illustrations of the Ming-Qing Transition." PhD diss., Washington University in St. Louis, forthcoming.

Watson, Burton, ed. and trans. *The Columbia Book of Chinese Poetry: From Early Times to the Thirteenth Century*. New York: Columbia University Press, 1984.

Wu Huiyi 吳蕙儀. "Nouvelle identification d'une traduction chinois-français (1735)." *Carnets du Centre Chine*, July 12, 2012. http://cecmc.hypotheses.org/7299. Accessed January 28, 2016.

Wu, Yenna 吳燕娜. "The Bean Arbor Frame: Actural and Figural." *Journal of the Chinese Language Teachers Association* 30.2 (1995): 1–32.

————. "The Debunking of Historical Heroes in *Idle Talk under the Bean Arbor*." *Selected Papers in Asian Studies* (Western Conference of the Association for Asian Studies), n.s., no. 43 (1992): 1–27.

Xu Fuzuo 徐復祚. *Huadangge congtan* 花當閣叢談. Taipei: Guangwen, 1969.

Xu zangjing 續藏經 (*Wan Xu zang* 卍續藏). 150 vols. Hong Kong: Yingyin Xu zangjing Weiyuanhui, 1967.

Xu zhiyue lu 續指月錄. In *Xu zangjing*, vols. 84–85, no. 1579.

Zeitlin, Judith T. *Historian of the Strange: Pu Songling and the Chinese Classical Tale.* Stanford, Calif.: Stanford University Press, 1993.

————. *The Phantom Heroine: Ghosts and Gender in Seventeenth-Century Chinese Literature.* Honolulu: University of Hawai'i Press, 2007.

Zeng Yandong 曾衍東. *Xiao doupeng* 小豆棚. Edited by Xu Zhenglun 徐正倫 and Chen Ming 陳銘. Hangzhou: Zhejiang Guji, 1986. Also available at Zhongguo zhexue shu dianzihua jihua, http://ctext.org/wiki.pl?if=gb&res=479952.

Zhang Dai 張岱. *Xihu mengxun* 西湖夢尋. Beijing: Zhonghua Shuju, 2007.

Zhang Dainian. *Key Concepts in Chinese Philosophy.* Translated and edited by Edmund Ryden. New Haven, Conn.: Yale University Press; Beijing: Foreign Languages Press, 2003.

Zhang Daoqin 張道勤. *Qianyan*.前言. In *Xihu jiahua deng sanzhong* 西湖佳話等三種, edited by Zhang Daoqin. In *Zhongguo huaben daxi* 中國話本大系. Nanjing: Jiangsu Guji, 1993.

Zhang Feifei 張菲菲. "*Doupeng xianhua fayin*" 豆棚閒話發隱. MA thesis, Chinese University of Hong Kong, 2003. http://etheses.lib.cuhk.edu.hk/pdf/003946199.pdf.

Zhang Mangong 張滿弓, ed. *Gudian wenxue banhua: Xiaoshuo. Zazhu* 古典文學版畫。小說。雜著. Kaifeng: Henan Daxue Chubanshe, 2004.

Zhao Jingshen 趙景深. *Xiaoshuo luncong* 小說論叢, Shanghai: Rixin Chubanshe, 1947.

Zheng Zhenduo 鄭振鐸. *Zhongguo wenxue yanjiu* 中國文學研究. Part 1. In *Zheng Zhenduo quanji* 鄭振鐸全集, vol. 4. Shijiazhuang, Hebei: Huashan Wenyi, 1998. http://www.doc88.com/p-25029606451.html.

Zhiyue lu 指月錄. In *Xu zangjing*, vol. 83, no. 1578.

Zhongguo guji shanben shumu (Zibu) 中國古籍善本書目(子部). Shanghai: Shanghai Guji, 1994.

Zhu Yizun 朱彝尊. *Ming shi zong* 明詩綜. Beijing: Zhonghua, 2007.

Zhuangzi. *The Complete Works of Chuang Tzu.* Translated by Burton Watson. New York: Columbia University Press, 1968.

Contributors

LANE J. HARRIS (University of Illinois PhD, 2012) is associate professor of history at Furman University.

ROBERT E. HEGEL (Columbia University PhD, 1973) is Liselotte Dieckmann Professor of Comparative Literature and professor of Chinese at Washington University in St. Louis. He is the author of *The Novel in Seventeenth-Century China* and *Reading Illustrated Fiction in Late Imperial China* and the translator of *True Crimes in Eighteenth-Century China: Twenty Case Histories*.

LI FANG-YU (Washington University in St. Louis PhD, 2015) is assistant professor of Chinese at New College of Florida.

LI QIANCHENG (Washington University in St. Louis PhD, 1998) is associate professor of Chinese at Louisiana State University and the author of *Fictions of Enlightenment: "Journey to the West," "Tower of Myriad Mirrors," and "Dream of the Red Chamber"* and the variorum edition of the 1641 novel *Xiyou bu*.

MEI CHUN (Washington University in St. Louis PhD, 2005) is the author of *The Novel and Theatrical Imagination in Early Modern China*. She is currently an independent scholar.

LINDSEY WALDROP (University of Oregon PhD, 2016) wrote her dissertation on *Doupeng xianhua*. She currently teaches at a private academy in Florida.

ANNELISE FINEGAN WASMOEN (Washington University in St. Louis PhD candidate in comparative literature) is the translator of the novel *The Last Lover*, by Can Xue.

ALEXANDER C. WILLE (Washington University in St. Louis PhD, 2014) is a postdoctoral fellow in Chinese at Washington University in St. Louis.

XU YUNJING (Washington University in St. Louis PhD, 2015) is assistant professor of Chinese at Bucknell University.

ZHANG JING (Washington University in St. Louis PhD, 2006) is associate professor of Chinese at New College of Florida.

CPSIA information can be obtained
at www.ICGtesting.com
Printed in the USA
BVHW071227040220
571349BV00001B/6